JIMMY
STEWART
A Wonderful Life

EAT HEALTHY WITH KENSINGTON

COOKING WITHOUT RECIPES
by Cheryl Sindell   (1-57566-142-X, $13.00/$18.00)
Unleash your creativity and prepare meals your friends and family will love with the help of this innovative kitchen companion. COOKING WITHOUT RECIPES includes intriguing culinary strategies and nutritional secrets that will stir your imagination and put the fun back into cooking.

EAT HEALTHY FOR $50 A WEEK
Feed Your Family Nutritious, Delicious Meals for Less
by Rhonda Barfield   (1-57566-018-0, $12.00/$15.00)
Filled with dozens of recipes, helpful hints, and sample shopping lists, EAT HEALTHY FOR $50 A WEEK is an indispensable handbook for balancing your budget and stretching your groceries while feeding your family healthy and nutritious meals.

THE ARTHRITIC'S COOKBOOK
by Collin H. Dong, M.D.   (1-57566-158-6, $9.95/$12.95)
and Jane Banks
Afflicted with debilitating, "incurable" arthritis, Dr. Collin H. Dong decided to fight back. Combining traditional Chinese folk wisdom with his western medical practice, he created a diet that made his painful symptoms disappear. Today, used in conjunction with regular arthritis medications, this groundbreaking diet has provided thousands of Dr. Dong's patients with active, happy, and virtually pain-free lives. It can do the same for you.

Available wherever paperbacks are sold, or order direct from the Publisher. Send cover price plus 50¢ per copy for mailing and handling to Penguin USA, P.O. Box 999, c/o Dept. 17109, Bergenfield, NJ 07621. Residents of New York and Tennessee must include sales tax. DO NOT SEND CASH.

JIMMY STEWART
A Wonderful Life

With an afterword by his daughter, Dr. Kelly Stewart Harcourt

Frank Sanello

Pinnacle Books
Kensington Publishing Corp.

http://www.pinnaclebooks.com

*For my co-authors, Shelby and Porkchop,
a rescued dog and a morbidly obsese kitten, who,
fearing abandonment by their new owner, refused to
leave his side during the entire composition of this work.*

PINNACLE BOOKS are published by

Kensington Publishing Corp.
850 Third Avenue
New York, NY 10022

Copyright © 1997 by Frank Sanello

All rights reserved. No part of this book may be reproduced
in any form or by any means without the prior written consent
of the Publisher, excepting brief quotes used in reviews.

If you purchased this book without a cover, you should be aware
that this book is stolen property. It was reported as "unsold
and destroyed" to the Publisher and neither the Author nor the
Publisher has received any payment for this "stripped book."

Pinnacle and the P logo Reg. U.S. Pat. & TM Off.

First Printing: July, 1997
10 9 8 7 6 5 4 3 2 1

Printed in the United States of America

CONTENTS

Preface

> "*How can you be accused of exaggerating Jimmy Stewart's monumental goodness when even the Pope confesses he's a big fan?*"
>
> —a retired movie studio executive

> "*Marlene (Dietrich) . . . had the art department make a life-sized doll of Flash Gordon that was, uh, correct (anatomically) in every way. Then she walked into his dressing room, handed over the gift and locked the three of them in together.*"
>
> —Joe Pasternak, producer,
> *Destry Rides Again* (1939)

> "*I was too busy.*"
> —James Stewart, denying the above incident in the presence of his wife, *Vogue*, 1989

Only the jaded and cynical will scoff at calling movie star James Stewart a secular saint. His intrinsic goodness and lifetime of kind acts did not, I believe, come from religious conviction, although he was a staunch Presbyterian for much of his life. The tenets of that branch of Protestantism suggest that salvation is not achieved by good deeds, which Stewart, the most beloved man in Hollywood, was famous for. Unlike Roman Catholicism, Presbyterian doctrine (aka Calvinism) implies that good works are no ticket to heaven; instead according to John Calvin, God indicates future salvation by bestowing material riches on those he plans to grant admission to the Pearly Gates. That's the Protestant Ethic in a nutshell, which seems to contradict God's dictum that the meek shall inherit the earth. Maybe Calvin thought God meant the *rich* meek.

It may not have been a coincidence that as a good Calvinist, Stewart spent a lifetime amassing worldly wealth—as much as his more famously rich contemporary Bob Hope—because it proved that he was one of The Elect, those fortunates whom Calvinism described as "saved." Much more likely, Jimmy Stewart was just a terrifically nice guy whose behavior was instinctual, not spiritual, motivated by congenital kindness rather than Calvinist doctrine.

In a dog-eat-babies industry where the joke goes, "You can tell who your true friends are—they're the ones who stab you in the *front,*" the *gemütlich* life of James Stewart was all the more remarkable. I believe he truly deserves the moniker "Saint Jim," even though his religion doesn't recognize the Roman Catholic equivalent of pagan Roman demigods, i.e. saints. After immersing yourself in 50 years' worth of magazine and newspaper clips and a handful of interviews with his few surviving contemporaries, it's virtually impossible to call James Stewart anything but Jimmy. In a 1970 interview, a reporter for the *Los Angeles Times* agreed, saying, "He's hard of hearing, a reluctant member of the 'toupe troupe,' yet he's so endearingly boyish it seems impossible to affix for respect either Mister or General. [His rank when he retired from the Air Force Reserves.] One cannot even call him James. He is, and will forever be, Jimmy Stewart, American *boy.*" Stewart was 62 at the time.

The actor was the most beloved figure in Hollywood. Colleague Robert Horton (TV's *Wagon Train*) pulled out all the stops and went even further, saying, "Stewart may quite possibly be America's most beloved man."

He was certainly one of the happiest until his wife of 44 years, Gloria Hatrick McLean Stewart, died in 1994 of lung cancer. Stewart, once a *bon vivant* octogenarian man-about-town with his still handsome septuagenarian wife on his arm, became an almost Howard Hughes-like recluse, turning down awards (and still numerous job offers). He didn't plan to suffer Gloria's absence for long. Two years after her death, he confided to his Irish maid, Anne Coyle, that he had decided not to replace his pacemaker when the device exhausted its life span. John Strauss, 83, Jimmy's long-time and only publicist, told me, "When people are as close as Jimmy and Gloria were, when one of them 'goes,' the other usually follows soon after."

But until Gloria's death, the story of the actor's life could have been aptly named after the film that was his personal favorite and mine: "Jimmy Stewart: It *Was* a Wonderful Life."

—Frank Sanello

West Hollywood, California, 1997

Introduction

He Never Met a Fan He Didn't Like

> *"He's the friendliest, most accommodating star in Beverly Hills."*
>
> —The Map to the Homes of the Hollywood Stars

Jimmy Stewart was the last of his breed. And what a glorious, endangered species it was! All his co-stars from Hollywood's Golden Age—Henry Fonda, John Wayne, Marlene Dietrich, even Grace Kelly—had passed from the scene while he was still reporting to the movie set or raising money for innumerable charities.

In 1991, *Life* magazine compared him to the last of an almost extinct species, a living, breathing artifact from the Dream Factory's finest design era: "Fact: Of all the major male movie stars of the Golden Years of Hollywood, say the mid-1930s into the postwar 1940s, Stewart is the only one still with us. Yes, Ronald Reagan is with us, but he doesn't fit; he's a B actor who made President. All the rest—Tracy, Cooper, Gable, Cagney, Astaire, Fonda, [Robert] Taylor, Wayne, Bogart, Flynn, Power, Grant—are gone. This sad attritional fact alone is enough to regard the man as a living national treasure."

Jimmy, typically, pooh-poohed such hagiography and told *Life,* "If they write, 'He gave people a lot of pleasure' as my epitaph, I'll be very pleased."

His 79 films gave pleasure for more than half a century and continue to do so. His personal favorite (and mine) was *It's a Wonderful Life.* The classic film and the fact that he loved it above all his other (some superior) work supply us with a Rosetta Stone for deciphering the psychology of a man who was less than voluble about his emotional life. "Dad has always been a man of few words about anything. Even when we asked him about his parents or his childhood, he wouldn't be very revealing," his daughter told me in 1966. When it came to self-revelation, Jimmy didn't believe less is more. Less was *the most.*

The 1946 Christmas perennial, *It's a Wonderful Life,* was inspired not by a book or stage play but by two simple sentences in a Christmas card director and close friend Frank Capra showed Stewart: "Just remember, no man is born a failure." And, "Nobody is poor who has friends."

James Maitland Stewart's life and career proved those sentiments—and then some.

Until his wife died, Stewart lived a *fabulous* life, embodying the film's theme that no man is a failure: He starred in some of the greatest films ever made and worked with A-plus-list directors. He earned five Oscar nominations and won one, plus one honorary Oscar. Before settling down to one of the happiest and longest-running marriages in Hollywood at the ripe old age of 41, he romanced some of Hollywood's most beautiful stars. Somehow, in between making nearly four-score films, he managed to become a World War II hero, flying 20 bombing missions over Germany. He entered the Army a private and retired a brigadier general! After "retirement," he continued to work in the movie business for another two decades—his last film in 1991, as a voice in a Steven Spielberg cartoon. And sometimes, late at night, you can still hear his signature drawl in voiceovers for Campbell Soup or tire commercials, the latter a personal favor for a close friend, magnate Leonard Firestone, whose company was in big trouble. One of the wealthiest stars in Hollywood, Stewart had long ago stopped working *for a living*. He didn't need to hustle chicken soup or radial tires to raise the mortgage or put his grandchildren through graduate school. A combination of the Protestant Ethic and the pure joy of working kept his nose to the grindstone until, with ill health and the loss of his life partner, he finally said, "Enough."

As for the other theme of *It's a Wonderful Life*, "No man is poor who has friends:" by that standard Jimmy Stewart—even without his airlines, real estate, oil wells and stock portfolio—was the richest man in Hollywood, perhaps in the world. The notoriously difficult Bette Davis once said he was the "nicest superstar" she ever worked with.

Another buddy put it best: "We think of the Stewart character in the movies as open, kind, and honest, just like the boy next door. Well, Nancy and I and his friends can tell you that's not just some screen character—that's the real Jimmy Stewart." That encomium courtesy of the 40th President of the United States.

Speaking of Ronald Reagan, when another addled bigwig, retired studio chief Jack Warner, was told in 1966 that Reagan was running for governor of California, the addled ex-tycoon shouted, "No, no, no! *Jimmy Stewart* for governor. Ronald Reagan for *best friend*."

Near the turn of this century in the era of Madonna and Lollapaloozas, fan mail still arrived at the 89-year-old superstar's Beverly Hills office at the rate of 500 letters a week, many from youngsters who had fallen in love with his films on video. "I get fan mail from the kids of old fans. They see my movies on video. I answer 'em all and get a kick out of it," he told the *Saturday Evening Post* in 1988, explaining why he still went to his offices every single day at age 80.

Stewart took a hands-on approach to another movie star chore: the fan mail often requested an autographed photo. "I sign all the autographs myself. Fans aren't customers: they're partners. I have a responsibility," he said. And in the days before celebrity stalkers carved up Theresa Saldana and gunned down Rebecca Schaeffer, Jimmy was accessible enough to allow the local *Beverly Hills Citizen* to publish his home address in an article. (For the record, it's 918 N. Roxbury Drive, Beverly Hills.)

When the annoying Hollywood tour bus drove past his home several times a day, he was known to step outside and wave to the starstruck fans, who often saw him out front washing his 1987 green Volvo. At other times, he invited fans in who had purchased a map to the stars' homes and had the temerity to ring his doorbell. Reporters frequently mentioned in interviews that he answered the door himself. The six-member Stewart family never employed more than two servants.

How did the frail senior tolerate such an invasion of privacy? This was clearly no Sean Penn or Alec Baldwin. Jimmy Stewart never punched out a paparazzo or sued the *National Enquirer.* "Privacy, schmivacy" was his motto. "I feel I belong to the public. I don't feel that my private life is my own. I must devote some of my life to my audience. Long ago someone told me that even though I might become a star in movies, always remember this: 'Never treat your audience as customers—always treat them as partners.' I've never forgotten that. It's a tremendous piece of advice."

One of the nicest guys in Hollywood was also one of the shrewdest. Stewart was directly responsible for the fact that today's superstars, once weekly wage slaves under the thumb of studio bosses, can now earn $20 million a picture.

Chapter 1
Small Town, Big Men

James Maitland Stewart II was born in the unlikely-named town of Indiana, Pennsylvania, (pop. then 9,000) on May 20, 1908. Stewart biographer Jhan Robbins called Indiana "a set right out of an old Stewart movie: overtly patriotic, friendly, financially stable."

The tiny town of Indiana may be only an hour's drive from the big city (Pittsburgh), but emotionally and spiritually it's smack dab in the middle of the American heartland, with all its old-fashioned virtues and values. James Stewart grew up breathing those values along with the oxygen and exhaust fumes from those new-fangled horseless carriages that were always backfiring and terrorizing the "dependable vehicles," horses.

You can see the ancient, worn-out Allegheny Mountains from the Stewart house in a tony neighborhood oddly called Vinegar Hill. The Stewarts lived in a sprawling 19th-century house with high ceilings, perfect for the only son of the house, whose eventual height neared 6'4". It was even more accommodating for his dad, Alexander, who topped his son by one inch. Jimmy would later describe his boyhood home in a first-person account in *McCall's* in the 1960s as "a rambling house of no particular architecture." Jimmy was being his usual modest self. Photos of the place in other magazines show a sumptuous, white Palladian villa that was a lot closer to a mansion than the bungalow he described. The front porch, with its wicker furniture, was a frequent family gathering place to discuss current events in the days before TV made family conversation an obsolete art form. In the parlor, one of Jimmy's younger sisters, Virginia, would play the piano; his other sister, Mary, the baby of the family, was an expert violinist. Jimmy played the accordion, and no one ever mentioned "expert" and "accordion" in the same sentence when describing his contribution to family musicales. In fact, his ineptitude would become famous as horror stories about his lack of musical talent followed him from Indiana to college to Hollywood, World War II, and 1950s TV appearances.

While Jimmy was the spoiler of these family get-togethers, his mother Elizabeth was the star of the show. Neighbors recalled hearing her achingly beautiful soprano voice wafting out of the Stewart home, accompanied by competent piano-playing and the worst accordion noise ever inflicted on the human ear. Out of deference to his wife's superior talent, the usually loud-mouthed Alexander forced himself to sing quietly so he wouldn't drown out Elizabeth Stewart's exquisite *bel canto*. Jimmy described this pairing of diametric opposites: "Her name was Elizabeth but he always called her Bessie . . . and he clearly adored her. Though small and gentle and not given to contention, she frequently had her way over his, because she possessed patience and endurance." On trips to Yellowstone or Washington, D.C., Alexander, always in a hurry about everything else, would force himself to drive slowly because he knew high speeds terrified his delicate wife.

Alexander found it harder to keep other impulses under control, creating chaos for Mrs. Stewart's dinner plans. If a customer at the hardware store seemed a particularly interesting conversationalist to the proprietor, Alexander wouldn't hesitate to invite a total stranger home for dinner, unannounced. One night, Jimmy recalled, his father's intellectual curiosity overwhelmed his sense of smell. A foul odor emanated from four dinner guests, who, it turned out, worked for the circus that had just come to town. They must have been in charge of cleaning out the elephant cages, but Alexander Stewart didn't care. For some reason they fascinated him and ended up sitting downwind of Jimmy and his aristocratic mother. The circus folk had asked to buy supplies on credit, and the big-mouthed— and equally big-hearted—Alexander figured they could use a good home-cooked meal in one of the nicest homes in Indiana, regardless of their personal hygiene.

Jimmy remembered that these roustabouts didn't hesitate to use profanity, which shocked his devout mother and delighted her children.

The circus was in trouble, and it went bankrupt before its engagement in Indiana ended. To pay his debts, the circus owner offered Alexander payment in kind—in this case a 14-foot python. As much a showman as his son would later become, Alexander immediately saw the promotional possibilities. Years later he would put his son's 1940 Best Actor Oscar in the hardware store's front window, but for now, he used the snake to lure curious customers inside. Not for nothing was his father the most successful entrepreneur in town. Soon customers were lining up to get a peek at the monstrous snake. The brilliant gimmick fizzled when the python tried to attack a female customer. Although plate glass separated the two, and the python ended up with a bruised head from crashing into it, the woman, a Miss Fullerlove, fainted from fright. When she came to, she marched straight over to the police station. The police had no compunction about telling the richest man in town that this live "manikin" had to go. Now.

Dad agreed, but found it hard to comply. None of his employees would go near the snake under glass. Finally Alexander and his best friend, Doc Torrance, somehow managed to chloroform the snake. The ultimate fate of the unfortunate reptile remained a secret, Jimmy recalled, but the two men failed to keep secret that they almost chloroformed themselves in the attempt.

In his brilliant 1985 oral history, *Everybody's Man: Jimmy Stewart,* Jhan Robbins returned to Indiana and interviewed D. Hall Blair, one of Jimmy's closest childhood friends. Blair

provided an outsider's perspective on the elegant Mrs. Stewart
which proved that Jimmy's recollections of his mother hadn't
been filtered through rose-colored glasses or filial love. Blair
said Elizabeth Stewart was a woman of aristocratic bearing
(and heiress to a banking fortune), but with no aristocratic airs.
Blair recalled, "She was a very dignified lady, a strong church-
goer. Mrs. Stewart had finished college," rare for even a well-
heeled woman of her day, "and she would talk to us about the
value of a good education. Her lectures were heeded. All three
Stewart children graduated from college at a time when less
than one percent of the population owned a sheepskin. Jimmy's
friend remembered the youngster regretting that he had not
inherited his mother's brains. As his brilliant college, film, and
business careers would later show, Jimmy did indeed inherit
Elizabeth Stewart's intelligence. He also inherited her reticence
and halting speech. His father, by contrast, was a blowhard
with an opinion on everything, which he was always happy to
volunteer whether asked to or not. Jimmy adored his father,
who called him "Jimbo," but he emulated his mother. It was
a lucky roll of the genetic dice. Mrs. Stewart's gentleness
couldn't help but influence her son's acting style, a style that
helped make him one of the most beloved of movie stars.
Had Jimmy resembled his dad, Hollywood might have been
subjected to a small town incarnation of Brando or Burt Reynolds.

Most tellingly of Indiania's old-time values is the amazing
statistic that in a town of only 16,000 today, there are 41
churches! Although figures aren't available, you almost suspect
that when Jimmy was born and the population only 9,000 it
still had 40-some churches even then.

The town's predominant style of architecture is *haute* Victorian, with enough gingerbread *boiserie* to fill a Currier & Ives
engraving. Iowa's fictional Madison County has nothing on the
covered bridges of Indiana, Pennsylvania.

Jimmy's childhood sounds a lot like his character George
Bailey's in *It's a Wonderful Life.* His real-life father, Alexander
Stewart, however, owned an immensely prosperous hardware
store instead of the bankrupt savings and loan in *It's a Wonder-*

ful Life. And unlike Stewart's George Bailey, who never earned enough money to go to college, Jimmy could afford to attend a tony prep school, Mercersburg Academy in his home state, and then his father's own alma mater, Princeton.

It was perhaps from his father that he learned the tough goodness and grace that suffused both the actor's life and his films.

A family friend and prominent citizen of Indiana grossly simplified this father-son relationship by comparing it to something out of a Mark Twain novel. The 19th-century author didn't even begin to skim the surface of this complex relationship, although their neighbor, Frank Moore, insisted, "Jimmy had a straight, small-town upbringing. He did many of the things Tom Sawyer was supposed to have done, perhaps more of them." Jimmy never tricked anyone into painting a fence for him, but his father used a lot of psychological tricks to teach his son lessons in life and forgiveness.

"With his temperament," Jimmy once wrote, referring to his father's famous bombast, "it was amazing how patient he could be with us kids and how subtle in his discipline. I don't recall a time when he stood across my path; he always walked beside, guiding me with his own steps."

Alexander's parental finesse was perhaps best demonstrated in the affair of the killer dog. At the age of 10, young Jimmy found himself in a murderous rage. Seventy years later, the emotion was still vivid enough for him to tell a reporter from *Life* magazine that he had wanted to annihilate the neighbor's dog because it had killed Jimmy's beloved Golden Retriever, Bounce. Sounding more like Jimmy's evil twin, the actor recalled, "I vowed to kill that dog in revenge. I vowed it day after day in the most bloodthirsty terms. I never quite did it, but I was making myself ill with my own hate and frustration." Precociously, the 10-year-old had already intuited that suppressed anger was as unhealthy as aggression. One night after dinner, his father confronted his conflicted son bluntly. "You are determined to kill the dog?" Dad asked. "All right, let's stop talking about it and get it done. Come on."

Alexander apparently knew something about psychology,

specifically reverse psychology, for when Jimmy accompanied
his dad to the alley behind the store, he found that Alexander
had already captured the killer mutt and tied it up. "He got a
deer rifle out of stock, handed it to me, then stepped back for
me to do my bloody work. The dog and I looked at each other.
He wagged his tail in a tentative offer of friendship, and his
large brown eyes were innocent and trusting. Suddenly the gun
was too heavy for me to hold, and it dropped to the ground,"
he told *Life* in 1991.

Finally, his father untied the dog, which ran over and licked
Jimmy's hand. The dog followed them home, and Jimmy ended
up adopting the killer. "No word was ever said about what
had happened. None was needed. Dad had taught me I wasn't
really a killer, and I didn't have ever again to try to work it
up or pretend. It was a great relief."

Jimmy was both right and wrong about the lessons he learned
that night. He never could "pretend" to be a killer, and in very
few of his 79 movies did he ever shoot anyone, rarely in fact
even playing a villain.

A photo from his boyhood reproduced in *Life* shows how
close father and son were. Dad had just returned from World
War I. Next to him stands his boy, wearing the mock-doughboy
uniform he refused to take off until dad came back from France.
Patriotically, Jimmy staged two plays during this time, serving
as writer, producer, director, and actor. Never as a professional
would he have the egomania to wear so many hats on a movie
set.

When his father returned from Over There, over here Jimmy
did his childish bit for the war effort with a little hometown
propaganda filled with enough jingoism to make the America
First crowd proud. "When I was eight I put on a play in our
basement," he recalled in a magazine interview more than half
a century after the war. "It was called *Beat the Kaiser.*" I
wrote it and played all the male parts, and I made my [two]
sisters play all the female parts. I was afraid that Dad was
getting sick as he sat there watching us. It wasn't until years
later that I realized he just looked the way he did—sort of

swelled up and red—from trying so hard not to laugh at Jimmy's rabid jingoism.

During the war, Alexander was too old to fight, but he enlisted anyway, as an ordnance officer. And he sent a lot of ordnance home as souvenirs. (In this pre-Watergate-Whitewater era, people were a lot less fastidious about helping themselves to freebies.) A drama teacher at Jimmy's prep school speculated that if his father hadn't "sent him all those helmets and stuff, he would have never become an actor."

Years later, Jimmy remembered all the booty dad sent home from the trenches. "Dad shipped home endless supplies of gas masks, German helmets, and swords. He provided all the props!" The denouement of this cellar epic suggested that Jimmy, had he chosen to, could have had a career as a special effects wizard instead of movie star. "The climax of the play was the electrocution of that weary villain [the Kaiser] by a gigantic dummy dry-cell battery, borrowed from the front window of the family-owned hardware store."

There was enough surplus for the future actor-entrepreneur to stage a sequel called *The Slacker*. Instead of the German Emperor, the main character was the Eisenhower of the First World War, General "Black Jack" Pershing, who decorated the hero (Jimmy, of course) at the climax with a medal fabricated from a soda-pop bottle top.

Besides stimulating a latent taste for theatrics, the Great War would leave a lasting impression and have serious repercussions on Jimmy's life when the Second World War broke out 20 years later. Jimmy would be part of five generations of Stewart men who fought—and some who died—for their country.

It all started with the founder of the family's considerable fortunes, James Maitland Stewart, Jimmy's grandfather. He started the "J.M. Stewart & Co." hardware store on Indiana's main thoroughfare, Philadelphia Street, in 1843, 1853, or 1863, depending on whether you believe Louella Parsons, Hedda Hopper, or some unnamed Boswell of Hollywood lore. Regardless of when he actually set up shop, the original James Stewart took time out from hustling screws and shotguns to sign up for the Civil War.

His son Alexander was just as gung-ho and willing to inter-
rupt his career when his country called, even when the call was
an egregious act of American imperialism, a little land grab
known as the Spanish-American War. In 1898, the U.S. decided
to lighten Spain of some real estate, namely Cuba and the
Philippines. Alexander didn't care if he was fighting for God,
motherhood, and apple pie or a slice of an oil-rich archipelago
like the Philippines or the sugarcane fields of Cuba. Like Teddy
Roosevelt, who gave up his post as Assistant Secretary of the
Navy to rough-ride up San Juan Hill, legend has it that Alexander, an undergraduate chemistry major at Princeton when the
Maine blew up in Havana harbor, left his Bunsen burner on in
the middle of chemistry class to enlist. The scholarly warrior
was in the middle of writing his senior chemistry thesis as well.
As Jimmy would recall with pride a lifetime later, "The ruthless
way the Spaniards were treating Cubans began to bother Dad.
He didn't even turn off his Bunsen burner. He just went."
Alexander's son proudly claimed, despite the absence of any
historical record, that Dad actually trotted up San Juan Hill
with the future president. This myth is not mentioned in any
other biographies or newspaper accounts. Jimmy's memory
was, however, more accurate when he reported that his father
returned from his imperialistic adventure just in time to graduate
from Princeton. While the other graduates wore mortarboard
and black gowns, Lieutenant Stewart showed up in full uniform—and lots of medals!

(Years later, his son would perform the equivalent of the
Bunsen burner incident but without creating a fire hazard,
dumping an Oscar-winning, multi-million dollar career to serve
his country. But that heroic tale is approximately 50 pages and
25 years down the line.)

Dad earned a degree in civil engineering from Princeton, a
"gentleman's degree" which Alexander had no intention of
using. The hardware store was so prosperous that he immediately left New Jersey and returned to Indiana to milk the family's cash cow.

When World War I broke out, Alexander didn't let a little
thing like being over-the-hill stop him from signing up, and he

landed a captain's commission. One of Jimmy's profoundest childhood memories involved accompanying his mother to New York to see his father sail off to France from New York harbor. Just before Captain Stewart embarked, he took his son to hear the perpetrator of the war, President Woodrow Wilson, speak at Carnegie Hall. Sixty years later Jimmy would still speak with awe about the creator of the League of Nations, the 21st President of the United States. Could the 10-year-old have had some clairvoyant inkling that the next time he came in contact with a commander in chief, they'd be playing golf together in Beverly Hills?

Long before he hit the links with Richard M. Nixon, Jimmy had another close encounter of a more remote kind with a head of state. Actually, Wilson's successor, President Warren G. Harding, was dead by the time Jimmy came in contact with him. Sitting in his Beverly Hills mansion nearly 70 years after the event, the actor recalled the incident as though he had been teleported back to Indiana in 1923. That was the day the funeral train bearing President Harding's body passed through an intersection 20 miles from the Stewart home. Dad rousted Jimmy out of bed at 2:30 in the morning and told him to get dressed. Jimmy was 15, but he didn't argue with the old man. Soon they were driving to the train track crossing where the funeral cortege would pass. Alexander didn't even bother to wake his wife and two daughters; this was purely father-son bonding. And it worked. A lifetime later, Jimmy was able to describe in detail to a reporter from *Life* magazine exactly what happened.

By the time of his death, Warren Harding's administration had been disgraced by so many scandals he made Richard Nixon look like Honest Abe. If the 22nd President of the United States hadn't died of a heart attack during a cross-country whistle-stop tour in San Francisco, Harding almost certainly would have been impeached. But the man was a Republican, and so was Alexander Stewart, who wanted his son to witness the historic, if sad, passing of a disgraced politician. Only a few other die-hard fans of the luckless politician showed up at 2:30 in the morning to catch a glimpse of the dead president. Alexander, like his son the future actor, had a sense of drama and wanted to commemorate the event. He took out two shiny new pennies and handed them to the teenager. Jimmy recalled, "He said, 'Now, son, go over there and set them on the rails . . .' "

The funeral train passed by and left in its wake two pennies flattened like copper pancakes—defacing, by the way, a much more upstanding Republican, Abraham Lincoln. Alexander permitted this little act of desecration for the sake of memorializing the event. He kept one penny and gave Jimmy the other as a keepsake. Alexander called them "lucky pennies," although the event they commemorated, the death of a failed president, seemed anything but lucky. The imagery and the incident were so powerful they remained with the younger Stewart well into the 1960s, when he wrote this first-person account for *McCall's*.

"As we drove home, I examined [my penny] and found the Indian's features had been spread and the few feathers of his headdress had become a great plume. On the other side, the two slender stalks of wheat had grown and burst, as if the seed had ripened and scattered." At the age of 15, Jimmy had the eye and ear of a poet for imagery and metaphor. The penny was just one more tangible bond with his father. "For years, Dad and I carried those coins flattened by the *weight of history*. And the knowledge that what was in my pocket was also in his made me feel very close to him."

For the symbolically minded, the coins however might also suggest the prickly side of their relationship—literally. Besides creating an impressionistic Indian's head, the train's wheels also serrated the edge of the coin, which promptly sliced up Jimmy's pants pockets. After sanding down the rough edges, Stewart recalled, "I took it everywhere with me. And then one day I lost it. Couldn't find it. I looked all over the place. It was very upsetting. You see, that coin was a link with my dad during all the years we were away from each other, me out here, he back there in Pennsylvania running the hardware store."

The coins and their bonding effect may have ameliorated a bit of the guilt Jimmy felt for not joining his father in the family business as the fourth generation to sell nails and screws instead of celluloid dreams.

Jimmy reconnected, so to speak, after his father died in 1961, aged 89. Going through the old man's things in his desk at the store, he discovered that Alexander, unlike his forgetful son, had held on to *his* penny.

"After he died, I was at the store, just sort of sitting there, pulling out drawers and looking through old piles of receipts, and right in front of me, staring up at me, was my dad's penny. I let out a whoop." And promptly expropriated the legacy of a 15-year-old shivering in the early hours at a train track, bonding with his father.

Chapter 2
Life With Father

Jimmy Stewart had a complex relationship with his father, but not a troubled one.

The love his father felt for his son, in an era when men were told to be strong and silent and wear their emotions not on their sleeves but deep within their macho ids, was profound but not demonstrative. One of the most telling anecdotes Jimmy ever recounted about their relationship was casually mentioned in an aside about his experiences in World War II. In a letter from home, just before Capt. James Stewart flew his own plane to war-torn England, Alexander Stewart told his son that he loved him for the first time. Jimmy was 32 at the time.

While the elder Stewart was not demonstrative, he was far from being aloof. Like many masculine men in the pre-Alan Alda/Robert James Waller era, Alexander Stewart demonstrated his love through actions, not words.

In a movie magazine interview decades later, Jimmy hinted at his father's silent approbation. The female reporter asked the No. 1 box office star, "But your father's proud of you . . . ?" Even more haltingly than usual, Jimmy stammered, "Oh, I suppose so . . ."

Instead of hugs and hosannas, Alexander liked to stimulate

his son's imagination and never discouraged him from the most outlandish plans—invaluable personal tools for a man who would one day crack the toughest of professions, Hollywood stardom, and help bomb Nazi Germany into the Stone Age.

When Jimmy was 10, he announced he was going *alone* on safari to Africa. A less imaginative parent might have looked up from his newspaper and said, "Don't be ridiculous. Go outside and play ball." Instead, the senior Stewart threw himself into his son's impossible dream. Dad brought home steamship schedules so Jimmy could book passage to Africa. They poured over intoxicating brochures describing exotic safaris on the Dark Continent.

Just as he sent Jimmy gas masks and German helmets from France during World War I, Alexander wasn't above humoring his son's fancies to the point of over-indulgence. He took time off from running the hardware to store to help his son actually build reinforced cages for all the wildlife Jimmy planned to bring back alive from safari!

"When at the age of 10, I announced that I was going to Africa at the end of the school year to bring back wild animals, my mother and sisters pointed out my age and the problems of transportation and all such mundane and inconsequential facts.

"But not Dad. He entered right into the project, brought home books about Africa, train and boat schedules for us to study, knapsacks and water canteens and even some iron bars, which we used to build cages for the animals I was to bring back.

"As the day of departure approached, I was becoming a little apprehensive." His thoughtful father came up with a way for his son to back down without losing face as a great white hunter *manqué*.

Alexander showed him a newspaper story reporting a wreck on the railroad which was to take him to Baltimore en route to the savannahs of the Serengeti. "By the time the train tracks were repaired, he and I were off on some other project that seemed more exciting even than wild animals."

The 10-year-old great white hunter never went to the Dark

Continent during his childhood, but Africa in a way came to him. Jimmy's favorite annual holiday wasn't Christmas or Halloween, but the day every summer the circus came to Indiana, Pennsylvania. The mesmerized tyke would volunteer to help unload the animals. His favorite circus "stars" were the elephants, a love affair that would continue into adulthood when he could finally afford to go on countless safaris well into his 60s. Another employee of the circus, however, also had a long-lasting effect on the youth. To his delight, during the sad departure of the circus, one of the clowns left his accordion behind. Jimmy appropriated the instrument and taught himself to play it. To the dismay of high school, college, military, and movie colony friends as well as 1950s TV audiences, Jimmy would show that people are just as capable of having tin hands as they are tin ears.

Children have short attention spans, and Jimmy's ran out before his dad's. Soon the curious youngster had lost interest in tigers and lions and turned his mind to the new wonders of the age: aviation and a futuristic device called the wireless, which could actually transmit the human voice invisibly through the air to every home in America.

The future combat war hero built life-sized model planes and tried to fly them. In fact, when he was a little boy and ignorant of Newton's gravitational principles, he tried on a box kite and launched himself off the roof of his house. Fortunately for the future of cinema, Mr. Stewart happened to be passing by, and the 4-year-old aviator's crash was cushioned by his dad's body. (In *War and Peace,* another great imaginer, Leo Tolstoy, would confess in a footnote that as a child he too thought he could fly—without even bothering with a kite—and threw himself out of the second-story window of his aunt's mansion.)

At 11, Jimmy created mock radio sets out of oatmeal boxes and materials from the hardware store.

Again, Dad played muse—and bankroller—to his son's latest inspirations. Jimmy built airplane models and crystal sets, genuine proto-radios with a homemade antenna and wireless transmitter. The superbright child taught himself Morse code so he could decipher news broadcasts from nearby Arlington, Pennsylvania. (In its infancy, Marconi's invention could only transmit Morse code. Years later it would graduate to human voices and Hootie and the Blowfish.)

Alexander Stewart may not have been emotionally demonstrative, but when it came to indulging Jimmy's every wish, his behavior verged on spoiling his only son. "The Stewart family was knit close," a family friend recalled years later. "It was pretty apparent to everyone in town that they all liked each other. However, I think that Mr. Stewart was slightly partial to his son."

When he was 12, Jimmy strong-armed his dad into buying a rare, very expensive Magnavox radio, the first in their hometown. Anticipating the keen interest he would show in politics as an adult, Jimmy lusted after the radio—not to catch Rudy Vallee croon over the airwaves, but to hear the first broadcast of the Presidential election returns on Pittsburgh's KDKA station. The future Beverly Hills Republican would hear the announcement that Warren G. Harding, also a Republican, had beaten Democrat Al Smith.

Alexander and Jimmy complemented one another, but they didn't mirror each other by any stretch of the imagination. In a fatuous comparison in the *Saturday Evening Post* in 1951, a journalist correctly wrote that "you have to understand Alexander Stewart to understand his son." But not in the way the *Post* writer went on to explain: both men had a "slow, solidly American way of sorting their thoughts out mentally before spilling them verbally. [These traits] are part and parcel of the personalities of both Stewarts, father and son."

In 1951, Alexander Stewart would have another 10 years to live, but obviously the *Post* reporter never met the man. He was accurate in describing the son as "slow . . . to sort out" his thoughts "before mentally spilling them verbally." By 1951, James Stewart had become an American icon and the richest man in Hollywood, in part because of his endearing tortoise vs. the hare approach to acting.

Alexander Stewart, however, was the antithesis of his son.

Where Jimmy was reticent and shy, foolish Alexander didn't hesitate a second to rush in where wiser angels feared to tread.

A resident of the Stewarts' hometown with no ax to grind would tell a magazine reporter, "Jimmy's father was basically a loudmouth. He shot from the hip and asked questions later. When he had an opinion, he didn't hesitate to share it with anyone who would listen and even with a lot of people who really didn't care to. He was the richest man in town, and his opinion carried considerable weight, regardless of its intrinsic merits." And this man described himself as "a friend" of the elder Stewart. The image that emerges is of a lovable blowhard whose kind heart made up for a lot of gale-force windiness.

The soft-spoken younger Stewart didn't inherit his father's bombast, but he did absorb a much more helpful personality trait: a work ethic that penetrated to the bone. "My dad went to work every day until he was eighty-eight," Jimmy would later proudly say, failing to add that his father spent a grand total of one year in retirement before he died at age 89. "My father taught me that. I believe there's no substitute for hard work. I sort of tried to follow in his footsteps in that respect."

In a nostalgia-drenched interview with *Parade* magazine in 1984, Alexander's son basically said he owed everything to his dad: "The biggest influence on my life was my father. I tried to take after my father in what he believed in." Family friends, however, said that physically and emotionally Jimmy much more resembled his mother. He even inherited her stammer, which would become his iconic trademark on the world scene. Dad never met a verb or a noun he didn't like, in the words of another "family friend."

Still, as much as he differed from his father externally, internally they were soulmates: "I was very close to him, and I don't think I've ever made an important decision in my life without thinking about how he made *his* decisions: Decisions about school, work, the importance of church and values, even my decision about going into the Army."

Typically, Jimmy wasn't about to stiff his mother's contribution in this newspaper *bildungsroman,* even though Elizabeth Ruth Jackson Stewart had been dead for 11 years when he went on the record with his version of *I Remember Mama*. While the Stewart side of the family represented three generations of mercantile wealth, his mother's family were American aristocrats, charter members of the Gilded Age of Whitneys and Vanderbilts. Jimmy's maternal grandfather was S.M. Jackson, the state treasurer of Pennsylvania and founder of the Apollo Steel and Apollo Trust Companies. (An article in *Life* in 1945 desperately tried to shoehorn the real Jimmy into his screen personae: "Jimmy Stewart's background is as typically American as his appearance."

Of his aristocratic mother's influence, Jimmy said, ". . . my mother was just as important in her way—to me and my [two] sisters too. She stopped Dad from being *overboisterous*. She was the only person he would listen to about anything. And there were times when we kids sure appreciated that. He would raise his voice about pretty nearly anything—*but never to her.*"

While Mom was riding herd on her loudmouth husband, Dad was making sure his son learned lessons that would prevent him from ever leading the life an idle playboy, a role Jimmy could have luxuriated in with trust funds from his mother's side of the family.

As a very old man, Jimmy dredged up Proustian remembrances of the hardware store's past. The madeleines baked by Proust's aunt had nothing on the pungent aromas that emanated from the J.M. Stewart & Co. "The pervading smells of my childhood were metal, leather, oil, and fertilizers. I always felt my dad had the hankering for me to go into the store with him, but he also knew that wasn't the way to raise kids. When I was young, I wanted to hang around the store just to be with him." (And absorb all those earthy scents.) Hard work was part of the family credo. Nepotism was not. "He wouldn't let me do that, though, when I got older. He made me get out and get a job—and get it on my own."

One summer Jimmy had a godawful sounding—and dangerous—job with the State of Pennsylvania Highway Department, painting white lines down the middle of the road.

For another job, his father broke the rule on nepotism and asked his good friend, Sam Gallo, owner of the local movie theater, to give his son a job as projectionist. This may have been the beginning of Jimmy's lifelong love affair with the movies, but his incompetence as a projectionist was not an auspicious indicator of his future success in the medium.

In the silent era, the movie projector was cranked by hand—in this case Jimmy's. The projectionist had to do double duty as "colorist." Color of sorts was added to the black and white footage by inserting tinted gels in front of the projector's lens. Barely visible marks on the film indicated which color and when the gels were to be inserted. Jimmy, however, became so engrossed in one epic, *20,000 Leagues Under the Sea,* he "missed his marks" and forgot to change the gel. The black inky underwater lair of the giant octopus was bright green "for an awful long time," Jimmy remembered.

One summer Jimmy loaded bricks for a construction company. Unlike his dreamy projectionist job, he took this blue-collar task as seriously as he would later attack a major film role. Addie Ross, his next-door neighbor, said, "Like everything else he did, he gave those jobs all his energy, never went to work halfway," except perhaps when he was mesmerized by the image of the screen, a fascination that would last the rest of his life. The neighbor praised the well-behaved youth for never missing a church service, which he attended with his mother, the congregation's organist, and his father, who sang—loudly and badly—in the choir. "Jimmy was always the most steadfast boy I've ever known, as well as being the most unpretentious. He must have gotten his modesty from his mother. Alex certainly didn't have any to spare." Addie Ross may have had a crystal ball. Years later some of the biggest barracudas in Hollywood would use the same terms, modesty and unpretentiousness, to describe the personality he inherited from mom.

Jimmy was so square, he stayed in the Boy Scouts well into high school, when membership was considered kids' stuff. On top of that, in his estimation, he made one lousy scout. "I was in Boy Scout Troop 3 in Indiana. I couldn't get past second class scout because I had to take the swimming test. Part of the test was saving another boy in the water. I never could do that. I'd go in to save the other guy and then somebody would have to come in and save me.'' Jimmy, the hopeless swimmer, would get to live out a Walter Mitty fantasy years later in *It's a Wonderful Life,* when he saved his on-screen brother from drowning in a frozen pond.

His career in the Boy Scouts wasn't all outtakes from a particularly nerdy Woody Allen movie. The proto-actor was popular with his fellow scouts because he was a master magician who had all the ham necessary to make such hoary tricks as sawing a woman in half seem fresh and exciting.

While his father's work ethic was an invaluable legacy that would keep the workaholic actor busy on movie and TV sets well into his 80s, Alexander's implied criticism in another area left Jimmy with a sense of inadequacy that would haunt him almost as long.

Jimmy Stewart was a classic ectomorph all his life. There are three basic body types, although no one is purely one or another but rather a combination of two. Lucky mesomorphs are typically athletes with naturally broad shoulders and narrow waists and hips. Any Calvin Klein model is a good template of this body type. The poor endomorph is pear-shaped with narrow shoulders, a thick waist, and even broader hips, forever condemned to the ''before'' picture in the diet ads. Alfred Hitchcock's famous TV profile was an endomorph in a nutshell—or bushel.

Kate Moss and George Bush are ectomorphs. So was Jimmy Stewart. They have narrow everything—shoulders, waists, hips. Their limbs are long and stubbornly resistant to any assaults by barbells and dumbbells.

Alexander was more than stubborn about accepting his son's body type. On a return trip home after World War II, Jimmy would look outside at the sunporch with a mixture of fondness and inadequacy. There was his beloved toy train set, bought by his father in an antique shop a quarter century earlier. Right next to this fabulous toy was an unpleasant reminder that Jimmy was and would always be an under-muscled beanpole: at the same time dad bought the train set, he had also bought his son a set of weights. ''My father gave me the weights years ago,'' he told a reporter from *Life* magazine shortly after the war.

Although his skinny chest could have been pumped up with enough military decorations to give him fake pecs, Jimmy sheepishly added, "He's always been worried about this lanky body of mind and figured that a little exercise would add some pounds to it." A few years later, gossip columnist Hedda Hopper would visit Stewart's bachelor pad in Brentwood, California, and note a similar set of weights on Jimmy's back porch. Hedda: "So are you exercising?" Jimmy: "No, to be truthful about it I never lifted a weight." So what were the barbells doing out back? Jimmy explained that his father was coming for a visit, and the then 40-year-old superstar had remained intimidated enough by Alexander's opinion of his body that he wanted the old man to think he was still working out!

Decades before eating disorders would become the daily diet of Oprah and Ricki's talk shows, Jimmy Stewart would suffer from what psychologists call a "dysmorphic body image." But unlike anorexics who look in the mirror and see fat where others see skeleton, there was some justification to Jimmy's feelings of physical inadequacy. And it wasn't just Dad telling him to pump it up. At several points in his adult life, his scarecrow physique would cause serious career problems.

Maybe Alexander wasn't being insensitive by pushing weight training on his son. Maybe he was actually prescient and foresaw all the havoc Jimmy's skeletal silhouette would wreak in war and peace, on screen and off.

Jimmy never really did pump up, but he didn't give up either. The 125-pound weakling even managed to shine as a "miniature" athlete at prep school. How Jimmy gained admission to this tony prep school is typical of the elder Stewart's "Mama Rose" approach to anything his son ever did, whether it was enrolling in a boarding school with no openings or getting a role in a movie over the objections of a producer and director. When it came to pushing his son's career, Gypsy Rose Lee's mama had nothing on Alexander Stewart.

Chapter 3
Lightweight Preppie

After ninth grade, Alexander decided it was worth parting from his only son in order to assure him a top-notch education. He, of course, decided what was top-notch—an ultra-exclusive institution called Mercersburg Academy in their home state. The school had impeccable academic credentials. Graduation from it assured entrance into the Ivy League college of your choice. Even more important, it was a rock-ribbed Presbyterian school with church services several times a week.

There was only one problem: the sophomore class was already filled. The dean of students didn't stand a chance against the proprietor of the J.M. Stewart Hardware Store. "They should have known better," recalled Bill Hastings, a reporter for the *Indiana Evening Gazette*. "Once Alex made up his mind about something, there was no way of stopping him. Nobody but nobody dared to contradict him."

One of the greatest ironies of the younger Stewart's life was that he was infinitely more successful than his father in every arena, and yet Jimmy was about as pushy as a marshmallow. A friend would later speculate on Jimmy's amazing success in spite of his passivity. "He'd just 'aw-shucks' you to death until you gave in. It was actually more effective than Alex screaming at you, and a lot easier on the ear."

A classmate from those days remembered both Jimmy's tentativeness and his tenacity once he made up his mind to do something, even if it meant flying in the face of reason and a scary line of fullbacks. "I'm sure he enjoyed his stay," Steven Brown said in *Everybody's Man*. "He was pretty easygoing, much like he is today. However, his speaking style was even slower than it is now, if you can possibly imagine that. I remember when he tried out for varsity football . . . Why, it seemed that he didn't have strength enough to even finish a sentence, let alone charge a line. In his embarrassed, hesitating way, he asked, 'Is . . . this . . . the . . . place . . . a . . . fella . . . gets . . . picked . . . for . . . the . . . football squad?'" The coach laughed in his face, but then kindly recommended something called "lightweight football," where the halfbacks averaged 120 pounds soaking wet. Even with that kind of diminutive competition, Jimmy was picked to play a position with the least physical contact: center. "We nicknamed him 'Elmer' because of his gawky, small-town qualities," Brown said.

In an in-house newsletter published by MCA-Univeral in 1985, the studio went out of its way to flatter Stewart in an interview. He had generously agreed to go on a world-wide tour (at the age of 77) to promote the studio's video release of some of his 30-year-old classics. In an orgy of flackery, the newsletter claimed that the prep school boy also "ran track, excelled in high hurdles and the high jump." This Jack Armstrong-type extra curriculum never occurred, but the man who claimed to have two left feet was too polite to correct his idolator-interviewer. The newsletter was correct when it said young Stewart drew cartoons for the school yearbook. Jimmy loved to draw, a talent which would serve him well when he chose his college major—or rather, it chose him.

Collier's magazine in 1947 offered a more accurate and less flattering résumé of Jimmy's high school years. The magazine mentioned that Jimmy was a slow reader. In those pre-psychobabble days, the terms dyslexia and learning disorder hadn't even entered the public consciousness, much less the

DSM-IV. Whatever the reason, the magazine made it clear that James Stewart was no scholar. In fact, it insisted that he "only graduated because a Latin teacher had a kind heart and was fond of Jimmy." Jimmy sang in the Glee Club and had a bit part in the senior class play about the French Revolution, called *The Wolves.* For some reason, the teenager wore a beard in the production despite the fact that men were clean-shaven during the so-called Enlightenment. He held on to the beard to play Lincoln in another Mercersburg production.

The shabby academic record rings true. In those days, all movie magazines were fanzines. There were no tabloids to unmask rock stars who shoot smack while pregnant. *Confidential* hadn't even been born, much less sued out of existence. And the *National Enquirer* empire was merely a dream for a police reporter named Pope.

Plus, Jimmy's college career was a near replay of prep school, a rerun whose ending was reshot on an upbeat note.

As for *Hard Copy*-type exposés of his academic weaknesses, Jimmy was harder on himself than any reporter.

"I wasn't that smart," he told Hedda Hopper point-blank in 1956. (Hedda, one of the meanest *gossips* in Hollywood, wasn't making this up. She adored Jimmy and probably quoted him only with great reluctance.) "I came near to flunking out of every school I was ever sent to. I had a terrible time with my studies and had to go to summer school the first year [after college]. I barely skimmed through . . . I tried everything, but I couldn't find anything easy enough."

Chapter 4
Rich Legacy

Jimmy's matriculation at Princeton speaks volumes about his relationship with his father and the family's status.

In his typically self-effacing way, Stewart always called the family business a "hardware" store. But from other descriptions and photos of the place, it sounds more like a full-service department store, a solely owned Wal-Mart that sold everything from shotguns to pocket knives, pots and pans to major appliances like stoves and iceboxes.

Whatever it was, it was certainly more prosperous than the cash-strapped savings and loan Jimmy ran in *It's a Wonderful Life*.

At least half a century old by the time Jimmy was born, the J.M. Stewart Hardware Co. of Indiana, Pennsylvania, on Philadelphia Street, founded by Jimmy's namesake, James Maitland Stewart, was a cash cow. It financed both Alexander Stewart's and Jimmy's education at Princeton.

When Jimmy attended the prestigious Ivy League institution in the late 1920s and the early years of the Depression (Princeton B.S. 1932), tuition and board hovered around two grand a year. That was an enormous outlay at a time when the average salary in the U.S. was $15 *a week*.

Despite the modesty and unpretentiousness that characterized his entire life, James Maitland Stewart II, prep school and Ivy League graduate, grew up rich.

How did such a dim-witted (in his own words) student gain admission to such an academically rigorous institution? He was what all exclusive colleges call a "legacy," a euphemism for the fact that his old man went there. Even today, many "legacies" are admitted over much more qualified persons. JFK, for instance, got into Harvard even though he was a C student. Same for FDR. JFK, Jr. was apparently such an academic washout that even his illustrious pedigree kept him out of Harvard and he had to settle for Brown.

Jimmy didn't want to pull strings to be admitted to Princeton. He didn't even want to go there. His first choice was the Naval Academy at Annapolis. Jimmy had dreams of someday becoming a military man, which he would finally do, despite his father's best efforts at academic meddling.

And while his father might be content to gently teach him lessons about being kind to killer dogs, when it came to his son's college career, Alexander became a pit bull.

Every biographer and magazine writer reported that the elder Stewart dragooned Jimmy into his alma mater.

Forty years after the fact, Jimmy wasn't averse to a little mythologizing about his father's "influence" on his college choice. In a first-person account in the early 1960s in *McCall's,* Jimmy offered this revisionist history:

Alexander Stewart's "oblique way of influencing me was demonstrated when it came time to go to college. Dad had graduated from Princeton, and it was his passionate hope that I would follow him there, *though he never said a word of this to me.*

"What he did do, however, was to make out my itinerary when it came time for me to visit the various deans of admission. (Shades of their imaginary safari when Jimmy was 10. Although this time the trip [to Princeton] would actually take place). I visited, in order, the University of Pennsylvania, Yale, Harvard, and finally Princeton. I came home with the freshest, strongest impressions of Princeton, *and that became my choice.*"

Years later, after Alexander's death, Jimmy, forgetting this doublethink, would tell a reporter, "I wanted to go to Annapolis. Dad wanted me to go to Princeton. I went to Princeton."

Despite an academic career that started out rocky, Jimmy at least behaved himself on campus. True to form, the elder Stewart had been just as bombastic in college as he was on Philadelphia Street.

Stewart recalled that as soon as he arrived at Princeton, the headmaster of his dormitory came up to him and said, "My father knew your father, and I'm keeping my eye on you!"

The headmaster was justified in his surveillance. Jimmy later learned, from college folklore that happened to be fact, not myth, that his father had played what today might be called the John Belushi role in *Animal House*.

In his magazine memoir, Jimmy was much too diplomatic even to imply that Dad's pranks were probably fueled by alcohol. In one of his pranks, as part of a venerable if inexplicable tradition, Dad and a few other undergraduates dragged a cow to the top of Nassau Hill. What they did with the animal once they hauled her up there, Jimmy left to the reader's imagination.

The closest—and it wasn't very close at all—Alexander's excruciatingly polite son came to late night cow-herding was to appear in a class play . . . in drag!

Shy, reticent Jimmy had somehow wangled his way into the Triangle Club, one of Princeton's most prestigious "eating clubs," an Ivy League term for fraternity. The Triangle was actually an association of WASP student actors. Jews and Catholics need not apply, as Jack and Bobby Kennedy—not to mention Grace Kelly's father—would discover when they failed to be invited into similar clubs at Harvard.

In one Triangle production, Jimmy showed early star power—and that was the opinion of a professional. Billy Grady, a talent scout for MGM in Hollywood, somehow caught a 1932 production at Princeton which featured Jimmy Stewart. Grady, who later became Stewart's unofficial Boswell, wrote in his diary at the time, "In that college show, he was one of a dozen guys dressed up to look like dames. But he was the only one of those Ivy League female impersonators *who didn't ham it up*. His restraint made him a standout.'' Even as a drag queen, Jimmy had intuited that less is always more, even when you're wearing a banana curl wig, hoop skirt, and way too much mascara.

There's no extant record of what Alexander thought of his son as a transvestite, but he couldn't have been pleased with his son's academic career at his alma mater. It's one thing to commit unnatural acts with a cow on a hilltop; it's quite another to flunk out.

Jimmy matriculated at Princeton with the intention of becoming a civil engineer, a nice practical degree, which he would never need to use because it seemed logical that Alexander's son would be the third-generation Stewart to run the family enterprise. A college degree was simply something a gentleman acquired, along with membership in the country club and a wife from an equally prominent family.

Algebra almost ''finished'' Jimmy off.

''College algebra was a killer for me. A professor friend of my father's told him, 'I've done everything but rewrite his exams. He can't spell. He's flunking his first year.' ''

The discouraging advice began almost immediately. Before the end of the first semester, a teacher summoned Jimmy to his office and said, ''Look here, old man, let's not fool ourselves. Frankly, do you think you have the slightest aptitude for mathematics?''

Another instructor, not a friend of his father's, was even blunter: ''Stewart, you do not have the slightest aptitude for engineering. I strongly suggest that you try something else.'' And yet another teacher said, ''Get out of engineering or get out of this school!'' Jimmy briefly switched majors to political science, but found he was as hopeless with Plato as he was with Pythagoras. In 1947, *Collier's* magazine hinted that the young man may have had a learning disability noting that Jimmy was an extremely ''slow reader, generally three books behind in his class.''

Jimmy's daughter doubted that her father ever suffered from a learning disorder, and she also denied the existence of his signature style of speech which has been engraved if not in stone, at least transferred to video. "I do not think that Dad ever had a stammer or a speech impediment, and he never struck me as having dyslexia," Kelly Stewart Harcourt told me.

A devout disciple of the Protestant Ethic, Stewart couldn't possibly have been goofing off instead of catching up on the syllabus. No doubt he devoted more time to reading than his dormmates, but some learning impediment slowed him down. It's almost as though he suffered from the visual equivalent of his verbal impediment, the stammer that would help make him a movie icon.

Alexander Stewart, who had been so wise and patient about the dog and the safari, was not at all understanding about an 18-year-old dunce. "My father was going to shoot me," Stewart recalls. "Then I took descriptive geometry—and liked it. I found it qualified me to become an architect. So I ended up studying architecture. But I was sure I would be going back to work in my father's hardware store after Princeton." Just like George Bailey, who took over the family business after his father died in *It's a Wonderful Life*.

Jimmy discovered he had a natural ability to draw. Unlike the professors who chased him out of the math building, several teachers praised his drawing ability. But rather than choose an impractical degree like art, or, God forbid, art history, which would have put Dad on the first train to New Jersey armed with a shotgun, Jimmy chose a practical outlet for his artistic bent: drawing pictures of buildings.

With the same work ethic he applied to painting white lines on highways and loading bricks, Jimmy decided to become the greatest architect who ever lived. Actually, the second greatest. "After several nights of hard thinking, I resolved to become a second Frank Lloyd Wright. It turned out to be a wise move. I liked it and began to study. My grades improved. I felt better all over. Even started taking an interest in the way I looked, matching socks and shoes *without holes.*"

Jimmy truly took his architectural studies seriously, as his skyrocketing grades showed. After graduation in 1932 he won the D'Amato architecture scholarship to study for a master's degree. But he was no grind. He found plenty of time to become if not the Big Man on Campus, one of the most liked.

The most liked *most* of the time. The klutzy undergrad didn't even bother to try out for the basketball team despite his 6'4" height. But he threw himself into the pep squad as a cheerleader. There, his self-admitted two left feet tripped him up. Every time he led the squad, the football team lost. It was no doubt pure coincidence, but the alumni weren't taking any chances. They first blamed the losing record on the cheerleaders' lack of motivational skills: you had to juice the fans in the stands before you could goose the players on the field. So Princeton hired a professional cheerleading coach from New York to shake up the pep squad and teach them the latest cheers. Jimmy, the most popular guy on the squad, was chosen to introduce the whiz kid from New York at a big rally. When the moment came, the future actor forgot his lines—actually, he even forgot the expert's name. Soon, Princeton was blaming the football follies on Stewart himself, and he was quietly asked to ''resign'' from the squad.

He immediately found a more nurturing campus group, which would also have a profound effect on the rest of his life and career.

Chapter 5

Mr. Stewart Goes to Princeton

Instead of a teddy bear, like *Brideshead Revisited*'s Sebastian, Jimmy took with him to Princeton the accordion abandoned by the circus clown years earlier. A fellow undergrad and future Broadway and film director, Joshua Logan, *(Camelot)* asked him to join the college's prestigious acting troupe, the Triangle Club.

It had been founded in 1881 by Booth Tarkington, the best-selling novelist whose characters would often be compared to Jimmy's boyhood.

Logan must have seen something in the gangly six-footer who couldn't even lead a football cheer properly without tripping over his feet. With typical self-deprecation, Jimmy insisted there was nothing special about his acting. "When I went down to audition, I was dressed in a devil's costume complete with a long tail," he recalled in *Everybody's Man,* Jhan Robbins' oral history. "I wore a mask and blew on a tin horn. The director kept shouting, 'Louder! And with more emtion!' It was real bedlam. I'm sure the reason I was selected was because they were hard up for talent." (Twenty years later he would explain his Oscar by suggesting the Academy felt sorry for him!)

In 1984, Dr. Lila Cavanaugh recalled the then unknown's performance even though she was only 13 at the time. "Jimmy sang and danced," the Boston pediatrician is quoted in Robbins' biography.

"The reason I particularly remembered him so vividly was because he appeared to be having such a good time while everyone else was trying too hard." (Shades of MGM scout Billy Grady, who would similarly comment on what a restrained drag queen Jimmy was.) "After the performance, I went backstage to see my brother, who was also in the play. He introduced me to Jimmy. I complimented him on his dancing.

" 'That's good to hear,' he said. 'My mother keeps telling me that I have two left feet. I can't wait to tell her what you just said.' " More likely, Jimmy couldn't wait to relay this "rave review" to his father.

Earning good enough grades to get the D'Amato architecture scholarship to grad school, the tireless student still found time to appear in three plays with the campus troupe: *The Golden Dog, Spanish Blades,* and *The Tiger Smiles,* all now happily lost to theatrical history.

Stewart also appeared in several plays written by Logan. The late director remembered that "Stewart genuinely liked being on stage, but it took him a long time to admit it. I finally asked him if he had ever thought about becoming an actor. 'Good God, no!' he shouted. 'I'm going to be an architect!' Well, he not only got a B.A. when he graduated, but an A.B.—Acting Bug."

At the time, Stewart insists he had yet to be infected with the acting virus. "I had never seriously considered becoming an actor even up to that day I walked across campus en route to get my degree in architecture. I figured I'd go home in the summer and work in my father's hardware store. Then go back to school and get my master's degree. That's when I ran into Josh. I suppose it was the most important moment in my life."

Stewart could easily have returned to Princeton in the fall for postgraduate work. It was the depths of the Depression, but Dad could afford it. Plus he had a scholarship, just in case his mercurial father suddenly gave up on higher education and

ordered him to report for work behind the counter. But before
returning for the fall quarter and graduate school, Logan invited
Jimmy to spend the summer with the University Players, a
group of novice actors that included a fellow named Henry
Fonda. Like New Haven, Connecticut, Falmouth, Massachusetts, on Cape Cod was used for Broadway tryouts—opening
out of town, as they still call it. Logan asked his fellow alum,
"Why don't you come up to the theater for a few weeks this
summer, bring your accordion and play in the tearoom?"

Rather than return to the hardware store for the summer
before starting grad school, Stewart had unsuccessfully tried
to find a summer job near the campus. It was the summer
of 1932, prosperity was nowhere around the corner, despite
President Hoover's insane optimism, and Jimmy found himself
unemployed. It was either tread the boards or hustle screws in
the family hardware store.

At this point, Jimmy made it clear he had no plans for "life
upon the wicked stage."

"I figured there wouldn't be any harm in playing around in
Falmouth for a summer before I started selling nails for life,"
he said years later.

The troupe played guinea pigs for Broadway in a small
theater in Falmouth. Logan must have regretted inviting Jimmy
to play the accordion in the theater's restaurant, the portentous-
sounding Falmouth Old South Silver Black Tea Room.

In his typically self-deprecating way, Stewart told *Vogue*
magazine in 1989, "After two nights playing accordion in the
tearoom, they asked me to stop. They told me my playing
spoiled their appetites." As the years went by, Stewart's vivid
imagination embroidered his awfulness and eventually he
would remember dinner patrons literally "running to the bathroom to be sick."

Jimmy may have been discouraged about his future as a
concert accordionist, but he felt sure he had found his niche in
the theater world. "By then I was with so many great people,
Hank Fonda, Margaret Sullavan, Mildred Natwick."

These were friendships of a lifetime. And more. Fonda would
remain his best of best friends until the actor's death in 1982.

And Sullavan almost became Mrs. James Stewart. At Princeton, Sullavan said, "Jimmy is a Booth Tarkington boy who just never grew up." Fonda remembered their first meeting in 1931, backstage at a Princeton production during Christmas week. Fonda, an aspiring actor, went backstage with Logan—Fonda to congratulate Jimmy on his performance, Logan to offer him a summer job on Cape Cod. Three decades later, Fonda recalled that fateful meeting. "Jimmy took the job figuring he'd go back to Indiana, Pennsylvania, and be an architect. Then he got an offer to [work in] New York and took it, figuring he'd go back home afterwards. He kept getting part after part until finally he decided he was never going back home."

After the accordion fiasco, the niche Jimmy found was sweeping floors, hauling props, and striking the sets. Eventually, he was promoted to designing them. Jimmy found his knowledge of architecture invaluable in his new avocation. In fact, New York columnist Ed Sullivan in 1940 said Stewart might have remained a set designer if the Falmouth troupe hadn't needed actors for bit parts.

His father was horrified when he told him he had decided to stay with the University Players, neither earning a postgraduate degree nor returning to help with the family business. It was 1932 and much of America was living real life scenes out of a future best-seller and screen classic, *The Grapes of Wrath*. Displaying the wisdom that went all the way back to Jimmy's murderous "dog days," Stewart Sr. realized his son would never find work as an architect during the construction bust of the Great Depression. Better an employed actor than an unemployed architect.

In fact, his father tried to find consolation by climbing way out on a limb of the family tree in order to convince himself that somehow Jimmy was actually following a Stewart tradition. When Jimmy broke the bad news to his father, "after the initial jolt he recalled that they had had a fourth or fifth cousin in vaudeville, sighed deeply and supposed it was all right," according to a 1947 *Collier's* interview. Or maybe the ever-optimistic elder Stewart hoped that the 22-year-old's acting aspirations were comparable to his safari plans when he was

10: something he'd eventually forget about and go on to other things, like the nuts and bolts of the family business.

Worse than Jimmy giving up his academic career, Alexander must have mourned the loss of his son as a partner in the family hardware store. A devoted son, Jimmy probably felt even more remorse than his father felt regret.

When Freud saw the stern visage of Michelangelo's Moses in the Vatican, seemingly staring right at him, the tourist from Vienna literally fainted from guilt at having abandoned his father's (Moses's) faith to create a secular religion called psychoanalysis. Similarly, looking through a yearbook from his father's college era, Jimmy found photos of his dad that seemed to haunt and scold him.

Jimmy was not the hysteric Freud could sometimes be. In a first-person account in *Collier's* in 1961, he stopped short of fainting when his father peered back at him from the yellowing pages of the yearbook, but the way he described his *angst* nearly half a century later suggested that Freud had no monopoly on guilt when it came to dumping dad's *weltanschauung*. Jimmy said, "As . . . I looked at his undergraduate pictures, his square young face both pugnacious and gay, full of thirst for adventure, I realized what it had cost him to return to the family hardware store in a prosaic little town. What had made him do it?

"I thought I knew.

"A great part of my father was the swashbuckling soldier of fortune; but there was a quieter and deeper strain, his desire for fatherhood. When he decided that these two sides of his nature were generally incompatible, he chose the second. I don't think he ever regretted his decision; certainly, he invested his fatherhood with all the excitement that was in him. Just to be near him turned ordinary events into adventure."

So back in "prosaic" Indiana, Pennsylvania, when his 10-year-old son wanted to go on safari alone, dad vicariously enjoyed the thrill of planning an itinerary neither he nor his 10-year-old would ever take. When Jimmy wanted to be the first kid on the block to hear the Presidential election returns of 1920 on radio, dad, remembering the life of adventure he had forsworn for family, coughed up the cash for another vicarious thrill.

Since by becoming an actor, Jimmy felt he had chosen "adventure" over family, he may have unconsciously punished himself, denying himself the pleasures of fatherhood until his 40s. In fact, decades later, he would deal with this issue on a Hollywood soundstage in *It's a Wonderful Life*. His character would make just the opposite career choice from the one Jimmy chose after Princeton. Maybe that's why Stewart played the role with such deep-felt conviction—enough to win him his fourth Oscar nomination. On screen, at least, he could expiate the "sin" he must have felt in abandoning the family business and deeply disappointing his dad.

Losing his son as a business partner was bad enough, but his choice of alternative career was downright embarrassing, in Alexander's set of values. Jimmy felt his father "could never bring himself to look upon acting as fit work for a grown-up man" even if a distant relative had also trod the boards. Acting was something you did in drag for college theatricals. The theater and magic of Hollywood had obviously not yet invaded the collective unconscious of Indiana, Pennsylvania—at least not the consciousness of the town's prime purveyor of nuts and bolts.

While his father was too psychologically astute to guilt-trip his son for rejecting the famliy business, he wasn't above eliciting a subtle twinge of remorse.

A notoriously soft touch, Alexander allowed the town drunk—basically a homeless man—to warm himself by the pot-belly stove in the corner of the hardware store during the harsh Pennsylvania winters. Years later, when James Stewart was an Oscar-winner and No. 1 box office star, tourists would visit the store the way they flock to James Dean's Indiana home today. When sightseers asked to meet the father of the "great man," his dad would point to the drunk nodding off at the stove, reeking of whiskey and say, "There's Jimmy Stewart's father. A very sad case. We try not to disturb him." His father knew these incidents would be picked up by the wire services, and his son would be sure to read about them all the way out there in Hollywood.

While Jimmy regretted disappointing his father, he didn't feel an ounce of loss about abandoning a promising career as a designer of buildings. He would create fantasies on the flimsiest of material—a form of acetate called celluloid—instead of concrete shrines to man's need to dominate the skyline. Still, his college major was an enriching experience that he never regretted even though he never made a living at it. Like an art history major who ends up selling insurance but uses his formal education to enhance visits to the local museum, Jimmy declared himself an amateur expert on the building boom that exploded in post-Depression, post-World War II Los Angeles. When Hedda Hopper asked him if he had any regrets about forsaking the fruits of his college education, Jimmy insisted he felt none. "No, but it certainly made me a critic of architecture. I have something to say about every building that goes up in California." That included the home he would live in for 44 years, which he described as belonging to the famous school of "plain Mediterranean Ugly."

Chapter 6

From Cape Cod to the Great White Way

"Jimmy Stewart lived a life that, in many ways, never had to break a sweat. He didn't ride waves all the way, he rode ripples. The way the Indiana string bean of our celluloid affections got into acting seems pretty much the way he got into everything else: right place, right time. Serendipity hitched to good looks and natural charm."
—*Life*, July 1991

A more fatuous analysis of Jimmy Stewart's career and work habits was perhaps never written. And the *Life* piece was supposed to be hagiography at the end of a sterling career. Instead, the magazine, a member of the Time-Warner family that puts out *People* and *Entertainment Weekly* anti-fanzines, implied that one of the greatest careers in film history was due to pure dumb luck that was probably also blind.

Nothing came easily to Jimmy Stewart. Not college, not "heavyweight" football, not even participation in the Boy Scouts. When his accordion playing made restaurant patrons scream "Ptomaine!" he did grunt work like hauling props and striking sets post-production.

A close friend who knew him much better than the *Life*

magazine reporter would say in 1956, "Don't think Jimmy just saunters through life. The truth is he works like a drayhorse over each job."

And no one ever handed him stardom on stage or screen on a silver platter. To beat a metaphor to death, stardom was more a life-preserver that Jimmy snatched at only after every other drowning actor had been safely rescued.

His first "starring" role with the University Players consisted of a whopping three lines. After literally sweeping floors on stage (so much for never "breaking a sweat"), his good friend Logan threw him a bone, a three-line walk-on as a chauffeur in *Goodbye Again*. Still, he remained forever grateful for the bone. "If it weren't for Josh Logan," he said years later, "I would have never become an actor."

In his comedy debut, "I was on stage for two minutes and forty seconds in the first act, but I always came out for the curtain call. I could hear the audience whisper, 'Who's that?' "

Goodbye Again earned rave reviews in its out-of-town tryout in Massachusetts. Coasting on its success, the comedy first moved to Off-Broadway and then to Broadway. James Maitland Stewart II, Princeton 1932, and his three lines went with the play to New York City.

By the time he got to the Great White Way, his role had been expanded to eight lines. They were enough to attract some ink from a reporter for the *New York Sun:* "It seems à propos to say a few words about James Stewart, who is on stage about three minutes and speaks no more than eight lines. Yet before this gentleman (even back then, as an unknown!) exits, he makes a definite impression on audiences because be makes them laugh so hard."

That was probably his first review as a professional, and the encomium stuck with him so firmly that at age 76, he remembered not only the rave, but the lines that earned it for him. And for once, Jimmy wasn't modest about his accomplishment.

"I remember that I was nearly two years in a play where I only had two lines. *Goodbye Again*. I played a chauffeur. I had to bring a book into the living room of a famous author and give it to the author's butler. My first line was, 'Mrs. Belle

Irving would sure appreciate it if she could have this book autographed.'

"My second line was when the butler brought me back the book and said the author couldn't do it—he was too busy. 'Mrs. Belle Irving,' I said, 'is going to be sore as hell.' That was all there was to the whole part, and I got the best mileage out of it I could. But every night, for two years.''

Like a joke translated from a foreign language, Jimmy's bit loses something—everything—in the "translation of time." But in 1932, it was funny to audiences, it was funny to the usually modest Stewart, and most importantly, it was funny enough to merit mention in the influential *New York Sun*.

Perhaps the most telling thing about the whole incident is the throwaway coda: ". . . every night, for two years." Jimmy was no playboy socialite treading the boards for a two-week outing in a regional theater during a summer stay in the Hamptons. He was in his friend's phrase "a drayhorse" who mostly sat backstage for two years so he could deliver a two-minute speech. If that wasn't "breaking a sweat," Arnold never pumped iron.

Jimmy spent three years on Broadway until Hollywood whistled, and that period wasn't all bouquets from charitable theater critics. His "good looks and natural charm" didn't stop him from getting beat up a lot (in print). As the *Ladies' Home Journal* not so lady-likely put it in 1987, "He appeared in numerous flops on Broadway in the 1930s."

In the 1960s, British actress Diana Rigg (*The Avengers*) collected all her venomous reviews in a bestseller, *No Turn Unstoned*. Jimmy could have written his own slender bestseller based on his three-year stint in the theater.

The most poisonous were also the funniest, and he earned them all for a 1935 drama, *Journey by Night*. To say poor Jimmy from Indiana, Pennsylvania was miscast as an Austrian prince is a mastepiece of understatement.

Of the production at the Shubert, one critic wrote, "Mr. Stewart, cast as a Viennese nobleman, wanders through the play like a befuddled tourist on the banks of the Danube."

The fact that Jimmy apparently made no attempt to ditch his

signature accent particuarly galled the press. One critic noted
dryly that he played a "Viennese aristocrat with a distinct
Indiana, Pennsylvania 'continental accent.' "

Another summed up the consensus: "He's about as Viennese
as hamburger."

Opening night was nightmarish, even without the fractured
accent. Jimmy managed to fracture the set as well. While his
sister sat in the audience horrified, Jimmy tried to make his
entrance through a door that refused to open. "The show must
go on" was Jimmy's motto, and he had to get on stage, so he
pushed on the door until it splintered and made his entrance
by squeezing through the crack in the door. Mercifully, Jimmy's
Nightmare from the Vienna Woods closed two nights later.

These critical torpedoes taught Jimmy a lesson he only par-
tially took to heart. For the rest of his career he would assidu-
ously avoid playing foreigners on film and stage. But the two
times he did, he didn't even try to fake a foreign accent.

At least he had his best friend to console him. Jimmy and
Henry Fonda both left Falmouth for Broadway at the same
time and shared a hellhole of an apartment near Times Square.

Fonda shared the general estimation of Stewart's ability as
an accordion player and one drunken night he dared Jimmy to
give an impromptu concert in Times Square. Fonda predicted
he would scare people away. Jimmy stood on his honor—and
his non-existent talent as a musician—posited a windfall. The
two men tipsily disagreed later on the outcome of the concert.
They did agree that within 10 excruciating minutes, 15 people
had surrounded the two drunks. Whether they were appreciative
concert-goers or a lynch mob was a source of debate as the story
became embellished over the next 50 years of their friendship.
Jimmy claimed the crowd coughed up 35 cents. Fonda thought
"threw up" was a better description and insisted the box office
was only 12 cents. Years later, Fonda would scale his estimate
downward to only eight cents. Sober, Jimmy claimed the incident never happened. Regardless of the details, there is documentary proof that as an accordionist, Jimmy was a disaster.
In his 1941 film, *Pot O' Gold,* he was once again called on to

play the instrument. The producer hired a professional to dub Jimmy's performance.

As a stage manager, Jimmy wasn't much more proficient. He was fired after ringing down the curtain during the climactic scene of *Camille before* the heroine died.

Jimmy's friendship with Fonda, which endured for 50 years until the actor died in 1982, could have been fictionalized as a play called *The Odd Couple* if Neil Simon hadn't done it first.

Fonda, like his daughter Jane after him, was a liberal. Jimmy, a lifelong registered Republican who played golf with Nixon *after* Watergate, campaigned for Ronald Reagan against the incumbent, Gerald Ford. The two men remained friends by agreeing to disagree—silently. Jimmy said of the relationship that lasted from 1931 to 1982, "Our political views have never interfered with our friendship—ever. We just don't talk about certain things. In fact, I can't remember ever having had an argument with him." Their friendship even survived the Vietman War.

Fonda thought too much of his best friend to denigrate him by calling him what he considered dirty words, "conservative" and "Republican." Fonda preferred to think of Jimmy as a humanist, not an ideologue, who just happened to vote for the GOP. "He cares about people regardless of ideology or identity. He feels the same way about cats and dogs. He likes mixed breeds."

There was also a curious competitiveness between the two actors, although from interviews it seems most of the envy emanated from the neurotic Fonda, not the laidback Stewart.

Jimmy's first starring role on Broadway, in *Yellow Jack,* was a hit with the critics and the public. Years later, Fonda confessed to *Parade* magazine, "The thing of it is Jim is a man who became an actor in spite of himself. I remember just sitting and looking at him in his dressing room [after the opening of *Yellow Jack*], studying him and wondering how in the hell he got so good. You see, I'd been at it for eight to nine years, playing literally hundreds of parts of all kinds and really working at being an actor, and here was this skinny son of a gun who hadn't really even tried hard for more than about a year or so, and I'd just seen him do about the most moving job I'd ever seen.''

The reporter from *Parade,* Cleveland Amory, had the temerity to repeat this damning with faint praise to Stewart when he interviewed him in 1984. With statements like the above, it was amazing their friendship lasted longer then Jimmy's marriage.

Jimmy wasn't offended by Fonda's belief that he was a ''natural'' rather than a disciple of the work ethic, but he did politely disagree with his best friend. Smiling, Stewart said to Amory, ''Hank was always telling that to people about how hard he'd worked and how I just *fell* into things. But the fact is that once we'd decided on theater, we all worked hard and we all starved a lot. I remember that I was nearly two years in a play where I only had two lines . . .'' History, failing memory, and PR inflation had enlarged the role in *Goodbye Again* to eight lines by the time of the *Parade* interview in 1984, but at 78, Jimmy still remembered the correct and self-deflating size of the role. Two lines, two years. And it would be a sucker bet to wager that the same man who fastidiously painted white lines on the highway and overcame a learning disorder to win a college scholarship showed up for every single one of those perfomances during his two-year stint.

Jimmy was probably the least solipsistic actor in the history of a business known for its inflated egos. He was so ego-less that accurate transcripts of his interviews show that he typically skipped the word ''I'' and would begin a self-descriptive sentence with a verb instead of the first person singular pronoun. This construction is common in some foreign languages, but not in English, with the exception of Stewart-ese.

Jimmy's lack of navel-gazing had a calming effect on the other struggling actors in his gang, especially those who were between plays. Fonda said, ''Jimmy was not career-obsessed— unlike the rest of his actor friends. He was never the eager beaver like the rest of us.'' Once, when Fonda became frantic during a particularly long period of unemployment in New York, Jimmy, the aviation buff, went out and bought his friend a model airplane and told him to assemble it. He also dragooned

Fonda into building and flying box kites in Central Park. Years later, facing similar unemployment in Hollywood after the war, Stewart and Fonda took up serious kite-flying. It was the pre-psychotropic age's answer to Prozac and Xanax.

According to Fonda, Jimmy didn't need to do a whole lot of kite-flying. "During the two years we shared an apartment near Times Square, he never went out and looked for a job. The parts just kept happening for Jimmy. They just got bigger and bigger."

Except for nerve-racking unemployment, their struggling actor days together seemed to include more fun than fear. Fonda remembered sharing an apartment not only with Jimmy but with their University Players' guru, Josh Logan, and another actor named Myron McCormick. An excellent cook, Fonda would serve elaborate Mexican feasts for parties of 20. Jimmy's repertoire, he recalled, consisted solely of French toast.

The apartment building would have shocked Jimmy's parents. The young actors shared a cramped railroad flat on 64th Street near Central Park West. "At the time, we barely had a toehold on Broadway," Jimmy recalled. "High rent was out of the question." Although he never came right out and said it, it appeared his father was willing to let his son give acting a try, but he wasn't going to bankroll his fantasies. No doubt, Alexander thought theatrical failure would soon send Jimmy home to hearth and hardware store. Nowhere does Stewart in 50 years of interviews and half a dozen biographies ever mention financial support from Mom or Dad during his salad days.

He and Fonda shared an apartment in a building that his father, had he known about its other residents, would have called a bawdy house. "Most of the other tenants in the building were hardworking prostitutes," Jimmy recalled, praising the girls for sharing his own ingrained work ethic, although in a different arena. "Hank told me they appreciated good music, especially my accordion playing. Whenever I practiced, he'd run up to me and say, 'The girls are rapping on the walls. They're demanding more.' When they weren't enjoying my accordion playing they were busy at, uh, work. It was impossible to leave our apartment without stumbling into a satisfied customer.'' Ironically, in their last film together 35 years later, Jimmy and Henry Fonda would play the unwitting inheritors of a Western whorehouse in *The Cheyenne Social Club.*

Although he would play pillars of the community in film after film, Stewart was no prig in real life. In fact, his bachelor life as a movie star in Hollywood would suggest just the opposite.

Jimmy's life in New York during these starving actor days sounded like something out of a Damon Runyon short story. Besides the hookers in the hallway, the building next door was even more colorful. It was a frequent meeting place for mobsters. Its most famous habitué was Legs Diamond. One night, their building's super told them if they had left the premises just a minute earlier, they would have witnessed a real life mob rub-out. ''Living there was literally a pistol,'' Jimmy said, but he was obviously not a fan of the NRA. ''When our lease ran out, we decided to move,'' leaving women behind of easy virtue and men with diamond studs embedded in their teeth.

Although this bonhomie took place during the depths of the Depression, Stewart recalled these years as some of his happiest. He had no sympathy for young actors 30 years later who were going through their own generation's national trauma, the war in Southeast Asia—and were pissed off at society instead of grateful to be working stiffs in the Dream Factory.

In the early 1970s, he told an interviewer, ''I wish today's kids [actors] would laugh a little more. I wish they wouldn't take themselves as seriously as they do. So many of them are completely undisciplined and selfish. When I got started, right in the heart of the Depression, theater was bright, gay, a lively, enthusiastic place, and young people had fun.'' Jimmy, unfortunately, had lost historical perspective. During the 1930s, escapist plays and especially fantasy movies offered people two hours respite from the Depression just outside the theater door. At the height of the Vietnam War, films and their politicized stars reflected the rage of napalming peasants, not Ginger Rogers' art deco penthouse in what French intellectuals dubbed ''white telephone'' movies. In the 1960s, moviegoers in effect wanted to "remember the Alamo" (and My Lai). During the Depression, they wanted to forget the Dow-Jones average that day.

But unlike many of his superannuated fellow stars, Jimmy never really became a curmudgeon. In fact, well into his 80s, without a trace of sarcasm in his voice, he would tell a reporter that his favorite actors of "the young crop" were Tom Cruise and Jim Carrey.

Jimmy spent a scant three years in New York before Holly-wood hijacked him. He would regret the brevity of these instructive, formative years for the rest of his life. In 1983, at the age of 75, he told a jammed news conference for a TV movie he was starring in, "At this point in life, when you start looking back, one of my regrets is that I didn't do more stage work. That's partly because it's a great, exhilarating, uplifting thing. But it's also because *you never stop learning to act.*" This from a man who had five Oscar nominations and a Tony on his résumé. "It isn't that kind of a racket," he said of a craft he felt at 75 he was still a journeyman in. "You never have the thing licked. And stage is great training for every part of it—timing, tempo, all your instincts about how to react without overdoing it . . . It's funny, but projecting your voice to the last person in the second gallery is wonderful training for the movies, where you talk like we're talking now." Jimmy didn't get a chance to explain that paradoxical statement because his co-star in the HBO movie, *Right of Way,* Bette Davis, monopolized the rest of the press conference and constantly interrupted him.

If there was one thing that did bring out the curdmudgeon in Stewart, it was the proliferation of acting classes and their half-baked theories. He was too much of a gentleman to tongue-lash Stella Adler, but if Stanislavsky had been around, Jimmy would have chewed his ear off. There is no record of the actor having met Stan's American avatar, Lee Strasberg.

Although he didn't spend much time in the theater, the stage was Jimmy's classroom, not some so-called master class taught by an actor who couldn't find work. "The most important thing about acting is to approach it as a craft, not as an art and not as some mysterious type of religion," he told *Women's Wear*

Daily in 1977. "You don't have to meditate to be an actor. And for heaven's sake! Stay away from acting schools! The only way to learn to act is to act. Acting schools take up all your time. Sure a lot of successful people came out of acting schools . . ." (Meryl Streep, M.A., Yale, 1975; Sigourney Weaver, B.A., Stanford, 1973; and Bruce Willis, A.A., Montclair State College, New Jersey.) "But they knew how to act before they went in. They had talent, you see. All they needed was a chance to acquire the skill. Acquiring the skill is what acting is all about."

Stewart practiced what he preached. Although he had only two (or eight) lines in *Goodbye Again,* depending on who was counting and reminiscing, he didn't waste all this downtime. He perched just out of audience view in the wings watching the play's star, Osgood Perkins (father of Anthony). "I saw every performance for over a year. I learned a lot that way. It's the best kind of experience. That's why I'm glad of the chance to get back again," he said on the set of 1983's *Right of Way.* At 75, he felt he still hadn't finished his acting education.

Stewart practiced what he preached—although like everything else—in moderation. Even after he became the top box office attraction in Hollywood, he would make infrequent forays back to "school"—the theater—well into his 70s. Typically modest, he insisted he was no Katharine Hepburn or Laurence Olivier, who seemed to use their $9,000 a week studio paychecks to finance their union-scale stage performances. "I didn't plan like Frederic March or Olivier to shuttle back and forth between stage and movies. I haven't had enough experience," he said. "I was in nine shows before I went to the Coast and most of them didn't last long. The longest-running play, *Goodbye Again,* I had nine lines in." (He did star in one play, *Yellow Jack,* which was his ticket, as they said in those days, to the "Coast.")

Hedda Hopper, then the dizziest entertainment journalist, claimed she sent the young actor on his way to Hollywood and the rest was history—at least in her mind. In fact, she claimed she stopped him from chucking it all and going back home to sell thumbtacks. In 1951, with the wisdom of hindsight and Jimmy's record as a major star, Hopper in her syndicated column recounted how she steered the unlikely actor in the right direction.

During an audition in the 1930s at the home of the great actress Katherine Cornell, Hopper, then an aspiring actress herself, followed the awkward youth out of the house, perhaps hoping to get lucky. Hopper later reported that she told him, "Young man, you ought to be in pictures." He said, "What with? This puss of mine?" "What's the matter with it?" the hoydenish Hopper asked. Jimmy allegedly said, "Take another look at it, Miss Hopper, then you tell me." Frisky Hedda lectured him, "Actors need more than a handsome face. They need heart, spirit, and intelligence, and I believe you've got all three." Hopper, like so many other Hollywood memoirists, was not above a little historical revisionism.

She also had the worst memory since the Watergate plumbers testified before Congress. Hopper actually claimed to have discovered Jimmy twice. The geography kept changing along with the story. The second "discovery" took place when they were appearing together in a play, *Divided by Three,* in New Haven, Jimmy brings his fiancée home to meet his parents and their best friend. When Jimmy discovers that the family friend is actually his mother's lover, he calls her a "whore" on stage. At least that's what the script said. Jimmy didn't want to. The director reminded him that he was under contract and refused Jimmy's entreaties to be let go. "I can't possibly do that," he said in one last plea to the producer. "Under no circumstance could I bring myself to call any woman that—and not my mother. Especially with the girl I intend to marry standing beside me." Trouper that he was, however, Jimmy called his stage mother a "whore" every night for the entire run of the play.

In this version of Hopper's hazy memory, Stewart was so fed up with all this smut that he was again ready to go back to painting lines on the highway, but she dissuaded him: "The screen needs a young man as clean and sincere as you. Why aren't you in Hollywood?" As he [allegedly] said outside Katherine Cornell's New York townhouse, Jimmy demurred, citing his ungainly looks. "What would they do with this puss of mine? It's no Arrow collar ad," Hedda said in this revamped version of her original column. She encouraged him. "You're an actor . . . and besides, they could fix *that*," she added, unkindly agreeing with his assessment of his physical equipment. "Pictures desperately need someone like you," Hedda orated. " 'You project sincerity.' Again, Jimmy laughed it off, but he looked less tense. I could tell that I had planted a seed."

In contrast to Hopper's "recovered" memories, Billy Grady had documentary proof that *he* was the one who discovered the Broadway actor and launched his Hollywood career.

Grady was a talent scout for the Tiffany's of movie studios, MGM, which boasted with typical flack-hack restraint that it had "more stars than in the heavens." Grady's job for the studio was to add future stars to this firmament by trawling Broadway prosceniums and finding the next Barrymore or Gable. Like a latter-day Boswell, Grady actually kept a journal of these stage Johnsons. After Stewart's star turn in *Yellow Jack,* in which Stewart gamely, lamely, played an Irishman, Grady would presciently comment on Jimmy's future.

He wrote in his journal: "Could not give him much for his brogue, but he was convincing." Grady fortunately missed his "hamburger" performance as a Viennese aristocrat in *Journey by Night.* Or maybe he was just diplomatic enough to expunge any embarrassing entries after the unknown become a known. Of Stewart's performance in the critically mauled *Divided by Three* in 1934, the armchair theater critic wrote, "I like this kid. Unaffected and sincere in all he does." Again, overcoming the Midwestern "Irish brogue" in *Yellow Jack,* Stewart elicited this journal entry: "He interests me."

Ironically, only a few days after his disastrous turn as the Viennese Big Mac, Grady, who perhaps missed the show, sent him a telegram in January 1935 inviting him to Culver City. Grady was so sure of his find, he didn't even suggest a screen test, instead guaranteeing Jimmy a supporting role in a film called *Murder Man.*

Grady's enthusiasm would be temporily misplaced and would almost cost him his job as a headhunter for MGM.

Chapter 7
Get Shorty . . . Er, Skinny

Grady was a cock-eyed optimist—or maybe just cock-eyed. He got Stewart a contract and persuaded the director of *Murder Man* to cast the actor in a small role as a newspaper reporter. That was hardly a stretch, especially since Stewart would earn his first Oscar portraying someone in that profession and had played reporters on Broadway more than once.

But Grady must not have read the script. The character was indeed a reporter, but his name, "Shorty," wasn't meant to be ironic. Grady had strong-armed the director to cast the 6'4" Jimmy in a role that the script described as a "nub of a man."

Grady pleaded with the director, "If you're willing to take a chance on an unknown kisser and change the character's name to 'Skinny,' I think I've got a great personality for you."

The open-minded director was sanguine about the change, but the producer, when he finally met Stewart, was out for blood—Grady's. The producer bolted to the head of the studio's office muttering words like "melon head" and "oaf" about Grady and "human giraffe" about his protégé. Then he asked L.B. Mayer to fire Grady and cancel Jimmy's contract.

Grady, who would understandably remain Jimmy's friend for life, didn't give up on his discovery. He finessed the apoplectic producer by saying, "Go ahead, can me, but why not do one day's shooting and take a look at the rushes?"

The producer, for reasons which remain unexplained, yielded to Grady's enthusiasm and decided to keep the casting agent—and his new hire.

MGM put Jimmy under the typical nerve-racking contract at "minimum wage." The standard contract was for seven years, which the actor would be held to even if he turned into the next Gable or Flynn. But the contract also had a renewable six-month option, which meant that if your films didn't perform well fast, the studio could dump you at any six-month point in the seven-year stretch. (TV actors on series sign contracts today that are similar. If the show's a Nielsen hit, the player, even an established actor, is stuck playing, say, the fat, stupid next-door neighbor for five to seven years. But if the sitcom settles into the Nielsen basement, the actor is just as likely to read of its cancellation—and his unemployment—in the trades with no severance pay.)

Don't cry too hard, however, for sitcom actors, or for Jimmy Stewart during his early days at Metro. Scale—or minimum wage—for a TV actor, no matter how small the supporting role, is almost $3,000 a week by union fiat. Scale in 1935 under the so-called tyrannical studio system was $350 a week, a very high income in the depths of the Depression when salesclerks were lucky if they brought home $12 in their weekly pay packets.

In *Murder Man,* the star of the film, Spencer Tracy, took time out to offer the newcomer some jejune advice: "Just say your lines, kid, and don't bump into the furniture." Tracy took to the deferential 27-year-old who looked like a teenager. A fellow workaholic, Tracy appreciated Stewart's seriousness and eagerness to learn and gave him wiser advice than avoiding the props. "I told him to forget the camera was there. That was all he needed. In his very first scene he showed he had all the good things."

Jimmy had ninth billing in *Murder Man.* Shot in three weeks, the crime drama cast Tracy as a private eye who provides investigative reporters (like Jimmy's "Shorty") with crime tips and gangster gossip. As Stewart told Dale Pollock in the *L.A. Times* on the eve of receiving the AFI Lifetime Achievement Award in 1980, his career had "nowhere to go but up."

And that's exactly the direction in which the hard-working neophyte went. In his first year alone, he appeared in nine films. Within five years, the studio had found a willing slave who was happy to appear in 24 films. Jimmy thrived under a system others compared to slavery, even if the chains were platinum and slave quarters were a handsome home in the best part of town.

The same youth who had happily loaded bricks in Pennsylvania and swept floors on Cape Cod rolled up his sleeves and whistled while he worked in this cushy coal mine. His crushing work schedule was invaluable training, not exploitation, in his mind at least. "This was doing all sorts of pictures—you'd do little parts in big pictures and big parts in little pictures. You'd be doing two pictures at the same time." That was literally true. Sometimes the stars would forget which film they had reported to. When George Saunders won the Best Supporting Actor Oscar for *All About Eve,* he confessed to the shocked Academy audience that he had been working on several films at the time, and he couldn't quite place the picture he was being honored for that evening in 1951 at the Pantages Theater on Sunset Boulevard.

Jimmy was just as overworked, although fortunately he never got as confused about what character he was playing as did Sanders, a playboy who never took his craft seriously. "It was a six-day week and we worked all the time," Jimmy said with relish, not resentment or exhaustion. "If you were under contract to the studio, you were there every day, 52 weeks a year. If you weren't in a picture, you were out on a publicity run for some picture you weren't even in!

"You were with the voice teacher, you were at the gym, keeping in shape, you were doing [screen] tests for new people coming along. And all of it was part of learning the craft." Jimmy recalled all these details as if they had happened yesterday, although he was describing them in an *L.A. Times* interview half a century later.

Relatively—and newly—rich, Jimmy was fobbed off on an in-house producer, Henry Rapf, who was ordered to "do something" with Metro's latest contract player after *Murder Man* wrapped. Rapf looked—up—at the 6'4" actor and exclaimed, "My God, you're skinny!"

Jimmy's second assignment at MGM was not to report to a another soundstage but to the studio gymnasium. As the best studio in town, MGM could afford the best personal trainer, a bodybuilding champ named Don Loomis. Loomis, a one-time Mr. America, had inflated Errol Flynn's chicken-breast chest and pumped up Gary Cooper's matchstick biceps. In terms of optimism and mind over matter, he was the Arnold Schwarzenegger of his day when it came to bulking up his protégés.

For once, Loomis's can-do spirit failed him. The trainer took one look at Jimmy and said to the producer, "Do you think I'm a magician?" Loomis may have been cruel, but his reaction was understandable.

Jimmy lied about his height, shaving off half an inch, but there was no way he could camouflage his physique without ordering a "fat suit" from the costume department, an idea he seriously considered. When Jimmy confessed that he weighed 130 pounds, Loomis was ready to resign from his job at the gym. "You're beyond hope," he told Stewart. Jimmy had inherited his father's optimism, if not his bombast. In fact, he wasn't outright begging. As he saw his film career slipping away, he pleaded with Loomis, "Please try. I'll cooperate. I promise."

Jimmy's patented charm won over even the macho gym rat, who insisted on a little test before agreeing to coach him. Loomis pointed to a smallish barbell and told Jimmy to pick it up. He huffed and puffed and finally managed to raise it only as high as his waist.

Loomis was ready to call the front office and tell the brass to send this kid back to prep school. Instead, he told Stewart, "I just had a little kid hoist it over his head a dozen times. Can't you do anything?" At least Loomis didn't claim the "kid" was Shirley Temple.

Jimmy's work ethic and enthusiasm overcame the trainer's

despair. They spent four days a week in the gym together. Loomis's feeding regimen would make Jimmy a candidate for Overeaters Anonymous today, but in 1935 it meant the chance to become a movie star. Loomis made his charge drink two quarts of whole milk and consume two pounds of bananas a day. For protein, he stuffed the actor with fish and enough red meat to give a British lord gout. With Jimmy as such a "difficult" student, Loomis earned every penny of his salary: After a year, the trainer managed to pack 13 extra pounds on Stewart's skeletal frame.

Henry Fonda, who had preceded his best friend to Hollywood by four months to reprise his stage role in *The Farmer Takes a Wife* on the big screen, was almost as hopeless an ectomorph as Jimmy. Both men suffered under Loomis's dietary tyranny and stuffed themselves in a desperate attempt to get their six-month options renewed.

"Hank Fonda also helped me gain some weight. He too was very skinny, and someone had told him that milk mixed with brandy was a good way to add pounds. We started with a lot of milk and a little bit of brandy, but Hank felt that we should add more brandy. Then some more. Soon the color got darker and darker. We used to drink that concoction for breakfast and by 8 A.M. we were half stoned," Jimmy recalled in the days before such behavior would lead to The Betty Ford Clinic, not a contract renewal.

Today substance abuse counselors would label this behavior incipient alcoholism, but for Jimmy and Fonda, it worked. Both men added enough weight to look near normal in suits. Mercifully, the style at the time called for padded shoulders, and even a 130-pound weakling could appear to be a mesomorph. Luckily for both men, nude scenes were decades away.

It took an entire year for the studio to feel Jimmy had sufficiently pumped himself up for anything larger than uncredited bit parts. But the brass were impressed enough after *Murder Man,* a cheapie potboiler, to give Stewart sixth billing in a big budget musical, *Rose Marie,* starring two of the studio's biggest names, Jeannette MacDonald and Nelson Eddy.

Jimmy's character in the 1936 film had the unusual name

of Flower, and it was one of his rare roles as a bad guy. He played Eddy's younger brother who gets in trouble with the law, and the Mountie (Eddy) has to get his man, even though it's his brother. Although Stewart was No. 6 on the roster, his performance was noteworthy enough to be singled out in at least two reviews. The *Observer* said, "A new screen actor, one Mr. James Stewart, plays the small part of the hunted young brother with considerably more than average promise. I think you will like him . . ." And then the critic added an opinion that suggested he had a crystal ball next to his manual type-writer: ". . . I am sure you will hear more of him." Less prophetically, *Variety,* which also took notice of his miniscule role, predicted the gangly youth would have a future playing teenaged character roles: "James Stewart, as MacDonald's brother, has a fleeting assignment, but gives it everything, looks like a character juve bet."

Despite those reviews, Jimmy lost the next role he tested for. The casting director who ordered up Stewart's screen test for the movie must have shared one of the famous Fonda brandy-milkshakes. Jimmy did a test for the role of an Asian in an adaptation of Pearl S. Buck's Pulitzer Prize-winning novel, *The Good Earth.* Not until Charlton Heston played a Mexican police detective in one of Orson Welles' crazier notions in *Touch of Evil* would an actor be so inappropriate for a role.

The film's lead, Paul Muni, an Austrian Jew and former star of the Yiddish theater, who had also been cast as an Asian, would sum up Jimmy's dilemma in those pre-politically correct days by saying, "He's awful tall for a Chinaman."

Forty years later, on *An All-Star Tribute to Jimmy Stewart,* which aired on CBS in December 1978, Stewart explained why such an unlikely casting decision had even been considered. In a rare moment of insensitivity during the post-Biafra, pre-Somalia 1970s, Stewart, still skinny, joked on national televi-sion, "I was the only one under contract who looked as though he'd actually been through a famine." Ouch.

Fortunately for Jimmy, the director of *The Good Earth* didn't have Welles' clout, and his screen test was laughed out of the projection room. But not before Stewart had put all his usual effort into the assignment, no matter how ill-conceived.

"They got the makeup department to design a special oriental mask for me. It took three hours to put on, but I felt it was worth it. I thought I really looked the part. Even my own mother wouldn't recognize me.

"Proudly, I paraded around the studio lot showing off. But everyone I met said, 'Hello, Jimmy.'" How the artistry of makeup has grown over the years. When Dustin Hoffman showed up in *Tootsie* drag at his son's prep school to test his credibility as a female, mothers welcomed the new "mom" with open arms. The reaction of Hoffman's unfortunate son to dad in drag went unrecorded.

A Scotch-Irish Pennsylvanian who looked like a basketball player instead of a Mandarin still didn't dissuade the director, who decided to dig a trench so that Jimmy could walk alongside Muni. This trick fooled no one, and the director did something pressure groups decades later would have to picket the studios to accomplish: he cast a real-life Asian as . . . an Asian. The actor who wound up with the job was 5'2".

Jimmy's inability to play a member of another race didn't hurt his reputation around town. In fact, another studio began clamoring for his services. Actually, an actress at another studio was doing all the hollering.

Chapter 8

Jimmy Tries to Bench Press an Actress

In Hollywood's so-called Golden Age, actors were not only chattel, they were *portable* chattel. The stars were traded like baseball cards by the studios. In fact, in the 1930s Jimmy would recall being "loaned out," as the phrase had it, to a studio— not in exchange for another actor but for the use of some soundstages. Without any bitterness, he recalled, "You didn't pick your movies. You did what you were told. Your studio could trade you around like ballplayers. I was traded once to Universal for the use of their backlot for three weeks."

At least they didn't trade him for a catering truck or "honey-wagon" for the ultimate feeling of being a piece of meat. The practice went beyond humiliation. It was also commercially exploitive. If Studio A really wanted Studio B's actor, Studio A would have to pay a lot more than the actor's regular salary for his services. But the actor didn't get to keep the difference. The studio did. And again, if you didn't feel like being loaned out like a slab of beef, the studio put you on suspension— without pay—until you came to your senses or the mortgage came due. And the time you spent on suspension did not count toward fulfilling your seven-year hitch.

But before we petition our Congressman for reparations for

the victims and their heirs, it must be noted that some of these wage slaves were earning the unheard of sums of $12,000 a week—in the middle of the Depression. So what if another studio paid their bosses $15,000 a week to borrow them and didn't share the difference? Even in today's inflated currency, for $12,000 a week I'd sing and dance in awful little musicals, as Jimmy and even a big star like Gable were forced to do at the command of their studio bosses.

Like a baseball player in the days before free agency, Jimmy found himself for his third film loaned out to Universal. Margaret Sullavan was a big star with big clout at the future home of Tyrannosaurus Rex and Spielberg. It was rumored that the beautiful actress had a thing for MGM's latest stud, whose skinny frame didn't seem to turn her off. What Margaret wanted, Margaret got, and she got Jimmy to co-star with her in *Next Time We Love* (1936). He played a foreign correspondent. Sullavan played his wife with a mind—and career—of her own, who refused to give up the stage to accompany him on postings abroad. Regardless of what she *wanted* to give him, Sullavan did provide Jimmy with his big break. *Next Time We Love* was his first leading role, a huge step forward after less than a year in Hollywood. "I think she was responsible for the first big leading part I had in the movies," he said, giving Sullavan full credit. The actress deserved it. She had been impressed by his talent when they co-starred in a production at Princeton. Sullavan admired his acting ability but forgot that he was a 130-pound weakling. Even after poor Don Loomis had spent a year troweling on 13 pounds, Jimmy was no weight lifter. Not even a woman lifter.

In Angela Dunn's 1983 newspaper series, Jimmy wasn't too embarrassed to recount this genuinely embarrassing tale of wimpiness. The script called for him to pick Sullavan up in his arms, and Jimmy discovered he couldn't lift her off the ground. "Under her breath she said, 'Pick me up! I'm not *that* heavy. Pick me up!' " The petite actress must have felt like an overweight blob when this 6'4" man couldn't raise her an inch off the floor. Jimmy confessed, "I couldn't get a grip . . . and Maggie yelled, 'Cut! This skinny bum can't lift!' "

Embarrassed and furious, Sullavan stormed off the set. Jimmy didn't say how he must have felt.

The head gaffer devised a way to salvage both stars' ego. He put Stewart in a shoulder harness attached to a piano wire. Robin Williams and Christopher Reeve would use the same contraption to fly as Peter Pan and Superman. Jimmy needed only to straighten up after bending down to pick up the dainty actress. When Sullavan returned to the set, she didn't see the piano wire or harness and didn't realize her leading man was wired for flight. As he bent over to hoist his burden, the gaffer jerked on the wire too hard, and Jimmy and Sullavan went flying through the air. Jimmy landed on his rear on top of the expensive camera. "Never lived it down," he said, although he was not too embarrassed to recall the incident for the sake of giving a reporter a good story nearly half a century later.

Sullavan's ego—and rear end—may have been bruised by Jimmy's lack of muscle, but she didn't hold a grudge—she carried a torch. They would star in three more films together.

The romantic speculation about Jimmy's casting would later prove to be stronger than rumor. After she divorced his best friend, Fonda, and then his agent, Leland Hayward, the beautiful Sullavan would put Jimmy in her blond bombsight—but miss the target by a mile. A beautiful movie star gunning for you . . . To paraphrase Mel Brooks's royal *bon mot* in *History of the World, Part I,* "It's great to be king . . . on screen."

Although Stewart was too much of a gentleman ever to comment on Sullavan's pursuit of him, her off-screen ardor may have added to his on-screen artistry. In a first-person account of visiting her famous brother in New York in *Coronet* magazine, Jimmy's sister Virginia said that Jimmy felt *Next Time We Love* was the "first film he thought he did a good job in." What Sullavan thought of Stewart's job performance went unrecorded except perhaps in her diary and daydreams. It's a safe bet that Stewart, the most loyal of friends, didn't touch Sullavan, who had been married to his best friend, Henry Fonda.

Unlike Sullavan, *Time* magazine did go on the record and praised Stewart for dumping an old stereotype. The reviewer may have been particularly pleased because the jettisoned stereotype involved the critic's own profession, journalism: "Stewart disregards a long-established cinema convention for such roles . . . ably introduces to Hollywood the character of a newspaperman who is neither a drunkard, lecher, nor buffoon."

Chapter 9

Stud Service

MGM reclaimed its contract player for his fourth film, and he was glad to be back when he found out who his co-star in *Wife Vs. Secretary* would be: Jean Harlow. It's hard for us today to fully appreciate Jimmy's enthusiasm, because Harlow has no counterpart today. You'd have to combine Marilyn Monroe's voluptuousness, Cindy Crawford's physical perfection, Madonna's sexuality, and Roseanne's comedic skills to approximate Jean Harlow's impact in the 1930s.

Even after Stewart had "bulked up" under Don Loomis' force-feeding, one studio executive still referred to the actor as a "human giraffe." The casting people capitalized on his ungainliness and unkindly used him as a fall guy to make their main guy look even better. MGM often cast Stewart as the gangly geek who lost the girl to the handsome leading man. In *Wife Vs. Secretary,* he "lost" Jean Harlow to Clark Gable. But the geek lucked out and did get one hot shot at the fabulous Harlow.

Sounding adolescent rather than 28, which he was at the time, Jimmy confessed, "Clarence Brown, the director, wasn't too pleased by the way I did the smooching. He made us repeat the scene about half a dozen times. I now have to confess that

I botched it up on purpose. That Jean Harlow sure was a good kisser. I realized that until then I had never really been kissed.''

In an interview given in his 80s, Stewart recalled the big moment: ''Harlow was a great kisser. We had to do a romantic scene in the movie, and I'd never been kissed that way in my life. I mean, boy, when Harlow kissed you, she *kissed* you. We had to do that scene over and over and by the time it was filmed, I was a very exhausted young actor.''

While the director of *Wife Vs. Secretary* was not enchanted with Stewart's purposeful incompetence, there's no record of Harlow complaining about her workload that day. In fact, when the actress gave Stewart such accomplished kisses, she may not have been acting. Although Jimmy had neither the matinee idol looks of Cary Grant nor the macho aura of Spencer Tracy, women found him irresistible. For more than a decade before his marriage in 1949, he was frequently referred to as Hollywood's most eligible bachelor.

Years later, Stewart was still just ''aw shucks-ing'' his reputation. ''If you're not married, you're an eligible bachelor. It's that simple,'' he told a magazine.

No, it wasn't. Jimmy was just that modest.

A confidante who was not identified by name claimed that his good friend was basically lying. ''For a man who was supposed to be shy with dames, he did OK. He got around,'' the fellow actor said. He was using the euphemism of the day for getting all the loving he wanted.

''He packed a potent appeal for some of Hollywood's tastier dishes,'' the unnamed friend reported. ''They found him different from the aggressive gents they usually encountered. Jimmy never phoned women. Never sent them flowers. He made none of the usual moves, even conversational ones. If they spoke to him, he replied. Otherwise, he just sat there and grinned. As a result, a number of the town's high-powered babes sent their cars to wait for him outside of his house. When they got him alone, they did their best to explode emotional dynamite under him.'' How this confidante knew about these female explosions was not explained, but the interview appeared in a reputable publication, the *Saturday Evening Post* in 1951. You can be sure the magazine did not illustrate Jimmy's reputed love life with one of its Norman Rockwell paintings.

In a town where men were expected to be wolves and the casting couch was a staple of interior decor in executive suites, Jimmy's style was unique—and immensely alluring to women who were used to being the prey, not the predators.

Still, Jimmy was not indifferent to sex. As he said years later with some pique, after his courtliness had practically been equated with eunuchhood, "There are those who remember me as no laggard in the romance department." And in his heyday he confessed that the magic of filmmaking was so overpowering, frequently on-screen romances overflowed off screen. "You know, you get about half stuck on every girl you're in a picture with. I got stuck on Harlow just from this—this one movie *(Wife Vs. Secretary).* I only had three scenes in the picture. She was so warm . . . really . . . really warm and giving . . ."

Jimmy was simply a gentleman from a small town in Pennsylvania. But that didn't mean he couldn't appreciate beauty. With the awe of a child whose nose was pressed up against the candy store window, Stewart described that earthly paradise, the backlot at MGM. "I remember not only the beautiful stars at MGM but the beautiful girls who were under contract. Contract players. Some were dancers or singers. Almost blinded you sometimes, walking among so much beauty, so much perfection of face and body." With that kind of line, is it any wonder that limos overflowing with beautiful women backed up outside his house?

Ironically, it took a man to distill the Stewart appeal and explain it. Bart Bull in the June 1989 issue of *Vogue* wrote, "A man left the movies feeling less capable than Clark Gable, less of a lady-killer than Cary Grant, but you never left a Jimmy Stewart movie feeling diminished. Nobody was less capable or apparently less of a ladies' man. What was most heroic about Jimmy Stewart was that he never tried to be a hero."

Even a gaga woman journalist in the unliberated 1930s conceded that in the physical department, Stewart was no Gable. "His nose, legs, and arms are all too long for beauty," *Colliers* said, then raved over his sexiness anyway.

With a commendable lack of machismo, Jimmy admitted that his charisma had a lot to do with the fact that he was so non-threatening. "Vulnerable" was the exact term he used, which was not then the overused touchy-feely adjective it has become today. How many men are so secure in their masculinity that they could say as he once did: "Even in a Western, people say when *I* get in a fight, they aren't sure if I'll win. But when John Wayne gets in a fight, they know all right!" In fact, in his second Western, Jimmy gets thoroughly beaten.

Appearing so innocent to women and non-threatening to men on screen showed just what a great actor Stewart was. On screen, he was Everyman. Off screen, he lived every man's fantasy sex life. In 1970, *Coronet,* not exactly the *Penthouse* of its day, was still rhapsodizing over these 40-year-old amours: "De Havilland, Dietrich, Rogers, Hayworth, and scores of others—all pursued him. He never phoned those girls *(sic).* He never sent them gifts."

Some 60 years after the fact, the envy in a good friend's voice is still almost audible when you read his description of Jimmy's allure: "He was the most pursued man in that community of beautiful dames. It must have seemed easy to hook Jimmy. He was so diffident, so awkward, so eternally grateful for the smallest of favors." When a reporter asked him why he just didn't take his pick and settle down, Jimmy responded, sphinx-like, "I have heard marriage well spoken of and have no objection to the idea."

Whatever his behavior in the privacy of his own bachelor pad, in public he was always the perfect gentleman. He never, ever kissed and told. One writer said approvingly, "If there are women in his life, he is not voluble about them, and they do not seem to enter into his plans for the future."

Another screen siren, Carole Lombard, once said, commenting on her husband's uninspired performance in the bedroom, "Gable was no Gable." With just the opposite implication, a lady friend who expected to experience the innocent screen character might have commented after their date, "Jimmy Stewart was no Jimmy Stewart." The actor seems to have been the Warren Beatty of his day (only much more discreet).

In 1989, *Vogue* magazine dug up yellowing magazine clips that reported Stewart was "romantically linked" to Rita Hayworth, Ginger Rogers, Dorothy Lamour, and Loretta Young.

One actress almost escaped him, but he really wanted just to worship rather than romance her. Greta Garbo was literally the girl (OK, love goddess) next door to him in the 1930s, but he never saw the mysterious superstar. Every morning before dawn, the movie queen would be picked up by her limo and whisked off to the studio, returning after dark. Stewart never even caught a glimpse of her face.

Then they happened to be working on adjacent soundstages, but the smitten actor was still out of luck. Garbo's sets were always closed, and a security guard was stationed outside her trailer. Stewart bribed a member of her crew to call on the house phone and let him know when she emerged from her trailer. When the news came, he rushed over to the set, bumping into a woman in his haste. The woman was Garbo. "I not only bumped right into her, but I knocked her down! That was my first meeting with Garbo, and I will never forget it."

There were witnesses to this famous smash-up, but another tale regarding Jimmy and the woman who "vanted to be alone" is pure apocrypha, though Jimmy claimed it was true. His best friend, Henry Fonda, said Jimmy was drunk. Jimmy often discussed with Fonda, his roommate in their Brentwood bachelor pad at the time, his plan to tunnel over to his glamorous neighbor's house since he was having such bad luck meeting her aboveground. Fonda insisted the conversations never took place, "like so many of Jimmy's stories." Jimmy himself conceded that his fantasies of excavating Garbo may have been fueled by something other than lust. "My memory of this is hazy at best," he said years later. "As you see, it's got to be a drunken idea. I can't be sure just how far it got, but I thought it was a wonderful, charming idea. At one time we thought of tunneling through our backyard to hers, popping out of the tunnel and saying, 'Hi, honey. We have no ulterior motives. We just wanted to see you in your long, lean flesh.'" He was lucky to have a (sober) friend like Fonda who was so much better at reality testing.

Although they remained best friends throughout their lives, Fonda found having the imaginative Stewart as a roommate a mixed blessing. "I was always the innocent party to his shenanigans. He kept getting me into all kinds of predicaments."

One was Jimmy's uncanny knack for hiring housekeepers from hell. They all seemed to think they were sorority headmistresses, not servants. One housekeeper firmly believed "her boys" needed a good eight hours sleep, so every night at 10 P.M. she would show up in the living room with their guests' coats— whether or not the guests were ready to leave. Another housekeeper seemed to think she was their personal Hays Code. If a woman caller sounded too sexy on the phone, the housekeeper forgot to relay the message. Yet another thought she was their story editor! When the studio messengered over a script, the woman would vet it before handing it over to her employers. If she deemed the storyline too risqué for her employers, they never saw the script.

Marriage, not dominatrixes masquerading as maids, finally ended the roommate situation. Jimmy had the last laugh. When he moved out of the Brentwood house to make way for Fonda's bride, New York socialite Frances Seymour Brokaw, he left the newlyweds with the latest housekeeper he had hired.

Fonda corroborated the stories of hellish housekeepers while dismissing the ones about digging to Garbo's. "It's fun to remember things," Jimmy insisted, even if they weren't true. "Hank says I exaggerate to the point where when I finish a story it's a complete lie."

Jimmy didn't contradict his friend's rude claim. In fact, he admitted doing a little needlepoint on the facts over the years. "Exaggeration is the plasa of this business," he said. While shooting *The Mortal Storm* in 1940 with Margaret Sullavan, the script called for him to save his leading lady from the Nazis while they were skiing to safety in neutral Switzerland. A stuntman did *all* of the two-left-footed Stewart's skiing. When the film came out, people stopped him, amazed, and said, "I didn't know you could ski." Jimmy confessed that he couldn't. A year later he "admitted" he had done "some" of the skiing.

And a year after that he was referring to *"The Mortal Storm,* where I did all that skiing in that scene."

While Stewart was having chaste knockdown affairs with Garbo and not so chaste collisions with every other beauty in Hollywood, the casting people still didn't understand his appeal to women.

The same year he made *Wife Vs. Secretary* and kissed Harlow off her feet, in his next film, *Small Town Girl,* Stewart was again set up to take the fall for the leading man Robert Taylor, cast opposite Janet Gaynor. The comedy involved a romantic triangle with Jimmy playing a role to which he was slowly gaining sole patent rights: the likeable boy next door who never gets the girl next door.

But while Taylor got the girl on screen, Jimmy quietly stole the show and earned some noisy raves in the press. One reviewer wrote, "In case somebody wants to see some really distinctive acting, there is Mr. James Stewart in one of those small-time, small-town parts that are the salt of any film which he essays." Another reviewer waxed even more enthusiastic, simply hailing Stewart as "the screen's brightest discovery."

He had been in Hollywood exactly one year and 365 banana milkshakes later.

Chapter 10
Chains O' Gold

Until the end of the 1930s, Stewart's career momentum slowed down. He alternated between leads in B pictures and supporting roles as dorks in big budget films. His movies from this period are mostly of interest to trivia buffs.

In 1936's *The Gorgeous Hussy,* he had a miniscule role opposite the reigning harridan of Hollywood, Joan Crawford. In the historical drama, he played one of Crawford's innumerable beaux. It was proof of the studio's casting tyranny that it could order a leading man like Stewart to play basically a bit part in one of its projects. Although the actress was as omnivorous off screen as Jimmy, she was one of the few movie queens he never dated.

After forcing him to make love to Crawford in a bit part in *The Gorgeous Hussy,* MGM did something worse: It made its contractee and his two infamous left feet sing and dance in 1936's *Born to Dance,* a misnomer if ever there was one when it came to Jimmy. Happily for Stewart fans, *Born to Dance* has yet to make it to video, but you can still see Jimmy's screen humiliation in 1974's *That's Entertainment,* which is on video. As proof of just how much sway the studio had over casting its stars, the compilation film shows excruciating clips of Jimmy singing and dancing opposite one of the best singers and dancers of the day, Eleanor Powell. Jimmy must have felt like Danny De Vito being ordered to go one-on-one on a basketball court with Shaquille O'Neal for a McDonald's commercial. Not only did Jimmy fail to benefit from the helpful assistance of Powell, but even the work of one of the greatest composers of all time, Cole Porter, couldn't stop Jimmy from looking like a gefilte fish out of aspic.

In a 1973 monograph by British film scholar Dennis John Hall, the academician apparently hallucinated when he watched the 1936 howler, because he wrote in *Films & Filming,* "As Eleanor Powell's sailor boyfriend, Stewart displays tremendous versatility within the bounds of his screen persona." (That's like saying Richard Simmons plays Arnold Schwarzenegger's identical twin convincingly within the limits of his physique.) "In his first big musical role, he's sincerely dramatic, shyly romantic, aglow with homely charm and surprisingly effective as a song-and-dance man." The scholar failed to uncover in his research that Jimmy's singing, like his accordion-playing in another film, was initially dubbed. Jimmy confessed to the *L.A. Times*'s Kevin Thomas in 1967 that when the studio executives attended a preview of *Born to Dance,* they said, " 'We're not going to have this big bum sing.' So they dubbed in a high-pitched voice with an English accent." After another preview, the producer said, "This picture's going to be such a big smash, let's put Stewart's own voice back in—he can't hurt the song.' "

Unfortunately, audio-animatronics would not be invented for another half century, so Jimmy's hands and feet couldn't be computerized and radio-controlled the way dubbing could mask a multitude of singing sins. (If Jimmy felt any embarrassment when he watched *That's Entertainment* in 1974, he needed to wait only a few more frames for a similar singing-dancing screen humiliation to be presented by Clark Gable.)

Jimmy was such a disaster as a song and dance man—with or without dubbing—that he wouldn't be called on to perform similar chores until 1970 in *The Cheyenne Social Club,* when he and Fonda warbled (mercifully, for the last time) on screen.

Luckily, Jimmy didn't need to be Fred Astaire to woo the

likes of Ginger Rogers and other reputed amours. To hype a movie, the studio would order its leading man and lady to go on very public "dates," with the paparazzi not only notified well in advance of the rendezvous but often put on the payroll to record these historic moments in advertising.

It's more than a coincidence that Jimmy was reported to be dating Ginger Rogers, Jeannette MacDonald, Virginia Bruce, Alice Faye, Heddy Lamarr (perhaps *the* most beautiful actress of her day if not the most talented), Eleanor Powell, and Lana Turner.

Jimmy's dating schedule was more the result of feverish churning of MGM's famous publicity machine than his rampaging libido. More often than not, but not always, the woman he was escorting to Ciro's or the Coconut Grove just happened to be starring in a film with him at the time of their date. *Colliers* flat out said Stewart's love life was the "creation of lady columnists" like Hedda Hopper and Louella Parsons, who perhaps lived vicariously, in print, through their imaginings of Jimmy's sex life. Tongue in cheek, *Collier's* reported that Stewart "found himself 'engaged' an average of twice a week, mostly by odd coincidence to the leading lady of his current picture." Even sophisticated male stars fell for this hype and didn't bother to conceal their jealousy over all the female attention Jimmy was reportedly getting—while they weren't. In an era when homosexuality was still the love that dare not even whisper its name in the media, Jimmy's rivals didn't stoop to innuendo. Instead, his envious contemporaries spread the rumor that these virtual busloads of lovely ladies simply wanted to mother, not marry, James Stewart. The shallow depths these rumors reached claimed women were not sexually attracted to him, but that he merely aroused their maternal instincts.

Jimmy's allure may also have been caused by his self-restraint or good old-fashioned manners. Gossip columnist Sidney Skolsky wrote, "He is the romantic type off screen as well as on. Yet he will go with an actress for weeks before he tries to kiss her."

Years later at the AFI tribute, Jack Lemmon hypothesized that Jimmy's attraction was actually a combination of evoking

maternal instincts and his gentlemanly behavior. Before intro-
ducing a film montage of Stewart's love scenes, Lemmon said,
"People don't think of him as the great screen lover, in retrospect. But he ended up with a who's who in Hollywood of the
great leading ladies. Hank Fonda said it's because they all
wanted to mother him." In that case, Hollywood must have
been filled with actresses suffering massive Electra complexes.
In fact, Grace Kelly at the same tribute confessed to having a
crush on him while shooting *Rear Window*. And she was a
good candidate for an Oedipal complex, a woman who sought
out older men as lovers, a reaction to her own cold, emotionally
aloof father. In 1954, when they made *Rear Window,* the 46-
year-old Stewart was about as sexy a "daddy" as a young
beauty could find. Unfortunately for her, he was already married.

This bizarre Oedipal imagery crops up in quote after quote
over 50 years of reportage. Frequently, it's men obsessing about
Jimmy's hold over women. Henry Fonda said, "Women wanted
to mother him. They were the aggressors. They showered *him*
with flowers." New York gossip columnist Earl Wilson
sounded very much like a female reporter for a woman's magazine like *Cosmo* when he wrote, "The American housewife's
dreamboat is Jimmy Stewart. They're mad about Clark Gable,
Eddy Duchin, and Victor Mature. But it's Jimmy they burn to
mother and smother in the oven of their lovin'."

Jimmy's rivals during his young stud days could have spared
themselves the aggravation and envy. Stewart was usually the
first to deflate all this Lochinvar lore. Self-deprecating anecdotes were his best weapon against the jealousy and the mythol-
ogy. "I don't have time to fool around," he lied to a reporter.
"Often I have to work on Sundays. Now, I ask you, how can
ardent love thrive under such conditions?"

Asked his opinion on nudity and sex in film, Jimmy sounded
like the poster boy for dysmorphic body image syndrome: "I
look terrible without any clothes on. I wore tights for *Ice Follies
of 1940* [he meant 1939]. I was supposed to be a champion ice
skater," but again his two left feet recast him in a less athletic
role as a horse's ass—literally. "I wound up as the back half

of a horse. Lew Ayres and I flipped for the position, and I lost.''

While Stewart patented the lovable *naif* on screen, sometimes his screen persona overlapped into his love life. While some women found his boyishness endearing, at least one considered it oafish. When Jimmy told his friend and discoverer Billy Grady that he had recently gone on a first date, Grady asked if he planned to continue the relationship. Jimmy said, ''I'm not sure. I don't understand her.'' In his Runyonesque patois, Grady related the rest of Jimmy's first and last date with the woman. ''I later find out on a moonlight night, they're parked in the car outside her house. The dame feels romantic and says, 'It's so lovely; the trolls must be out tonight.' If she'd said elves or pixies or leprechauns, Jimmy might have got it, but he didn't know what troll meant. So he asked her, 'Who are the Trolls—your neighbors?' The dame thinks he's putting her down and she storms into the house—alone.' ''

Jimmy was no lounge lizard either. More like a lounge loser. This is how he described his first visit to the swank Trocadero: As he emerged from a taxi in front of the club, his suspenders broke. ''Here I am, almost a movie star and here with me is a beautiful actress. It is a wonderful night, and I'm at *the* Trocadero. And what is happening to me? I am losing my pants!''

The Trocadero was also the site of another memorable first meeting with a girl, but not romantically. If he hadn't become a superstar, Stewart could have been a talent scout. He was like a pig sniffing out truffles when it came to ferreting out future greatness.

One Saturday night at the Troc, as it was known to its habitués, ''I was there [when] a little girl [an unknown] with pigtails got up and sang for an hour. Although most of us were drunk, you could hear a pin drop. Nobody who was there will forget. That little girl was Judy Garland.'' Interestingly, Jimmy remembered the unknown singer, but when a reporter reminded him in 1978 that after her Trocadero debut he'd co-starred with Garland in 1941's *Ziegfeld Girl,* Jimmy confessed that he not only didn't remember Garland, who had a supporting role, he didn't remember being in the film. Jimmy in 1978, age 70, was not suffering the memory loss but the aftereffects of workaholism. "I don't remember *Ziegfield Girl* because I was making *Pot O' Gold* at another studio, and I just walked in and out to film scenes with Lana Turner" (in *Ziegfield*).

Pot O' Gold may have stuck in his mind while the luscious Lana and *Ziegfield* didn't because of an embarrassing incident that seared the 1941 film into his memory forever.

As an indentured studio servant, Jimmy was making *Ziegfield* at night and *Pot O' Gold* during the day. Exhausted after the day's shoot, he would show up at the nighttime location of *Ziegfield* and ask the director, "What's my attitude here? Where have I been and where has Lana been?"

The two films became so entangled in his mind that at one point he found himself asking the director a question 10 times more embarrassing than "What's my motivation?"

"I came in late on the set that night and said, 'How did Lana die? Did I have anything to do with it?'"

Jimmy's forgetfulness was typical rather than embarrassing as it revealed the ridiculous sweatshop conditions he and other stars labored under. If George Saunders couldn't even remember the Iago-like gossip columnist, Addison De Witt, he played in his Oscar-winning classic *All About Eve,* Jimmy could be forgiven for forgetting whether or not Lana had died in a potboiler like *Ziegfield.*

Jimmy was reminded of *Pot O' Gold* in a much less pleasant way than receiving an Oscar for it. In 1955 when the studios were terrified that television would steal their audiences, Stewart recalled staying at a hotel in New York City and seeing "this godawful movie" on TV in his suite. "Awful! Someone squirting a selzter bottle. I thought, 'If this is the kind of stuff they're putting on TV, we haven't anything to worry about in Hollywood.' Then I got a little closer to the TV and found *I* was squirting the seltzer—it was *Pot O' Gold!*"

Little humiliations like being forced to sing and dance, and big pains like making two films at the same time, never soured Jimmy on the studio system. To the end of his career, even after he had helped destroy the studio's hegemony, he would remain one of its biggest defenders. His defense reflected so many of his personality traits and values—self-criticism and constant self-evaluation, a work ethic that was really workaholism, and good old-fashioned respect for authority, all of which he learned from his father.

Stewart was his harshest—and perhaps only—critic. In an interview with *The New York Times,* he said, "I know I'm forgetful. I know I have a stubborn streak. I think I have a sort of a mild straitlaced attitude about me. I approve very highly of discipline. An actor needs discipline. You hear so much about old movie moguls and impersonal factories where there was no freedom. MGM was a wonderful place where decisions were made on my behalf by my superiors. What's wrong with that?" A liberal rather than conservative Stewart might have deadpanned, "Waal, I think you call that totalitarianism."

Chapter 11
True Love, Parts I & II

The studio's backbreaking schedules may have made Jimmy's love life difficult, but not impossible. There were at least two women who were neither publicity matchups nor columnists' fantasies.

One date was definitely not the product of a Metro promotional push. In fact, a movie studio tried to keep them apart. In 1980, at the 40th anniversary of the New York premiere of *Gone With the Wind,* Olivia de Havilland displayed an amazing memory for detail regarding her serious romance with Jimmy. Although the liaison had ended nearly half a century earlier, her comments were so fresh it sounded as though the affair was a recent phenomenon.

The anniversary screening at the Los Angeles County Museum of Art goosed her memory of the original Hollywood premiere in 1940. Under contract to Warner Brothers, de Havilland had been reluctantly loaned out to MGM to play Scarlett O'Hara's rival for Ashley Wilkes' affection. (In return for de Havilland's services at Metro, Warners' got Jimmy to star in an awful little farce about alcoholism called *No Time For Comedy.* Hitchcock may have said actors were cattle. To the studio heads, they were literally chattel.) Jack Warner was willing to let de Havilland go to work for MGM, but he was damned if he was going to let one of his biggest stars promote his biggest rival's biggest film. Warner imperiously commanded her not to attend the premiere of the film in which she had a major supporting role. (And would win her an Oscar nomination.)

As de Havilland recalled in the *Hollywood Reporter*, "Curious, it was Jimmy (whom I didn't know) who took me to the opening of *Gone With the Wind* in New York—which Jack Warner forbade me to go to." Irene Selznick, the wife of the film's producer, David, was determined to play matchmaker— and get a little promotional sugar out of de Havilland's appearance at the Big Apple premiere. "Irene arranged for Jimmy and me to get together," the actress said. A major star in her own right, de Havilland recalled being starstruck at the prospect of going out with Hollywood's Un-Stud. "At that time he was an American folk hero, a latter-day Charles Lindbergh in a sense," she said.

Although Jimmy reportedly never phoned women or sent them flowers, he not only picked de Havilland up for the date, he met her at the airport. On the tarmac. "He even had a limo drive out on the airfield. We were both quite shy and ventured one word at a time in our conversation."

In her reminiscence, de Havilland suddenly jumpcuts from tongue-tied shyness to describing what sounds like a full-blown affair. "From then on, we went out on the town—*night after night*—to the theater and 21, where I had my first bourbon old-fashioned. We saw each other for months until people started quizzing us about when we were getting married . . . and *I* decided we should stop seeing each other." De Havilland was an accomplished heartbreaker. She also dumped the all-time Hollywood sex symbol, Errol Flynn, who suddenly embraced monogamy when he fell in love with her on the set of *The Adventures of Robin Hood*.

While her disposal of Flynn, a compulsive womanizer, needs no explanation, de Havilland's explanation for dropping the most lovable guy in Hollywood doesn't explain much: "Jimmy had a degree in architecture.'' OK, so maybe her mother told her never to date sailors or musicians, but *architects?*

De Havilland continued to beg the unasked question: ''He probably wanted to put more money in the bank.'' (He was earning $2,700 a week at the time and was famous for investing his money profitably.) Finally, she suggested the real reason, which was consistent with her rejection of Flynn. ''And he probably wanted to sow his wild oats.''

Or maybe, although it seems unlikely, it was just that Jimmy was such an absent-minded driver, or parker, actually. Fifty years after the romance ended, Jimmy found himself shooting an episode of his TV series outside the very house in the Los Feliz area of Los Angeles where de Havilland lived during their brief affair. Perhaps he remembered the house because of an embarrassing incident that may explain in part why he never got the Cary Grant roles except when Hitchcock hired him. He recalled pulling up to de Havilland's in his brand new La Salle. He was so excited about his date, he forgot to put on the parking brakes. The expensive car rolled down one of these hills and onto the main drag, Los Feliz Boulevard. Jimmy ran after it, then watched with horror as his La Salle bounced off several parked cars and fences, destroying front lawns until it came to rest by wrapping itself around a telephone pole. ''Most expensive car I ever owned,'' Jimmy recalled ruefully, although its cost represented less than one week's pay at the time. As much a lady as Jimmy was a gentleman, de Havilland was too polite to tell Jimmy what a moron she no doubt felt he was. Instead, she suggested sweetly, ''Why don't we take my car instead?'' Jimmy ignominiously sat in the passenger seat. De Havilland insisted she drive her white Packard to their destination.

The courtship turned out badly for de Havilland as well. By attending the *Gone With the Wind* premiere, which started the whole affair, she was suspended by the vindictive Jack Warner for 2½ months without pay. In de Havilland's estimation, it was well worth the slap on her savings account. ''The premiere allowed me a wonderful whirlwind affair with an American folk hero,'' she said 40 years later.

The other great love of his bachelor days was Ginger Rogers.

In a rare moment of candor after he was married, Jimmy fessed up—minimally: "We were an item." An unlikelier odd couple there hasn't been since Jack Lemmon and Walter Matthau shared a New York co-op. Louella Parsons had called Jimmy "the nicest superstar in Hollywood." Although it's not nice to speak ill of the dead, Ginger, the most famous termagant in Hollywood, anticipated Barbara Bush's famous rhyme about Geraldine Ferraro and "rich." Rogers seemed to have stepped out of her solipsistic universe long enough to return Jimmy's affections. In a nostalgia-drenched piece in *TV Guide* in 1970, a visitor to the set of his TV series wrote, "Ginger was crazy about him for a while." Jimmy, according to one report, was even more smitten. A reporter speculated that he remained a bachelor until his 40s because he was still carrying a torch for Rogers. According to another account, their affair lasted six months. "I think he loves Ginger," a friend said, "but she seems to *scare* him!"

Another witch that got away was the even scarier Bette Davis, whose daughter wrote a bestseller about her in 1985 that made *Mommie Dearest* read like *I Remember Mama*. Davis never got a chance to work with Jimmy during his bachelor days, so she never got a crack at him either—until 1973, when they were both working on a TV series on the backlot of their old home, MGM. During a joint luncheon interview with *TV Guide,* Davis was still miffed at getting stiffed by Stewart 40 years earlier. In front of the magazine reporter, Davis put him on the spot and said, "How come you never asked me out when you were one of the most sought-after bachelors in Hollywood?" Instead of saying, as her daughter B.D. Hyman would in *My Mother's Keeper,* "Because *you* were one of the meanest drunks in Hollywood," Jimmy gallantly replied, "I never knew you wanted to go out with me." Davis lamented, "It took me 41 years to land even a lunch date with him."

Chapter 12

Riding the Wave of Stardom

After a series of potboilers like *The Shopworn Angel* and *The Ice Follies of 1939,* Jimmy got lucky. He began to work with A-list directors like George Stevens in *Vivacious Lady* (1938). He also made a minor classic, *You Can't Take It With You* (1938), with the director who had a transforming effect on his life and career, Frank Capra. As Claude Rains says to Humphrey Bogart as Ingrid Bergman flies out of his life in *Casablanca,* "I think this is the beginning of a beautiful relationship." It was for Capra and Jimmy. He said of their first screen collaboration, "I just became completely engrossed and an admirer of Frank Capra, and I did as many pictures as he asked me to."

The *New York Daily Mirror* capsulized the heady but steady evolution of Stewart's filmography: "A couple of good things came out of the Depression—Jimmy Stewart for one thing. With each new movie he keeps getting better and better. He's the original perseverance kid."

Perseverance got him his best role up to that time. In 1939 Stewart finally broke away from the loser nerd roles in the political classic, *Mr. Smith Goes to Washington.* On loan to Columbia, the studio figured out what MGM had failed to: the gangly misfit was actually an attractive Everyman. As the

Saturday Evening Post wrote half a century later, "Suddenly the studio realized exactly what image Jimmy Stewart projected to the audience." And it wasn't the junk he had been doing for the past four years. His "foster home" found it had borrowed "a decent guy, an average fellow, the epitome of the honest, ideal American." Today, when screenwriters need shorthand to describe such a personality, they say something like, "It's the Jimmy Stewart character."

Mr. Smith was the second collaboration with his favorite director, Frank Capra. An amazing bit of trivia pops up in a news story from the period about a plagiarism suit in which Capra testified in favor of the credited author of the screenplay, Sidney Buchman. In the middle of his testimony, Capra let a shocker slip out when he mentioned casting the lead. "I first thought of Gary Cooper, but he was engaged in making another picture. I then thought of Jimmy Stewart and felt I had hit upon the logical man. He was the perfect character to portray a garden-variety citizen."

Maybe it was the solemnity of the real-life courtroom that made Capra so circumspect in his praise of Stewart's talent. Half a century later, he'd be more effusive in his estimation of Jimmy's artistry.

Capra told the *Boston Herald* in 1983 that there were three levels of actors. "The first kind, the majority of actors, go in and get paid for it and do it. Then there are a few who give great performances . . ." The third level, Capra said, is not a performance. "That's the level at which there is no acting at all. Jimmy Stewart is one of the very few actors who have achieved that level. He's tops."

Ironically, for the same reason Capra praised him, many film critics would pooh-pooh Jimmy's acting ability, calling him a typical movie star who basically played himself in film after film. Similarly—and more on the mark—charges were leveled at Cary Grant and John Wayne.

The normally sycophantic *Saturday Evening Post* in 1988 said, "From Westerns *(Winchester '73)* to mysteries *(Rear Window, Vertigo),* from biographies *(The Spirit of St. Louis, The Glenn Miller Story)* to sentimental fairy tales *(It's a Wonderful Life),* he like Cary Grant and all the old time movie stars never subordinated his own image to that of the character he portrayed.''

Cary Grant, for one, was sick of being the poster child for one-note actors. The actor had been dead for two years by the time the *Saturday Evening Post* decided to badmouth him, but earlier, he defended the movie star as auteur theory by saying, ''It's easy to hide behind a character. By contrast, the hardest thing is to be yourself in front of 30 million people. That's exposure of one's self.''

At the age of 78, Jimmy was still insecure enough about his talent to worry that his critics might be right. ''Sometimes,'' he said, ''I wonder if I'm doing a Jimmy Stewart imitation myself. I'm lazy. I don't act. I react.''

Two years before that self-deprecating quote, Jimmy was a bit more stalwart in his own defense. When asked for the umpteenth time if he was just playing himself, he politely responded, ''My favorite answer to that is Spencer Tracy's. Spence used to get that an awful lot, and finally, one day, he got fed up. 'Well,' he said, 'who would you rather have me play? Humphrey Bogart?' ''

Frequently Jimmy would quote Laurence Olivier, who unbelievably copped the same guilty plea. ''Actually,'' Jimmy said, ''I think I like Sir Laurence Olivier's answer to that question best: 'I always play myself . . . with *deference* to the character.' Well, that's a pretty good fella to take advice from. I guess that's what I try to do too.'' Jimmy was being modest. Sir Laurence, later Baron Olivier, was being insanely modest when he suggested he was playing himself on screen or stage—with or without deferring to the role. When Jimmy played a Budapest salesman in the film *The Shop Around the Corner,* perhaps remembering the barbecuing he took on Broadway for attempting a Viennese accent, he didn't even bother to drop his Pennsylvania drawl to attempt a Hungarian accent.

Olivier, by contrast, could imitate an unplaceable Mitteleuropean accent in *The Prince and the Showgirl,* an Oxbridge intonation for *Hamlet,* and an almost unintelligible Cockney ''haccent'' in *The Entertainer.* Today, Robert De Niro, as crazy as it may sound, is more like Olivier, playing an intellectual studio head in *The Last Tycoon* and scum of the earth in *Taxi Driver.*

So Jimmy didn't do accents. That still doesn't mean he was always playing himself. It's true Stewart didn't have Meryl Streep's linguistic bag of tricks (speaking German with a Polish accent in *Sophie's Choice)* or De Niro's ability to literally disappear into a role, gaining 50 pounds for an inflatable Jake La Motta. But what he lacked in diversity of mannerisms and *patois,* he more than made up for in the variety of roles he played in 79 films. *Vogue* called him "the most fully realized personality in film history. He has played the widest range of roles of an American actor. Roles so central to the times that to examine Stewart is to consider the American man. He's played senators and lunatics, regular joes and G-men. All of them different, *each a lot like Jimmy Stewart."*

It's hard to say if it was a compliment or not—although it was clearly meant to be one—when *Good Morning, America* ran an ad in *People* magazine for Jimmy's 1982 appearance on the show: "David Hartman interviews the greatest character Jimmy Stewart ever played. Jimmy Stewart."

Thanks. I think.

One wonders if that off-handed compliment in the *People* ad reminded Jimmy of Capra's similar compliment years earlier when the director called Jimmy a "garden-variety citizen" perfect for the title role in *Mr. Smith Goes to Washington.*

In his syndicated column, pre-variety show days, Ed Sullivan called Cooper's unavailability for *Mr. Smith* "18-carat luck" for Jimmy, then insisted it was even luckier for Capra and the movie: "It wasn't lucky, however, that Stewart played the role better than the older Cooper could have played it." This column was filed in 1940 and showed that Stewart was not only the darling of cooing female columnists like Hedda and Louella, but a favorite with hardboiled reporters like Sullivan. Even right-wing Walter Winchell worshipped Jimmy—frequently in his column.

It's hard to guess what must have hurt Stewart more: the left-handed compliment of being called "a garden-variety citizen" by Capra in his plagiarism suit testimony or learning he wasn't the first choice for the role that made him a superstar.

At least Stewart could console himself with the fact that Capra may have reflexively thought of Cooper because he had cast the actor three years prior in *Mr. Deeds Goes to Town,* a film with a near identical theme (even a climactic courtroom speech) that substituted the evil capitalism of New York for the evil politics of Washington. Jimmy could also console himself with the fact that although he and Cooper both won Oscar nominations for their films, *Mr. Smith* was a much bigger critical and financial smash.

It was also an instant classic, unlike *Mr. Deeds.* The political drama cast Stewart as Jefferson Smith, an honorable *naif* who is appointed to fill a vacated Senate seat by his state's corrupt party machine. Claude Rains played the state's senior senator with the same oily charm and menace he would display a few years later as the Nazi collaborator in *Casablanca.*

Stewart won the New York Film Critics Best Actor Award and his first of five Oscar nominations—in no small part due to his impassioned climactic filibuster speech in the Senate chamber, where he denounces the corruption he has discovered all around him.

The speech was "grueling," Stewart recalled. "The hardest thing for me was trying to fake the hoarseness in my voice as the filibuster went on."

Despite an excellent working relationship that would span decades and produce classic collaborations, Capra never coddled his star.

At the end of the first day of shooting, Capra told him it sounded as though he was *faking* laryngitis, which of course he was. Decades before Robert DeNiro would make himself morbidly obese to play an over-the-hill prizefighter, Jimmy Stewart proved himself one of the earliest "Method" actors. Driving home from the studio, he stopped at the office of an eye, ear, nose, and throat doctor and asked him, "Is there any way you can give me a sore throat?"

Chuckling, Stewart recalled the doctor saying, "I heard you Hollywood people are crazy, but *you* take the cake. It's taken me 30 years to learn how to *keep* people from getting sore throats, and now you come in here and want me to *give* you one? OK, mister, I'll give you the worst sore throat you've ever had in your life.''

Obligingly, the next day the otolaryngologist accompanied him to the set and every few hours swabbed the actor's throat with a corrosive mercury solution that swelled and irritated the vocal cords. *"I* could hardly talk, hurt something terrible. But it worked,'' Jimmy said, still grimacing at the thought of the long ago pain.

The pain and suffering paid off when he received his first of five Oscar nominations, losing to Robert Donat in *Goodbye, Mr. Chips.*

One demographic didn't share the general enthusiasm for drama. At a special preview of *Mr. Smith* for members of Congress and their wives in Constitution Hall, this particular audience didn't consider the film an instant classic. More like visual libel. They were furious when graft was portrayed as commonplace in Congress. Reporters in the audience were ticked off that they were portrayed as drunks in the pay of politicians. Mr. Smith, it seemed, had done something to offend everyone at the D.C. premiere. People began booing the film. After half an hour, they started to leave. Soon the theater was half empty. Jimmy was on location in Canada shooting a Western so he didn't witness the walkout. A senator who had also missed the preview nevertheless condemned the film on the floor of the Senate. ''I hear there's a picture that's derogatory about the Senate. I assign so-and-so to see the picture and make a report.'' The Congressional aide later made his report: ''I've been down to that theater four times and I can't get in.''

Mr. Smith's popularity then and now should not be surprising. It may be one of the most ''undated'' films ever made. Only a few years after Watergate should have made most Americans cynical about anything regarding Washington, the New York *Times* said, ''*Mr. Smith* seems rather radical in 1977.''

In 1939, the film was a huge hit despite the raw nerve it touched when its fictional depiction of corruption on Capitol Hill appeared too documentary-like for some politicians. While most of them contented themselves with walking out of the theater or badmouth-

ing the film on the floor of the Senate, one statesman went much
further and tried to get *Mr. Smith* banned overseas.

In an eerie foreshadowing of William Randolph Hearst's
attempt to block the release of *the* classic, *Citizen Kane,* only a
year later, Joseph Kennedy, the U.S. Ambassador to London,
personally phoned Columbia chief Harry Cohn and begged the
most vulgar mogul in Hollywood not to release the film in Europe.
Kennedy genuinely feared that *Mr. Smith's* negative portrayal of
the American political system (actually its politicians, not the
system, which Jimmy's Senator Smith glowingly embodied)
would be a blow to the morale of our allies . . . and it might be
construed as propaganda favoring the Axis powers. The irony is
rich. Kennedy would soon be recalled by FDR in disgrace from
the Court of St. James for urging Americans not to get involved
in "Europe's" war. Kennedy was as notorious an isolationist as
Jimmy's hero, Charles Lindbergh. Both men would be banished
to minor functionaries' jobs when the U.S. entered the war. As
punishment, Lindbergh, the Colin Powell/Norman Schwarzkopf/
Neil Armstrong of his day, wasn't even allowed to enlist in
the armed forces. As for Kennedy, once a serious presidential
contender and a huge financial contributor to the Democratic
Party, it has been claimed that FDR refused even to take the ex-
ambassador's phone calls! When it came to enemies' lists, Richard
Nixon had nothing on FDR. The wartime president simply wasn't
stupid enough to write his list down—although he did do a primitive
phonograph recording of confidential Oval Office conversations,
anticipating Nixon's own preoccupation with audiotape. Jimmy's
war-time activities would be slightly more hands-on.

In 1987, at the height of the Iran-Contra scandal, Jimmy was
invited to address the National Press Club in Washington as
the highlight of a screening of *Mr. Smith.* Although many
politicians were in attendance and the film had special resonance
in the wake of Iran-Contra, no one walked out this time. In his
speech Jimmy joked that his invitation to the event meant that
he had finally been forgiven for ruffling so many feathers almost
half a century earlier. "They invited me and my wife Gloria
to the National Press Club in Washington and said I was OK.
So I guess all was forgiven," he said. Asked if today Senator

Jefferson Smith would be a Democrat or a Republican, Jimmy, a lifelong standard-bearer for the GOP, showed that he was also a diplomat, saying he didn't know, "but I'm sure he'd be a conservative, though."

Despite his new status in 1939 as one of Hollywood's most respected actors, Jimmy had to suffer something akin to the casting couch, although it was more like the entire casting trailer. And he already had the job!

In contrast to de Havilland's dewy remembrance of things past, there's the raunchy story of the day Marlene Dietrich attempted to seduce Jimmy Stewart. In a tale that *Vogue* insisted was "well-documented," Stewart kept putting off Marlene Dietrich's entreaties on the set of the ground-breaking Western, *Destry Rides Again,* also shot in 1939.

Finally, the actress stormed his trailer and locked the door behind her. As a friend of the actress said years later, "If Marlene wanted a man—or a woman—they didn't stand a chance."

According to *Vogue,* Jimmy took it like a man—lying down.

In 1989, happily married to his wife of four decades, Stewart gallantly insisted in *Vogue* that the tale was apocryphal. Even though he was an unattached bachelor at the time and wouldn't meet the future Mrs. Stewart for a decade, Jimmy was too much the gentleman—and much too wise to rub his wife's nose in his premarital love life, especially since she sat in on the *Vogue* interview. "I was too busy," he said, dismissing his close encounter with Dietrich.

Wrong. Anyone who has ever visited a movie set knows how much down time there is for the actors while the cameraman and lighting technicians spend forever setting up the next shot. That's one of the reasons actors have trailers on the set. So they can have a private place to hang out while they're waiting to be called back to work.

Vogue stood by its "documentation."

In his 1985 bio, Jhan Robbins not only provided documentation but managed to dig up an eyewitness to the seduction. Or as close as one could get without being a Peeping Tom. *Destry's* producer Joe Pasternak was on the set the day Dietrich got her man. "The more exotic the woman," Pasternak told Robbins, "the more deceptively simple Jimmy became. When Marlene got on the set of *Destry Rides Again*, she took one look at him and said, 'That's for me.'

"Jimmy didn't seem to be aware of what she had in mind. He was in love—with Flash Gordon, the comic book character. That's all he seemed to read, all that occupied his attention.

"Marlene decided to take the initiative. She had the art department make a life-sized doll of Flash Gordon that was, uh, correct (anatomically) in every way. Then she walked into his dressing room, handed over the gift and locked the three of them in together," Pasternak swore in 1985.

Dietrich was not only aggressive, she was creative. If it took a *ménage à trois* with an imaginary space hero to bag her hero, the German vamp did what she had to do. The *Vogue* story did sound apocryphal, as Jimmy gallantly suggested in front of his wife, but Pasternak's account is so filled with detail—unlikely detail (a Flash Gordon doll!)—that one is tempted to believe the producer instead of Honest Jim. All Jimmy would say in his gentlemanly way was, "Dietrich was a toucher. Carole Lombard was not a toucher."

Whether or not Stewart was seduced by one of the most desirable women in Hollywood, *Destry* nevertheless turned out to be one of his finest films. Jimmy's enthusiasm was shared by cineastes. In a 1982 poll of cable movie channel subscribers, *Casablanca* and *Destry Rides Again* tied as the most "beloved" film of all time.

Besides being one of 1939's biggest hits, *Destry Rides Again* is historically noteworthy for a wagonload of reasons. It was the first comic Western. In fact, when the film was released, Universal was deluged with furious letters from fans for desecrating the venerated genre. Stewart in a 1982 interview for the film's screening on a pay cable channel, dismissed the whiners as "dyed in the wool Western fans."

Until *Destry,* sagebrush was serious stuff, involving what today would be considered serial murder, widespread alcoholism, and the treatment of aboriginal peoples that Pizarro and Custer would have approved of. Clint Eastwood suggested much of this in his revisionist classic, *Unforgiven.*

Destry was not only a flat-out farce, its lead was a woman in this most macho of film genres. The male lead was a doofus, Tom Destry, the sheriff who not only couldn't shoot straight, he wouldn't shoot at all. Jimmy played a gunslinger without a gun. On screen and in trailer, Dietrich was in charge as Frenchy, the saloon hall chanteuse whose stage gymnastics even topped her over-the-top eroticism in *The Blue Angel* and gave Madonna something to imitate 50 years later. Stewart was the wimp of the West hired to clean up a town where the concept of law and order was unknown. The sheriff had his work cut out for him because he refused to wear a gun. Besides being the first comic Western, *Destry* was and may well be the only *pacifist* Western—Gandhi as Wyatt Earp. The director of *Destry* was George Marshall, who specialized in broad farces starring Laurel and Hardy, W.C. Fields, Bob Hope, and much later Dean Martin and Jerry Lewis.

Marshall couldn't resist sending up Dietrich's by now self-parodic image of an emasculatrix first seen in the 1930 German classic, *Der Blaue Angel*, in which she drove men mad with her sexual allure, "like moths to the flame." Stewart was the perfect foil for this man-eater. Marshall ended up giving the picture to Dietrich at Stewart's expense.

That was an inexplicable gift. According to the American Movie Classic cable channel host, Bob Dorian, Dietrich was ranked 126th on the list of box-office attractions in 1939. She was suffering from the same malaise Katharine Hepburn was enduring, box office poison syndrome. (Jimmy would "cure" both actresses by working with them in blockbusters, *Destry* and *The Philadelphia Story.*)

Although Stewart's Tom Destry *was* the title character, *Destry* remained Dietrich's vehicle. When he showed up on the set, Stewart was a newly minted superstar, just coming off the career-making *Mr. Smith* and soon to win his first Oscar nomination. He was at the peak of his career, earning almost three grand a week, while Dietrich's career was already in freefall after one too many unintentional parodies of her femme fatalism. *Destry* was produced by Universal, then the Rodney Dangerfield of studios, and Jimmy, on loan from the No. 1 film factory, MGM, easily could have demanded that *Destry* focus on him, Tom Destry, not on Frenchy. The movie was, after all, called, *Destry Rides Again,* not *Frenchy Straddles a Chair for Erotic Effect.* Although one film critic, tongue firmly planted in cheek, wrote, "I think it was Lord Beaverbrook who said that Marlene Dietrich standing on a bar in black net stockings, belting out, 'See What the Boys in the Back Room Will Have,' was a greater work of art than the Venus de Milo."

And when Madeline Kahn sent up that chair-straddling scene in Mel Brooks' *Blazing Saddles* 35 years later, Kahn was spoofing what in 1939 was already a spoof of Dietrich's sexual voraciousness.

Instead of Jimmy, it was Dietrich who got the glory and the great scenes. She even "got" the girl, although not in the way she allegedly "got" Jimmy in his Winnebago. Even subtextually, *Destry* was not a sapphic Western. We'd have to wait until 1953 for Joan Crawford and Mercedes McCambridge to even hint at that kind of Western revisionism on screen.

In 99 percent of Westerns, old-fashioned or revisionist, the climactic scene is a fight, usually a *mano à mano* gun duel on Main Street between the two male protagonists. Marshall invaded this male preserve with his two female leads, Dietrich and Una Merkel. Instead of guns, Dietrich and Merkel engaged in a catfight, clawing and punching without resorting to firearms. Jimmy wasn't miffed that he was cut out of the fight. He was just impressed with what great brawlers his leading ladies were. "It's one of the best fights I've ever seen," he said. A Method actress before the Method was even known outside Moscow's Art Theater, Dietrich, Stewart said, rarely used a stunt double in these punishing scenes. "Less than 10 feet of film," he claimed, featured Dietrich's double. Merkel and Marlene "really beat each other up. I think it was because of Dietrich. And they got mad at each other because Dietrich was determined to make a good fight out of it. It's easy for us to put on pads." A proto-feminist, Stewart felt for the actresses who had to beat each other up, Dietrich in a tight-fitting dance hall hostess costume and Merkel in a gingham dress. "And of course," he added, "they couldn't have much padding because they didn't have suits and stuff like we had."

Chapter 13

An Oscar for Dad, A Career For Kate

We've already seen how the tyrannical studio barons worked their well-paid stars like mules and miscast them as horses' asses—literally, in *Ice Follies of 1939*. The gilt-edged abuse, however, didn't stop with inappropriate casting. On any given day a major star, even one with an Oscar nomination under his belt, might be commanded to play a supporting role. And the actor, under an unbreakable seven-year contract, meekly obeyed. (One holdout: Katharine Hepburn, who was always turning down roles and getting suspended *without* pay. She used this "down time" to return to her real love, the New York stage.)

Almost 40 years later, Jimmy was still defending this dinosaur of a system that paid him well but treated him like a piece of stegosaurus meat. He was also a big booster of the main culprits who ran the system. In a 1977 interview with *Women's Wear Daily,* he defended the practices and even the taste of these vulgar moguls. "I miss the big studios. A lot of people say they were impersonal factories, but that's not true. That's where the magic and the glamour were born. People like Harry Cohn, Darryl Zanuck, L.B. Mayer—they knew movies and they had an uncanny way of judging what was star material.

You can say what you like about Sam Goldwyn, but he loved the motion picture industry, and he put his all into it.'' *Women's Wear Daily* added, ''You can say the same thing about *James Stewart.*''

Jimmy was being his typically generous self when he praised the taste of famous vulgarians like Harry Cohn, about whom another apocryphal story has evolved into ''fact:'' A Jewish producer was pitching a script about the New Testament to Cohn. Cohn demanded, ''What do you know about the New Testament, you Jew? I bet you don't even know the Lord's Prayer. I'll bet you a hundred bucks.'' The producer nervously began, ''Now I lay me down to sleep . . .'' Cohn stopped him and whipped out a hundred dollar bill, saying, ''I didn't think the sonofabitch knew it.'' Most of the moguls were businessmen who had made their fortunes in distinctly unartistic enterprises like glove-making and junk-dealing, then put their cash in the most glamorous business in the world. Their lack of education and culture didn't faze the educated and cultivated Stewart.

Cohn may not have known his New Testament, but he was the one who greenlighted *Mr. Smith,* so maybe Jimmy wasn't off the mark when he praised the moguls for recognizing star material.

In his next film, 1940's *The Philadelphia Story,* the Oscar nominee again obediently played a supporting role. Jimmy's Macaulay Connor was a cynical gossip columnist for a proto-*National Enquirer* called *Spy* magazine. Jimmy and a photographer (Ruth Hussey) sneak into a socialite's home to get the scoop on her ultra-exclusive wedding.

As a burnt-out reporter, Stewart plays a man of the people who despises the idle rich, yet finds himself falling in love with the wealthy bride-to-be, Traci Lord, played by Katharine Hepburn. Stewart's Everyman was the perfect plebeian to play off Hepburn's patrician.

As in his earlier films, it was the other guy, this time Cary Grant, who got the girl, but Stewart won the Oscar that year (strangely, for best actor, not best supporting actor, which the role actually was). With typical modesty, Stewart downplayed

the honor. "I thought it was a sentimental reward for not getting
the award for *Mr. Smith* the year before."

Mr. Smith had made Jimmy a superstar. *The Philadelphia
Story* ratcheted his career a notch higher with the prestige of
winning an Oscar. Again, he owed his advancement to the
determined will of his leading lady. Just as Margaret Sullavan
had given him his first leading man role in *Next Time We Love,*
Hepburn put her imperious foot down and demanded that Jimmy
play the gossip columnist in *The Philadelphia Story.*

Hepburn was in a curious position in 1940. While she hovered
in Dietrich land at the bottom of the list of box-office attractions,
a national poll of theater owners had placed her at the top of
an even crueler list called "Box-Office Poison" after she had
starred in flop after flop over the past five years.

How did this box office spoiler have the clout to make casting
demands? In fact, how did she manage to land the lead in *The
Philadelphia Story,* which had been a huge Broadway hit by
one of America's hottest playwrights, Philip Barry?

Simple. Hepburn may have been poisoning the box office
but she was sweetening the well with wise business decisions.
Before Barry's play became a hit, she had bought the film
rights.

She was in charge. For once, MGM's Louis B. Mayer had
to roll over and wish he were dead. Mayer probably didn't
object a bit to her insistence on casting Stewart and Grant, two
of the hottest actors in Hollywood, but he must have wept when
he was forced to hire the Lucrezia Borgia of the box office,
owner of the film rights to the hottest ticket on Broadway.

The Philadelphia Story couldn't do all that much for a career
like Jimmy's that was already skyrocketing, but much more
importantly than the class and the clout the Oscar bestowed on
him, it represented a turning point in his father's condescending
attitude toward his son's career, which up to this time he still
refused to take seriously. It was almost as though the older
man was still expecting his son to leave Tinsel Town and sell
tarp in Indiana, Pennsylvania.

His father could be as masterful an actor as his son when it
came to hiding the genuine pride he eventually came to feel

about his progeny's superstardom. Alexander played it cool when Jimmy won his Oscar, pretending to be unclear on exactly what it was.

His father had genuine trouble, however, understanding the three-hour time difference between Pennsylvania and California. Stewart fondly recalled in a 1991 *Life* interview that his father had an annoying habit of calling him at 7:30 in the morning, right after he opened the hardware store. That was 7:30 Eastern Standard Time.

After spending most of the night partying hearty after winning the Oscar in 1941, Jimmy was awakened by his father at the usual time—4:30 A.M. Pacific Standard Time. Half-conscious, Jimmy recalled his father saying, ''I heard on the radio they gave you some kind of award. What was it, son, a plaque or something?'' Alexander was, as they say today, messing with his son's mind. The Oscar in 1941 was every bit as big a deal as it is today. While there was no Mary Hart to gush about the couture of the arriving celebrities on TV, radio announcers were just as awed over the airwaves about the biggest gala of the year.

Alexander completely gave himself away as the closet fan he was when he added, ''You better bring it [the Oscar] back here, and we'll put it in the window of the store.' ''

Jimmy, still his father's son, obediently packed up the statuette and mailed it home. ''It was there in the window of the hardware store for 20 years. He put it under a cheese bell,'' Stewart recalled. Only after his father died did he reclaim his prize.

It seems that Dad had been a closet fan from day one. Jimmy's sister Virginia remembered that her father refused to drive with her and her mother to Pittsburgh 50 miles away to see Jimmy in his first starring role, *Next Time We Love*. Her father didn't hold out for long. In a first-person account in *Coronet* magazine in February 1940, Virginia wryly noted that after a few more pictures starring Jimmy, her father suddenly began subscribing to movie fan magazines! ''Dad came home for lunch one day,'' Virginia wrote, ''with a fan magazine under his arm, bearing a full-page picture of his son. We realized, incredible though it was—that Jim was 'in the movies.' "

Virginia also recalled that their father was inordinately impressed when he received a letter from Shanghai, written by a Princeton alum, asking, "That wasn't the same serious little boy in glasses he had seen at Princeton reunions 15 years ago, was it?" Virginia summed up the *entire* family's eventual concensus. "We became movie fans. Picture magazines overran our house. In our home *Photoplay* had replaced *Atlantic Monthly*—irrevocably."

Eventually, his father gave up all pretense of indifference and turned the hardware store into a virtual Jimmy Stewart Fans Clubhouse.

The *Motion Picture Herald* in 1946 said archly, "It's the only hardware store in the country, as far as anybody knows, where an Academy award, their son's, is on display."

In 1984, you could hear Jimmy's own pride in his voice when he told *Parade* magazine how proud his father was of his success. "If I made a picture he liked, he'd go badger the local theater to give him posters and stuff. Eventually, J.M. Stewart & Co. got to be sort of a museum. People'd come around asking for 'Jimmy Stewart's father.' "

When Hedda Hopper asked Jimmy what his father thought of his success, Jimmy dismissed the question with irony, but underneath the answer was a hint that Jimmy still missed his father's approval: "He still doesn't believe it. He thinks that some day Hollywood will get wise to me and that'll be the end." Jimmy was joking. Or was he?

As usual, Jimmy was being too hard on himself and his dad. All the memorabilia in the store belied any disapproval his father attempted to feign.

Still, Alexander never stopped pushing his son toward further excellence. He believed in withholding just enough approval to get the best out of his son, whether he was a 10-year-old Boy Scout flunking his swimming test or a 32-year-old man collecting an Academy Award. Jimmy could always do better.

When hardware store patrons stopped oohing and aahing over the Oscar, Alexander moved it out of the window and put it at one end of the knife counter. Then he gave a visiting wire service reporter a quote he was sure his son would read in the L.A. papers. The statuette, Alexander told the UP reporter, was "out of balance and needs *another* Oscar for the other end of the counter." You don't need to be a psychologist to realize that that was his father's way of telling his son not to rest on his laurels but keep on trying for the brass ring—or golden statuette. Unfortunately, his father wouldn't be around to place Jimmy's second Oscar, which he received for lifetime achievement in 1985, at the other end of the knife case for "balance."

At about the time of all the Oscar hoopla, the Stewart family encountered the downside of celebrity, which every star who ever caught a paparazzi with a zoom lens shooting him in the bathroom knows. When Virginia and her sister Dorothy moved to New York and shared an apartment, a reporter interviewed them and totally misquoted the star's siblings. Virginia remembered that even the photographer "lied." "The snapshot made us look like we were colored girls," she wrote.

The press was so eager to link Jimmy with a woman, any woman, that when he emerged from a nightclub with his two sisters, a photographer screamed, "Get him with the girl." Virginia ran away, but Jimmy and his other sister were snapped "looking like frightened sheep." Embarrassed and outraged is more like it, since the accompanying caption grossly described his sister Dorothy as his "new girl."

While photographers chased the latest Oscar champ and Dad finally fessed up to being a fan, Jimmy's glory was diluted by the widely held belief that the Academy Award was a consolation prize for having lost the year before for *Mr. Smith* and *Destry*. Jimmy admitted, "I guess it could be true that I won it as a deferred payment. Come to think of it, I've always felt Bette Davis won an Oscar for *Jezebel* because she should have had it for *Of Human Bondage*. Other oversights, I suspect, have been made up this way. I suppose that's okay, since right usually triumphs eventually," he said, sounding more like Senator Smith than the winner of the Best Actor Oscar for 1940.

Jimmy didn't need a hit, but Hepburn did, and the commercial success of *The Philadelphia Story* allowed the actress to revive her career and go on to become perhaps our greatest and most enduring screen actress. Without her prescient purchase of screen rights to *The Philadelphia Story,* she might have been one of the stars of the 1930s like Grace Moore (Oscar nominee, best actress, 1934) or Luise Rainer (Oscar *winner,* best actress, 1936 *and* 1937) who burned brightly but briefly before vanishing into film encyclopedias.

Hepburn didn't cast Jimmy because he was a babe or a box office magnet. Besides being a great actress, she was a great businesswoman. *The Philadelphia Story* was a comedy, and Jimmy made her laugh. In 1984, Hepburn explained her casting decision to *Parade* magazine. "People like to laugh, and Jimmy is funny. He's funny on the screen without looking as if he's trying to be, and he's funny off the screen when he doesn't even mean to be."

Jimmy repaid the compliment by almost killing her.

Chapter 14

Back Seat Poison

Katharine Hepburn played a famous aviatrix in 1933's *Christopher Strong* and allegedly dated a famous aviator, Howard Hughes, at about the same time. But not even her experiences with that flyboy-turned-wacko billionaire could have prepared her for her brief time up in the air with an actor turned wacko aviator, Jimmy Stewart.

With the bankroll of a movie star, Stewart had bought a Stinson cub airplane and earned a pilot's license. "First thing I did when I got my first check," he says. Then he toted up more flying hours and lessons to get a commercial pilot's license.

During a break in shooting *The Philadelphia Story,* he invited his benefactress to go for a spin in the Stinson. Hepburn turned out to be the backseat driver from hell. She was just as pushy about flying as she was about casting her leading men. Unlike Jimmy, however, Hepburn didn't have a pilot's license. That didn't stop her from instantly deciding she was his co-pilot. Or maybe that Jimmy was *her* co-pilot.

Stewart acknowledged that Hepburn did know something about aviation. "Well, of course, she learned from Howard Hughes! And he was probably as expert a pilot as ever lived.

She and Howard Hughes were . . .'' In this 1983 interview with
the *Boston Herald*, Jimmy was still too much of a gentleman
to suggest that a "lady" might be living in sin with a man.
The interviewer, Angela Dunn, supplied a euphemism—"An
item?"—which Jimmy silently accepted, then went on with
his story. "I don't think she could fly, but she knew about
planes. I think she asked Howard, and I think he probably liked
to explain . . .''

Unfortunately, even the powerful Hughes never had the nerve
to tell Hepburn to shut up when somebody else was at the
controls. Jimmy and Kate took off from Santa Monica Airport,
and within five minutes she was demanding they return to the
ground. She had noticed that a gauge indicated the plane was
out of oil. Jimmy explained that the gauge needle was simply
stuck, and it always registered empty. "That's no answer,"
Hepburn said tartly. Jimmy knew for a fact that the plane had
sufficient oil. He didn't have a death wish. Hepburn had learned
from Hughes, however, that when the gauge says empty, you
land right away.

Accommodating as always, Jimmy agreed to ground the
plane even though he knew his "co-pilot" was dead wrong.
Things only went downhill—literally—from there. Not only
did she demand they land, she wouldn't let him turn the plane
around so he could do so. "She wouldn't let me turn . . . after
I took off . . . she wouldn't let me turn!" Jimmy repeated the
fact, still incredulous after 40 years. "We were over the Pacific
Ocean . . . and I was sort of wondering . . . the next stop's
China! If you kept going . . . She said, 'Don't turn. Don't
turn.' ''

Finally, she ordered him to "level off." At last he ignored
his leading lady and turned the plane around to approach the
runway. Hepburn said, "I think I've had enough." So had
Jimmy. She had apparently so rattled him that he forgot much
of what he had learned while earning his *two* pilot's licenses.
"I had quite a few landings in my life, but this was . . . this
wasn't a landing. This was a controlled crash. And she didn't
say anything. She didn't scream . . . and here's where it would

have been understandable ... I taxied up, cut the engine. She got out on her own. Got in her car and left. And never a word.

"Never a word since ..." Except, apparently, when the cameras were rolling on the remainder of *The Philadelphia Story.* It's a shame for movie lovers, although probably a blessing for Jimmy's mental health, that Hepburn was so ticked off she refused to ever work with him again. As they demonstrated in their one successful screen collaboration, he was the perfect passive yin to her domineering yang. Hepburn ended up doing some of her best work with her long-time lover, Spencer Tracy, in *Adam's Rib, Woman of the Year,* and *Pat and Mike.* Although Tracy fans will probably try to beat me up in an alley for writing this, Stewart was a far superior and more complex actor than Tracy, who had been his first mentor way back on *Murder Man,* Jimmy's film debut. Tracy and Hepburn were both tough and stubborn on screen and off. They were too evenly matched. Hepburn might have done more interesting work if she had played her dominatrix persona off Jimmy's gentle facade, which concealed a will every bit as steely as the Iron Lady's. Especially in the 1950s, as his career reached its apex and hers began to falter, he might have pulled another *Philadelphia Story* hit out of his hat and resuscitated her career, which didn't revive until the late 1960s when she ended up playing old mothers and aging queens. But her truculence and loss meant a gain for every other leading lady in Hollywood.

In the same interview about his near-fatal crash with Hepburn aboard Stewart also confessed that he got "stuck" on just about "every girl you're in a picture with." He then gallantly named a veritable laundry list of co-stars on whom he had platonic crushes. Pointedly left out of this encyclopedia of actresses was his cockpit co-star from *The Philadelphia Story.*

Chapter 15

Uncle Sam Doesn't Want You

Jimmy's decision to become a pilot and fight in World War II is filled with irony. Next to his father, Charles Lindbergh was the actor's all-time hero. It was Lindbergh's famous Transatlantic flight in 1927 that would prompt Jimmy to buy a cub plane and get both a pilot's and a commercial pilot's license.

When Stewart was 19, Lindbergh, only six years older, made his historic flight. Jimmy charted the course of Lindbergh's crossing in his father's store window with cardboard models of the Woolworth Building where Lindbergh began the flight. Using a tiny airplane, Jimmy slowly moved Lindbergh's Spirit of St. Louis across a map of the Atlantic as the pilot crossed the ocean. At the end of the map was a model of the Eiffel Tower, although Lindbergh actually landed in Le Bourget airfield.

The aviator wasn't just Jimmy's hero. He was America's. No single American today comes close to approximating the hero worship or capturing the public imagination which Lindbergh's flight accomplished.

The irony of Jimmy's adulation was that Lindbergh was a notorious isolationist who opposed U.S. entry into the war, agreeing with JFK's father, Joe Kennedy, that the embryonic

American Air Force was no match for the Luftwaffe which Hitler and Goering had been beefing up since 1933. Lindbergh led huge ''America First'' rallies, urging the U.S. not to get involved in a war that was Europe's, not America's, problem. In the late 1930s, America's Golden Boy was thoroughly discredited when he visited Nazi Germany and toured its munitions factories. Newsreels of the day capture the creepy image of Lindbergh flanked by a beaming Hermann Goering and Rudolf Hess. After the war, he must have cringed when he saw footage of himself shaking hands with Hitler himself.

After his death, Lindbergh's private correspondence was made public and revealed him and his best-selling author wife, Anne Morrow Lindbergh, to be anti-Semitic. In Lindbergh's defense, documents have come to light which also show that the aviator actually made the trip to Germany at the secret request of the U.S. Government, to gather information on the military preparedness of the Third Reich. FDR was livid, however, when Lindbergh returned and publicly predicted that Germany would beat the hell out of America if it came to war. That was not what the President wanted to hear—or at least not have disseminated publicly. Lindbergh was punished for his frankness when the War Department refused him a commission after hostilities commenced. Frustrated, Lindbergh secretly flew 50 missions in the Pacific in civilian togs.

Jimmy Stewart must have been shocked by his idol's behavior since he held diametrically opposed views.

In March 1941, seven months *before* Pearl Harbor, when ''Europe's problem'' became America's as well, Jimmy Stewart enlisted in the Army Air Corps.

Well, he *tried* to enlist. Jimmy met with more resistance than Lindbergh's attempt to join up, and Jimmy had never praised the Luftwaffe or told FDR to keep his nose out of European affairs.

So many things conspired to keep Jimmy stateside, it's amazing he managed to become Hollywood's most decorated war hero.

First there was MGM, which greedily squeezed three awful films out of him before he finally succeeded in heeding Uncle

Sam's call. Then the studio, which would later make ponderously patriotic war films, tried to turn its biggest star into a draft dodger.

When the studio learned he had tried to enlist, an executive told him, "Relax. We'll try to fix it so you won't be drafted." Another honcho said, "Hollywood needs you. And after all, no other star has joined up and we have a terrific new picture for you."

A friend recalled, "Jimmy got awful mad and went back to the draft board without telling MGM."

Jimmy had a right to be almost as mad at Uncle Sam as he was at Uncle L.B. He had already earned a commercial pilot's license even though he knew men with that kind of experience would be the first to be drafted. To make himself even more attractive to the army, he rented a 400 horsepower plane and racked up an additional 200 hours of flying time. He paid for these private lessons out of his own pocket at the enormous rate of $17 an hour.

MGM executives could have saved themselves all that trouble: The army still didn't want Jimmy.

At the time Jimmy was one of Hollywood's biggest stars, "a real-life American hero like Charles Lindbergh," in de Havilland's phrase. He had won the Best Oscar less than a month before he tried to enlist. His eagerness to join up was better advertising than Uncle Sam pointing a guilty finger at young men and demanding, "I want you."

And the Army wouldn't have to spend thousands of dollars teaching him to fly. He already had two pilot's licenses plus 200 hours extra flying time.

What did Uncle Sam want? Blood?

No, he wanted heft. Jimmy's old bugaboo, his scarecrow physique, came back to haunt him and get him declared 1-B, a deferred classification that amounted to 4-F. Jimmy Stewart immediately appealed the classification—and lost. Many other stars, including Frank Sinatra, who had ear and throat problems, were happy to sit the conflict out in the comfort of Beverly Hills. The closest they would come to the Pacific war was Malibu Beach. The ultimate hawk, Ronald Reagan, had hearing problems which kept him out of the trenches and in a movie studio making propaganda films for the duration. (In a very scary segment on *60 Minutes* about 10 years ago, before Reagan's Alzheimer's was publicly revealed, Reagan was shown reminiscing about what he claimed were his real-life war-time air battles. *60 Minutes* devastatingly intercut these "memories" with scenes from Reagan's films of that era. The President's recollections were actually based on his movies, not his military service.)

Jimmy flunked his first physical. Army regulations didn't make exceptions, not even for Academy Award winners. If you were 6'4″, you had to weigh a minimum of 148 pounds. Dripping wet, Jimmy tipped the scales at 133 pounds.

The press found out, and the newspapers were not kind. Jimmy later said, "Coast-to-coast headlines blared, 'Movie Hero Heavy Enough to Knock Out Villain But Too Light for Uncle Sam.' " The press has always had a fascination with stars' vital statistics. For a time in the 1980s, aided and abetted by Joan Rivers, variations in Elizabeth Taylor's waist measurement received the kind of scrutiny usually reserved by the financial press for NASDAQ.

The press reaction to Jimmy's ectomorphic problems was not only unkind, but inaccurate. The headline Jimmy specifically recalled 20 years after the fact, in *McCall's,* implied that he played tough guys on screen but was a 133-pound weakling in real life.

Jimmy's father read the same tacky headlines and didn't take a philosophical view of their inaccuracy. Once again showing he was the Mama Rose of the Stewart family, he phoned his son and said, "Jim, this is your father." Jimmy wrote in *McCall's,* "As if I could mistake his thunderous voice. Dad announced, " 'I'm coming right out to Hollywood.' " Jimmy said, "Dad, there's nothing you can do about the situation."

"I can punch a few noses among those reporters. Then we'll start [law] suits." His father hadn't fought in *two* wars without learning how to fight. Stewart Sr. was ready to take on the U.S. government and the Selective Service so his boy could do his duty to his country.

For once, Jimmy lectured his father instead of the other way around. "That wouldn't help things a bit. Only make it worse. You can't treat the press that way," said the actor, who was religious about giving interviews to promote his films. The press always got the red carpet treatment from this superstar, even though his father wanted to give its reps a bloody nose.

Dad wasn't through. "OK, I'll hire a public-relations man for you. I'll get the best there is in the business." The older man was amazingly media savvy for the owner of a hardware store in the heartland.

"No, Dad," Jimmy said, probably disobeying his scary father for the first and last time in his life.

"Well, by God, we've got to do something!" Alexander thundered long-distance from Indiana, Pennsylvania.

Jimmy finally, gently, hung up on his blustery father and put the phone call out of his mind. But not for long. Just as Jimmy recalled his father "gently nudging" him in the direction of Princeton when he had set his sights on Annapolis, "I realized [the phone call] hadn't been inconclusive at all; Dad had been walking beside me, nudging me in the direction he thought I should take. He had named all the alternatives I should take but one, leaving the proper decision obvious. Now we both knew what I had to do to retain my self-respect."

At this point in his 1960s magazine reminiscence, Jimmy engages in a little historical/mythical revisionism. Unlike most revisions of history, its purpose wasn't to save face. In fact, the following version of how Jimmy finally squeegeed his way into this man's army is much less dramatic than another version, much more fancifully described below.

Twenty years after the fact, Jimmy recalled in *McCall's*, "The next day, I went back to the induction center and begged them to forget the fact that I was underweight. I knew I could meet all the physical requirements if they would just ignore the scales. At last they agreed, and I became a soldier—just as my father had been in two previous wars," (and Granddad in the Civil War).

That was Jimmy's version. Contemporary newspaper and magazine accounts are more in keeping with Stewart's character. They also jibe with the ''by-the-book'' mentality that has pervaded the military before, then, and since.

Calling on the same industriousness with which he attacked the film studio when it rejected him for similar puniness, Jimmy once again called on the services of MGM's trainer to the stars, Don Loomis. After superhuman exertions, Loomis only managed to raise Jimmy's weight to 143 pounds—still five pounds under the legal limit. This time, even Fonda's famous brandy milkshakes didn't work.

Probably for the first and last time in his life, Jimmy tried to cheat on a test. He returned to the induction center and using all the charm that had made him America's favorite star, he told—begged—the enlisting officer, ''Listen here, why don't you just rerun the tests and, uh, 'forget' to weigh me.'' The officer was not starstruck, but he was shocked. The man said Jimmy's suggestion was ''highly irregular.'' Jimmy said, ''Well, war is highly irregular.''

Finally, Billy Grady, the talent scout, since promoted to head of casting at MGM, came to Jimmy's rescue once again. Grady was a magician. He also had a very creative imagination when it came to effecting the seemingly impossible. As ridiculous as this story sounds, Grady swore it was true. And there's no other published explanation for how Jimmy added those five crucial pounds. Grady in his patented Runyonese described the day he finessed his protégé's entry into the Army.

''Jimmy goes down for his next physical. And I'm there to take him in a studio car. He refuses to go in a limousine. He goes by trolley instead! I tail him to the place where they look Army candidates over. I sit there waiting. When the medical officer comes in, I ask him if Jim has made it. 'He's made it by one ounce.' What the officer doesn't know is that Jim is so determined to make weight he hasn't been to the bathroom for 36 hours! It's been torture, but it puts him over.''

Without referring to this alleged subterfuge, Jimmy simply explained his success by saying ''the draft was the only lottery I ever won.'' Again, he was being too modest. Jimmy wasn't drafted; he enlisted. But he was accurate when he claimed that he had won a contest of sorts. Before the war, it wasn't that easy to get into the armed forces. The country was still in a Depression, and many of the unemployed hoped to get a job with Uncle Sam. In fact, 16 other wannabes who volunteered the day Jimmy was finally accepted failed to pass the physical. It wasn't the lottery, but Jimmy was right to feel like a winner.

MGM wept. The country wasn't even at war, and one of its biggest box office draws was abandoning the studio. Patriotically, the same studio that had urged him to dodge enlistment now told him his seven-year contract would be waived for the duration of his stint. MGM wasn't exactly being noble or generous. The public backlash would have led to boycotts of the studio's films if it had refused to let its contract-player hero out of his contract.

But first the studio forced him to make three more quickies before he showed up at Westwood and Santa Monica Boulevards for a trolley ride to the enlistment center: *Come Live With Me,* a witless romantic comedy which had the saving grace of allowing him to make love on screen to the most beautiful woman in Hollywood, Hedy Lamarr; *Pot O' Gold,* the stinker which made him almost retch when he saw it on TV years later and didn't recognize the idiot (himself) playing the lead; and *Ziegfeld Girl,* which wasted Jimmy's star power by casting him in a small role at the expense of its three female leads, Lamarr, Lana Turner, and Judy Garland.

Even before he announced his intentions to give up career for country, Jimmy was doing his bit to fight the Nazi menace. As we will see in a later chapter, this early example of what would be called premature anti-fascism didn't get him into trouble during the McCarthy witch hunts. In 1940, while Joe Kennedy in London was still urging Americans to leave the Nazis alone and stay the hell out of the war, Jimmy was engaging in a little bit of anti-Nazi propaganda.

The Mortal Storm was an early propaganda film which prophetically warned of the Nazi menace while German-American storm troopers were still goose-stepping around Soldier Field in Chicago, doing bad imitations of Leni Riefenstahl. One film critic credited the drama with "bringing home the inherent evil of the Nazi system" at a time when there were still many

American apologists for the appalling fascist regime. Stewart and his former ''discoverer,'' Margaret Sullavan, play Bavarian lovers whose romance is interrupted when Nazis take over their town.

In contrast to Kennedy and Lindbergh, who was organizing America First rallies around the country, Stewart and Sullavan were already doing their bit for a non-existent war effort. As the film critic for *The Observer* in blitzed-out London wrote, ''Margaret Sullavan as the daughter of a university professor and James Stewart as her lover—both open rebels against the Nazis—act with a kind of unwilling intensity which is extremely effective.''

And the Army still had the nerve to turn him down until the eleventh hour.

While Jimmy and Sullavan were battling Nazis on screen, off screen they were taking a more active role in the still undeclared war. In August 1940, probably as a publicity stunt for *The Mortal Storm,* Jimmy, Sullavan, and her ex-husband, Henry Fonda, flew to Texas to raise money for Great Britain, which was about to begin the battle for its life in a near *Gotterdammerung* called The Blitz the very next month. At a Houston fundraiser, the Coliseum was sold out to see real-life stars like Jimmy and Henry Fonda do hokey magic acts and play a duet, with Fonda on the cornet and Jimmy on his lethal accordion.

Many other Hollywood stars and especially screenwriters took on the Nazis before Germany officially became America's enemy after Pearl Harbor. Amazingly, their prophetic patriotism would actually get them into trouble during the postwar anti-Communist hysteria. Exactly what did these stars and writers have against Hitler *before* the war, certain politicians wanted to know. Wasn't Hitler an anti-Communist when you opposed him? But that's a nightmare for another book, a nightmare which Jimmy with his impeccable patriotic credentials would escape. Many of his colleagues would not be nearly so lucky.

MGM, meanwhile, managed to squeeze one more bit of hype out of Jimmy's heroism—although by then he was safe and far away from Culver City, ducking flak attacks and Nazi fighter planes in Germany. In 1944, Jimmy's heroic efforts to gain weight and admission into the army were fictionalized—in *You'll Never Get Rich*. Another real life ectomorph, Fred Astaire, played a dance instructor who is drafted then rejected because of his weight. Somehow, he manages to gain six pounds and entry to the Army. Astaire's dance man ends up running a stage show for GIs in the film. Jimmy's wartime experiences would be significantly different—and not just because he couldn't dance.

Chapter 16
"Jimmy's Finest Role"

The *Saturday Evening Post* called his four years of wartime service simply, "Jimmy's Finest Role." The *New York Times* explained his motivation for enlisting perfectly: "Stewart's idealism and honesty didn't end with mere movie characterizations" as in *Mr. Smith*. "He practiced in real life what he preached on the screen."

This wasn't hype.

But first, MGM wanted to get some last-minute publicity out of the star it had tried so strenuously to keep at home and on screen. A huge going-away party took place on the backlot. When all the screen goddesses under contract to the studio were ordered to "report for duty" and plant lipstick kisses on the departing star. Joan Crawford, Lana Turner, and Judy Garland did their duty, then Jimmy did his, wiping off each successive kiss and writing the star's name under the imprint on his handkerchief. *Life* magazine noted that he kept the handkerchief.

Induction day was a pain in the neck, or more accurately a publicity zoo with the nightmarish quality of a Hollywood premiere, except that it was held near dawn.

At 7:30 A.M. March 22, 1941, James Maitland Stewart II,

actor, was ordered along with 19 other enlistees to show up at the corner of Westwood and Santa Monica Boulevards, a few blocks south of the UCLA campus. His pal Burgess Meredith and Billy Grady drove him to the corner in Westwood, which was a trolley stop. As Jimmy boarded the streetcar, a band of drunken UCLA fraternity boys played two ancient drums, a battered trumpet, and a rusty trombone. They weren't there to send off Hollywood's biggest star. They were performing a farewell song for their frat brothers, who comprised two of that day's 19 enlistees. The band played—or attempted to play— "You're in the Army Now," while waving placards that said, "So long, Yardbirds," the unofficial rank for one step below buck private.

The Hollywood premiere atmosphere grew more intense when the trolley delivered its victims to the induction center at 106 W. Third Street in downtown L.A. Several hundred fans had been alerted by MGM's publicity machine, and the 1940s version of groupies, bobby-soxers, tried to mob Jimmy as he fled inside. A wire service reporter filed this copy: "They were there to catch a glimpse of an actor portraying a real-life role without retakes."

The bobby-soxers were kept at bay, but a tsunami of paparazzi was let in with the enlistees. No doubt the studio had greased the gears of a big wheel at the induction center. There, the cameras faithfully recorded Jimmy saying, "I, James Stewart, do solemnly swear I will bear true faith and allegiance to the United States of America and will serve them honestly and faithfully against all their enemies whomsoever. I will obey the orders of the President of the United States and the officers appointed over me according to the rules of the articles of war. So help me, God." Journalists even recorded the name of the officer who administered the oath, Col. John A. Robinson, the district recruiting officer.

The paparazzi were finally kicked out, but the print and radio reps must have been allowed to stay, because newspaper accounts of the time duly reported with the detail of eye-witnesses that Jimmy was then stripped of his clothes and had a purple I.D. number painted on his stomach. Jimmy took and passed a physical exam—again—with a "good rating" and named his mother as his beneficiary in the will all the inductees were ordered to fill out.

In uniform, Pfc. J.M. Stewart received his first promotion. He was appointed group leader of the men, now grown to 41 souls, as they made their way from the induction center to Fort MacArthur.

Chapter 17

You're in the Army Now, You're Not Behind a Camera

Before, during, and after his service in the Army, Stewart almost religiously refused to talk to the press. While his ingrained work ethic made him duty-bound to promote the hell out of his movies as part of his studio duties and service his fans as "paying partners," military service was not a clause in his contract with MGM. And his natural modesty wouldn't allow him to capitalize on his stardom or use it to get a cushy berth in the armed services. Which makes sense. If he wanted special treatment, he could have gotten the most special treatment of all, a deferment. (Errol Flynn claimed New Zealand citizenship. Others, failing to find a good excuse, ended up entertaining rather than fighting alongside the troops. Syndicated columnist Robert C. Ruark maintained that "for most of the War, any movie actor who didn't want to get in this mess could duck [active service]—as so many did—on grounds of public morale, merely by entertaining the troops. Only a handful of movie stars and athletes actually fought: Gable went in way over age on purpose; baseball player Ted Williams did three hitches. Mostly they organized bands, played ball, entertained troops or worked a safe billet in a back area, such as the U.S.A.'')

The military brass didn't want Jimmy to entertain *per se*. Perhaps they had seen *Born to Dance* or heard him play his accordion somewhere and knew that "An Evening With Jimmy Stewart" would probably do more propaganda harm than the Luftwaffe blanketing Britain with counterfeit pounds or defeatist pamphlets.

The more sophisticated War Department officials knew exactly where Jimmy would be most effective—as a superflack for the entire war effort. When Stewart enlisted, higher-ups begged him to become what was known as "an information officer." Today, that's the handsome, picture perfect officer you see briefing the press on the network news during a crisis in the Gulf or Bosnia. Norman Schwarzkopf instinctively knew the star-making effect such a job would have and somehow, while organizing Desert Storm in Iraq managed to find time to brief Dan Rather, Tom Brokaw, and Peter Jennings almost every night at 7 P.M. Schwarzkopf knew what he was doing. He not only parlayed his media celebrity into a best-selling autobiography post-Gulf, but upon retirement landed a six-figure salary doing a butcher impersonation of Charles Kuralt's "On the Road With . . ." series for the *NBC Nightly News*.

Jimmy already had a six-figure salary, and he had had enough media attention for a lifetime. He didn't join the Army to become Colonel Superflack. If war came, he wanted to fight. Defending one's country was generational and practically genetic among Stewart men. As he later succinctly put it, "Eventually, I talked them into letting me become a pilot" instead of a press agent. "I realize a movie actor is an offbreed of cat to the military establishment, but there's nothing that says an actor can't be a man who can do an effective job as an officer with duties that normally befall an airman. I still believe I can be more useful as a combat officer," he told UPI before hostilities began.

It may be the ultimate testament to Jimmy's clout as Hollywood's hottest star that he in effect had the power to disobey orders. No one in the War Department apparently had the cojones to simply order Jimmy to whore for the military. If such a command had come down, Jimmy—prewar—could have resigned from the service. The ensuing PR nightmare ("Army Insists on Superstar Treatment for Reluctant Superstar") would have made those counterfeit pounds sterling dumped over Britain look like manna from heaven by comparison. Once the war began, it was too late to order Jimmy into the flack department. He had already become an accomplished pilot.

A few months after his brass band induction into the Army, Jimmy was still treating military service like a camping trip. The war hadn't started yet, and he wasn't as press shy—or maybe just plain traumatized—as he would become after the war turned grim and the bodies started piling up.

In a cornball first-person account for the Associated Press from his first billet at Moffett Field near San Francisco, Corporal Jimmy Stewart of the 9th Air Base Group described a life in uniform that sounded more like *Sgt. Bilko* than *All's Quiet on the Northern California Front.*

Jimmy reported that his principal feeling on his first day at "summer camp" was literally nausea. "You have it for about a week. It's the same feeling you have before a race or before you play in a football game or go in and ask the boss for a raise." (Jimmy hadn't experienced the latter feeling in years. His high-powered agent, Leland Hayward, did all the begging for salary increases. And after star turns like *Mr. Smith* and *The Philadelphia Story,* Hayward probably did a lot more demanding than begging, even from the terrifying L.B. Mayer.)

Jimmy first thought his sinking feeling was unique, because of all the nauseating attention from paparazzi and bobby-soxers. Then he asked around and found out his fellow inductees were also feeling butterflies.

His nervous stomach vanished within three days, but exchanging his upscale existence for the lifestyles of the low-born and unknown took longer to get used to. Some of Army life was nothing new. Reveille was at 5:45 A.M, which didn't faze him at all, since he was used to getting up only slightly later—6:30—for early morning calls to the movie set. Autocratic directors and 12-hour shoots to save money had a boot camp flavor of their own.

Time was the luxury this wealthy recruit had to forfeit. Although pre-induction he rose at 6:30, he spent the next hour luxriating in the shower, shaving, reading the newspaper and studying his lines for the day's scenes. In boot camp, he was allowed 15 minutes to wash up. There was no time for reading the paper and no script to bone up on.

For the first and only time in his military career, Jimmy complained about this aspect of Army life. "I think I have a legitimate beef on this score. I'm almost 10 years older than most of these fellows in my barracks. They can get away with shaving once a week, but it's every day for me."

Inhaling his food was another problem for Stewart, who chewed and swallowed as slowly and deliberately as he stammered. Jimmy discovered that if he didn't bolt his food and eat every morsel on his plate, KP duty was the punishment.

In sum, boot camp was no day in the park, but it wasn't an internment camp either. "The work and drill is pretty hard, but don't let anyone tell you it's too hard. It isn't. And you have plenty of time to rest and relax," he wrote in his syndicated account for UP.

The optimism and good spirits that suffused boot camp before the war became a deadly affair impressed Jimmy. He said he talked to hundreds of fellow GIs, "and I've yet to hear any grumbling."

This bit of nostalgia which ran in the Los Angeles *Times* and other AP subscribers on June 1, 1941, is recounted in such detail here because its chirpy tone would contrast dramatically with newspaper accounts of Jimmy after he had experienced the full horror of war in bombing raids over Germany and France. Before the war he could write and joke about comrades-in-arms too young to shave on a regular basis. As the war heated up, there was nothing amusing about the dozens of these comrades who didn't return from bombing raids.

And then he refused to talk about his military experiences, much less write about them.

But until Pearl Harbor, Jimmy continued to treat the service like a frothy MGM musical with reveille instead of a Richard Rodgers score. A month and a half after the above wire story,

1935—Jimmy Stewart, the young matinee idol.

1938—The World War I romance *The Shopworn Angel.*

In *The Shopworn Angel,* leading lady Margaret Sullavan reportedly had a crush on her handsome leading man.

1939—Stewart won his first Oscar nomination as the crusading senator in *Mr. Smith Goes to Washington.*

In *Mr. Smith Goes to Washington,* Jean Arthur cheers him on.

1940—
The Philadelphia Story
with co-star
Katharine Hepburn.

Katharine Hepburn had cast approval and chose both Cary Grant and Stewart as her leading men in *The Philadelphia Story.*

1945—Stewart left the Army Air Corps with the rank of Lieutenant Colonel. He had it written in his studio contract that his war record never be used to promote a film.

A rare photograph of Stewart in pilot's uniform.

1946—*It's a Wonderful Life.* Stewart hugs his
leading lady, Donna Reed, who plays his wife.

Co-star Donna Reed
and Stewart pose for
It's a Wonderful Life.

1949—In *The Stratton Story* Stewart played a one-legged ballplayer.

The Stratton Story featured June Allyson as the sympathetic wife.

1949—The happy newlyweds: Jimmy and Gloria Stewart.

1950—Stewart won his fourth Oscar nomination for
his role in *Harvey*.

In *Harvey*, Stewart is featured with Josephine Hull as his
long-suffering aunt, Veta Louise.

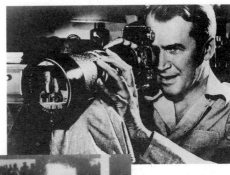

1954—*Rear Window* featured Stewart in a Hitchcock film.

In *Rear Window*, Grace Kelly played the fashion-plate who thought the 46 year-old star was a real dish.

1954—In *The Glen Miller Story*, he studied the trombone for months, and the director dubbed his music anyway.

Jimmy Stewart as icon of the American man.

1955—In *Strategic Air Command*, Stewart played a pilot of a jet loaded with nuclear-tipped warheads.

Strategic Air Command featured June Allyson as his wife yet again.

1958—In *Vertigo*, Stewart was reunited with Hitchcock.

1959—Stewart and his wife Gloria, a big game hunter, en route to India.

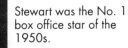

Stewart was the No. 1 box office star of the 1950s.

p2570-29

1968—*Firecreek*. Henry Fonda and Stewart didn't work together on screen until they starred in this film.

In *Firecreek*, Stewart was typecast as the good guy.

Well into middle age, Jimmy Stewart personified the American cowboy with numerous roles in Westerns.

Jimmy Stewart with his wife, Gloria, and their daughter, Judy.

Jimmy Stewart with the honorary Oscar he received in 1985.

1992—At 84, Stewart posed for the Desert Palm
Achievement Award at the Palm Springs Film Festival.

he was back at his typewriter, composing *shtick* about Army life so hokey it would make *No Time for Sergeants* seem like Restoration Comedy for its sophistication. In a July 13, 1941, AP story, Jimmy devoted seven column inches to a lame anecdote about a Private Simpson who had the improbable shoe size of 15A. The Simpson story went on so long with so little payoff that you begin to suspect that Honest Jim never used a ghostwriter for all this wretched whimsy. Why, that would have been plagiarism, and plagiarism was out of the question for a man of integrity like James Maitland Stewart II. The ghostwritten *Profiles in Courage* would win JFK a Pulitzer and Martin Luther King's doctoral dissertation would "borrow" heavily from Paul Tillich and earn him the title Doctor King, but Honest Jimmy was content to speak in his own voice. The ultimate proof of Jimmy's sole authorship was the fact that even if a studio flack had stood in for him, the writing would have been superior. Fortunately for Jimmy's sterling film career, unlike so many other wannabe star-auteurs, he never tried his hand at screenwriting.

There was one much more polished pre-war piece that ran in Sidney Skolsky's syndicated column. It purported to be a reprint of a letter Jimmy sent his agent Leland Hayward complaining about unfair treatment in the Army. (Skolsky was an embarrassing hack, the Hank Grant/Army Archerd of his day, who is remembered, if at all, in a trivia footnote, as the man who hired an unknown starlet to be his driver, a woman by the name of Norma Jean Baker.) The letter sounds spurious for several reasons. Jimmy was never one to complain, and it was way too amusing for the actor's ham-fisted style. Most importantly, the column ran under Skolsky's own by-line, unlike the Stewart by-lined pieces for AP.

Dated May 2, 1941, the alleged letter to Hayward from Jimmy, datelined like the AP stories from Moffett Field, began:

"Dear Leland,
    Enclosed find $2.10, which commission, owed you by me from my salary of month just passed. Leland, I would _____ ____ __to a little matter with you . . . Now, Leland,

you know me, I never complain about anything, but I am not happy [with] the dressing room they gave me. It's a great big barn, but I wouldn't mind that because you know me, but the thing is that they put 30 guys in here with me.''

Jimmy (probably Skolsky) went on to complain about his wardrobe while he was ''on location at Moffett Field. I don't know if you realize it when you read the script, but I just have one change all the way through this thing.'' Ironically, Jimmy would literally have many ''costume changes'' during the war as he was rapidly promoted through the ranks, with each promotion carrying some new insignia or ''fruit salad'' on his chest.

Money was another source of irritation in Skolsky's impersonation of an atypically greedy Stewart, in particular his buck private's salary of $21 a month.

''Now I could go up to the front office and raise hell myself, but I remember when I signed with you, you said any time I had any problem to just come to you and you would go up and talk to them about it once and get it straightened out. So I hope you will attend to this at once.

Your client and pal,
Jimmy Stewart.''

The Skolsky letter pretended that Jimmy was your typical egomaniacal star, expecting special treatment. The bizarre fact of the matter was that a lot of people acted as though he really did have those expectations. Just as it's almost certain that he rejected the services of a ghostwriter, it's definitely a fact that he spent much of his time in the Army before and during the war ducking special treatment. That didn't stop everyone from trying to give it to him anyway, from MGM offering its clout to win him a full deferment to other, even more outrageous freebies and free rides.

There was even a starstruck general whose behavior sounds as preposterous as Jimmy's purported temperament in the Skolsky column. The big difference is that this general actually existed, whereas Skolsky's "Jimmy" was almost certainly the sole creation of the columnist's hack humor.

In one of the AP stories quoted above, Jimmy mentioned that he didn't mind the early roll call. It wasn't that much different from the indentured servitude of a movie shoot. But just in case Jimmy objected, the general told him point-blank: "Don't worry about putting in your hours. Sleep late if you want to." Even the presumption that Jimmy expected star treatment infuriated the usually laid-back actor. Except that he feared a court martial for insubordination, he probably would have blown his stack when he overheard two officers discussing his presence at Moffett: "They probably sent [Jimmy] here to be photographed with the general. I suppose we've got to handle him with kid gloves."

In 1941, Pfc. James Stewart was still a superstar with clout. And he knew it. It was constantly being flung in his face. But the only time during his entire stint that he used this clout was to get rid of it. As we've seen, Jimmy spent his own money to get ahead of the learning curve and earn a pilot's and a commercial pilot's license. When it came time to take the pilot's *and* the instructor's exam, Jimmy's private tutoring allowed him to ace both tests easily. With such impressive credentials, if his name had been Mike or Bob Stewart, he would have been shipped overseas faster than you could say Queen Mary, but Jimmy was too much of a PR bonanza to be sent overseas like the men who, in those callous days, were called "expendables," and historically known as "cannon fodder."

If they insisted on treating Jimmy like a star, he was going to act like one—but only briefly and for a specifically non-starlike reason. He picked up the phone and called a few Washington friends in high places from his Princeton days. (Obviously not the same crowd that had booed and walked out of *Mr. Smith.*) The word eventually trickled down. Stewart was to be given exactly the same treatment others were getting.

An amusing trivia coincidence. A future Oscar-winner, Walter Matthau, served as a staff sergeant under Col. Stewart in the 453rd Bombing Squadron. Forty years later at the AFI Lifetime Achievement Award ceremony, Matthau would deadpan at the podium: "He only asked for one special favor—that he not be given any special favor. He won his officer's commission not by pulling strings in Washington nor on the strength of his civilian prominence but by the unspectacular method of meeting official requirements."

The only person out of the loop Matthau described seemed to be the same loony general who had suggested Jimmy throw away his alarm clock.

This superior called Jimmy into his office and said there was no reason "things couldn't be made a little easy for him. For example, what would he like to do for a start?" Like no character he had ever played on screen, Jimmy stared at his commander with visible contempt. "Please treat me exactly as though my name didn't start with an 'S.'"

Rebuffed, the general finally got the message and got more than a little ticked off that his repeated overtures to become the unofficial president of the Jimmy Stewart fan club at Moffett Field were constantly rebuffed. A few days later, Jimmy was placed in charge of cleaning out the chicken coops on base.

Being a superstar is a dirty job, but somebody has to do it.

His fellow enlistees were just as starstruck as the general, and they too had trouble keeping their fan-aticism to themselves. A twentysomething barracks at Moffett recalled looking at the older man in the bunk next to him and thinking, "There's the guy who won the Oscar for *The Philadelphia Story* and got to kiss Katharine Hepburn. Just think, that buck private has kissed the most beautiful women in Hollywood on screen and gotten paid [almost three grand a week] for it."

Soon, his fellow non-coms overcame their awe and shyness and began to pester Jimmy for autographs. Jimmy was polite but firm. Like the curmudgeonly Paul Newman (in peacetime), he refused to give autographs or sign magazine covers. The inordinately polite actor, especially after his "training" at MGM, found it "excruciatingly hard to refuse requests for autographs and photos from fellow enlistees. *But he did,*" the *Saturday Evening Post* reported.

Soon, his fans got the message and stopped asking. Jimmy apparently turned them down with such finesse he never engendered any resentment. Today, Jimmy could open a celebrity etiquette school and force celebrity delinquents like Sean Penn and Alec Baldwin to enroll.

The general and the non-coms had been effectively neutralized, but Jimmy was still besieged by interview requests and cameramen hiding in the bushes on base. (Where was camp security? Thank god Jimmy was never stationed at Los Alamos or *Variety* and Hedda Hopper would have gotten the blueprints for the atomic bomb before the Rosenbergs and the Russians stole them.)

For a respite from reporters, Private Stewart went to see Col. George Usher, the commanding officer of Moffett Field. Usher, as we shall see, did a good job of hiding his admiration, which was probably as strong as the more upfront general's. But Usher said simply, "How can I help you, Stewart, to help get you out of the spot you're in?"

"The biggest help, sir, would be no publicity. No interviews. No publicity stills. No radio appearances," Jimmy said.

"I can fix that," Usher said. The colonel kept his promise and became the PMK of the Army Air Corps. No one, not even *The New York Times,* was allowed to interview a guy named Private J. Stewart.

While the press was thus effectively kept away, that didn't stop Usher from acting like Jimmy's No. 1 fan. Usher didn't insult Jimmy the way the unnamed general did by suggesting he become a slacker and sleep late. But the colonel did engage in inappropriate fraternization with an enlisted man and became the superstar's unofficial mentor. As long as the colonel didn't try to get Jimmy to shirk his duty, Stewart put up with this unsolicited buddy relationship. Usher would frequently call the Oscar-winner into his office for "chats." He also gave Jimmy tips on how to advance his career in the military and urged him to take extension courses and earn enough flying hours to apply for an officer's commission in the Army Air Corps. That was advice Jimmy was delighted to take, and had in fact, entered the Army with that plan in mind.

Presciently or maybe clairvoyantly, Jimmy was already getting ready for the Big One. By 1936, he had racked up 200 flying hours and even learned how to survive a plane crash! While friends like Bing Crosby and Bob Hope were burning minimal calories on the golf course, Jimmy was burning rubber—and not always willingly.

Jimmy had an apparently sadistic flight instructor at this time who wanted to see how his student would react in a crash. The instructor decided to simulate a crash—without telling his pupil it was a simulation. As we've surmised, the teacher was perhaps a graduate of the Marquis de Sade *École Militaire.*

The instructor surreptitiously held back the throttle, causing the tiny plane to plummet. Jimmy would have to respond by making a forced landing. Instead, he nearly crashed the plane. The instructor was ready to chew his student out for not pulling back on the throttle and raising the plane a safe distance off the ground. After Jimmy had somehow managed to land the plane, the instructor discovered the fault was not Jimmy's, it was Professor Death's sadistic streak. The throttle had gotten stuck and Jimmy *couldn't* pull up. The fact that Jimmy was able to ''crash'' the craft safely was testament to his talent, not his incompetence. The instructor, on the other hand, should have been shot. It's a shame Kate Hepburn wasn't in the backseat to beat him up.

After the war, a researcher would find symbolic significance in what to all intents and purposes was a stupid prank by an instructor who should have had his license yanked: ''The incident was small but the implication was allegorical: from make-believe to reality without dropping a stitch,'' the *Saturday Evening Post* said glowingly.

Within a few years, under even more torturous conditions, Jimmy would be severely tested and would prove his mettle again and again.

Chapter 18
The Real Thing

When the War in Europe ended in May 1945, the biggest war hero from Hollywood, hands down, was James Stewart. As his exploits grew, news outlets from the Los Angeles *Times* to *all* the wire services sent war correspondents to Europe in search of the elusive big game known as Jimmy Stewart. With few exceptions, their prey successfully eluded them for the duration. The few times he spoke to the press was when he was cornered on a military base, and the star-turned-soldier was too much the gentleman to say, "Piss off, sir." There were other occasions, mercifully few, where he was ordered to attend press conferences. Jimmy Stewart, the former MGM contract player who would show up for the opening of an envelope if the studio ordered him to for PR purposes, gave a masterful impersonation at these military press conferences of someone undergoing root canal—without anesthetic.

When Jimmy's theater of war "went dark," he still refused to discuss his wartime experiences. In desperation, the *Saturday Evening Post* hired one of Jimmy's commanding officers, one Col. Beirne Lay, Jr., to compose a 5,000 word, two-part series, headlined, "Jimmy Stewart's Finest Performance." Obviously, the colonel or the *Post* was as starstruck as everyone else to call Jimmy's hellish military exploits a "performance." Starstruck or not, Lay turned out to be not only a competent military man, but a crackerjack journalist who told an inspiring story of Jimmy's "performance" in the European theater of war. In fact, just as the acting bug had bitten the Princeton architecture major more than a decade earlier, the "writing bug" infected Lay, who became a Hollywood screenwriter after he mustered out.

By now a corporal, Jimmy had taken Colonel Usher's advice to heart and in his spare time and with his own spare change, paid for the additional 300 hours of flying time he would need to log to take the officer's exam.

When exam time came, Jimmy discovered stage fright wasn't the only terror he would know. His nervousness before the test made appearing on stage in front an audience of a thousand seem like a play he put on in the basement at age 10. Jimmy also suffered stage fright in the air, but he didn't freeze during the exam. In November 1941, a month before the country would really need pilots, Jimmy went up in the air, an examiner beside him and butterflies in his stomach. His stage fright was misplaced. He executed each of the test instructor's commands flawlessly. After less than half an hour, the examiner grew bored by all this perfection, so he ordered Jimmy to simulate a crash landing. Jimmy did even that exquisitely. Maybe his 1936 instructor had been sage, not sadistic. After 30 minutes in the air, the instructor said, "Take her in. You're OK."

Jimmy was now a qualified pilot, but his country didn't really need him—yet. The havoc at Pearl Harbor was a month away, the U.S. was at nervous peace, and Corporal Stewart found himself standing guard in front of a giant hangar for a dirigible. This was truly a make-work assignment, since there was no enemy—yet—to sabotage the big balloon. Jimmy must have been wondering by then if maybe making jingoistic pro-war pictures at MGM might not have been a better war to serve his country.

On Jan. 19, 1942, Jimmy was still garrisoning the balloon coop, but at least by now there was a potential enemy to keep away from the hangar. On this day, however, his duties would

suddenly become much more important than preventing puta-
tive Japanese invaders from puncturing a weather balloon.

Jimmy's commanding officer walked up to him with a broad
smile and a long white envelope, Lay wrote. The letter inside
contained Corporal Stewart's commission as second lieutenant.

But the envelope contained even more important information:
orders to report immediately for active duty at the advanced
flying school at Mather Field in Northern California. Lay
reported that Jimmy's enlisted friends were not jealous of his
promotion to the officer corps. They realized he hadn't pulled
strings to get a job more exciting than baby-sitting a balloon.
It was all those extra hours of flying time (and the movie star
savings to pay for them) that allowed him to pass the exam
and qualify for this "grad school" in the air. Whether or not
they resented the fact that their pre-war salaries as soda jerks
or gas station attendants wouldn't pay for expensive private
flight training was never recorded for posterity—at least not
by the *Post*. Jimmy, however, was so modest and discreet
about his wealth that his fellow non-coms probably wouldn't
begrudge him the opportunity to participate in the most famous
element of the American dream, getting ahead by getting a
good "education."

Jimmy began "grad" school with a four-hour refresher
course on formation flying at Mather, followed by advanced
flying school for instructors. Like his meteoric film career, from
the tall "Shorty" in *Murder Man* to *Mr. Smith* and an Oscar
nod in four years, Stewart was on the fast track of flying.

After only a four-week course, Jimmy got certified as an
instructor. But for the first time, his achievement was met with
skepticism. Not simply because he was a star, but because his
more seasoned colleagues considered him a "mail-order pilot
who had never undergone the regular Army course of pilot
training," Lay wrote. But the colonel-turned-journalist failed
to mention—and Jimmy's skeptical colleagues didn't seem to
realize either—that the country was at war, and "four-week
wonders" were a necessity.

Any residual skepticism disappeared, Lay added, when
Jimmy "became an excellent instructor" after only one month:

Lay did his homework for the *Post* piece and found out about Jimmy's own learning problems—especially with killer algebra—at Princeton. Stewart's handicap, if that's not too dramatic a term, was actually a boon for the new instructor, armchair psychologist Lay posited, because it gave him empathy for other slow learners at a time when being a slow learner could get you killed. "A fundamental trait of character helped him," Lay wrote. "He was conscientious. From his own difficulties with some subjects, like navigation (or engineering at Princeton), he sympathized with a student who had to learn the hard way."

You can be sure Jimmy took extra time with slow learners so that when they graduated from his class, they were up to speed. A less dilligent teacher might have lost patience or—more disastrously—just passed the jughead along to become the next instructor's problem.

A year after enlistment, Jimmy still found himself getting the star treatment, but for once, it was a boon, not a bane. One star struck general, Kenneth McNaughton, urged Jimmy to enroll in bombardier school at Kirkland Field in Albuquerque, New Mexico. The general actually may have been more savvy than star struck, since he got double duty out of Stewart, who was promoted to first lieutenant in New Mexico at the ripe old age of 34. At Kirkland, Jimmy would continue to teach flying while learning about one of the most important inventions of the war, the Norden bombsight and related bombing techniques. The Norden ranked right up there with radar in helping the Allies beat the far better prepared and armed Axis powers. Before the state-of-the-art bombsight allowed pinpoint accuracy, aerial bombardment had all the finesse of wildcatting for crude. Sink a drill bit and pray you strike oil. Open the bomb bay doors, and pray you hit an oil refinery. After his fast-track stop at Albuquerque, Jimmy could not only fly a plane, but step out of the cockpit and wipe a munitions plant off the map. Whether he was a Democrat or a Republican, Mr. Smith was becoming a real Renaissance man in the art of warfare. Five hundred years earlier, he probably would have taken a refresher course on siege warfare from Leonardo.

Armed with what would now be the equivalent of a doctorate in all things aeronautical, Jimmy was ready to go where the action was—an English airfield. The way he got there suggests the Renaissance man moniker wasn't just hype.

The by then Captain J. Stewart, the *L.A. Examiner* reported in its November 29, 1943, edition, flew *himself* across the Atlantic. It must have been the ultimate adrenaline rush to personally retrace the route his childhood hero Charles Lindbergh had flown 15 years earlier. The *Examiner* said he piloted the big four-engined American Liberator himself on the last 900-mile leg of the Transatlantic flight. Today, we complain about stale peanuts, cramped seating, and in-flight movies starring Pauley Shore. In those days, plane cabins were unheated and unpressurized. All they lacked was Bette Davis urging the men to fasten their seatbelts because it would indeed be a bumpy, not to mention oxygen-deprived, flight.

Jimmy, however, could comfort himself from all this discomfort with the recent memory of his father's farewell, just before he flew off to England and perhaps death.

Jimmy's first-person description of this parting in a 1960s issue of *McCall's* deserved a Pulitzer. If not for style, which was excellent, but for the way in which this most private of public figures unashamedly revealed himself and his complex relationship with a difficult but doting dad.

"Dad came to the farewell ceremonies in Sioux City, Iowa, and we were very self-conscious with each other . . . At the moment of parting, he studied his shoes a moment, then looked at the sky. I knew he was searching for a final word of advice, of love, something to sustain me . . .

"We embraced; then he turned and marched quickly away. Only after he had gone did I realize that he had put a small envelope in my hand . . . That night, alone in my bunk, I opened it and read: 'My dear Jim boy, Soon after you read this letter you will be on your way to the worst sort of danger . . .''

Stewart Sr. wasn't engaging in hyperbole or armchair warriorism. He had known exactly this "sort of danger" in not one but two wars.

"Jim, I am banking on the enclosed copy of the 91st Psalm

... I am sure God will lead you through this mad experience ... Good-by my dear. God bless you and keep you. *I love you more than I can tell you.* Dad.''

Now comes the part of his reminiscence that should have won him a Pulitzer if there were a prize category for self-revelation: Stewart wrote, ''Never before had he said *he loved me.* I always knew he did, but he had never *said* it until now. I wept.''

So when is NBC or Disney going to shoot *The Jimmy Stewart Story?*

If they do, they will have to do it without an autobiography for reference. Jimmy held to two rules during and after the war. During it, he refused to talk about Hollywood. Back in Hollywood, he refused to talk about the war.

Chapter 19
Over There

When the *L.A. Examiner* reported that Jimmy had taxied himself across the ocean, it also snidely noted that he was the first actor to be assigned to actual combat flying on a regular basis. Although Captain Clark Gable had preceded him and flown five bombing raids, the over-the-hill star was primarily Over There to make a propaganda movie or two. Although he inexplicably entered the service as a captain when Jimmy, a college grad unlike Gable, enlisted as a buck private, Gable's war "effort" was more like a civilian "ride-along" in the backseat of a cop car to promote good community relations.

When Jimmy arrived at the English air base, which was never identified for security reasons in news reports of the time, he didn't waste a minute or a frame of film doing any promotional *cinema verité*. Maybe Gable's million-dollar smile helped fight the war in a truly effective way—selling bonds, bolstering morale at home, and getting men to enlist—but Jimmy's approach to getting the job done was typically more hands-on.

After only 10 days of training in England, he was assigned his first bombing raid over the Third Reich. The target was the crucial naval installation at Kiel. Stewart was in charge of a squadron which flew at 27,000 feet above the enemy target.

Maybe it was beginner's luck, but on his first mission, Stewart's squadron returned to base without a single loss.

Over the next 16 months, Jimmy would fly 19 more missions with ever-increasing authority and more men under his command. He led a "group," which consisted of 36 planes, then a wing (three groups), an air division (four groups), and finally in Colonel Lay's complex technical terms, "the whole enchilada, the entire Eighth Air Force."

Jimmy's second mission was a no-brainer over Bremen, Germany. The raid went flawlessly but no tough decisions were required, Lay said, on "what turned out to be a routine flight." The Bremen mission was routine in that Stewart didn't encounter any German counterattacks, but the target was a gold mine— actually, a steel manufacturing plant—for driving a stake into the heart of Germany's industrial might. With a population of nearly half a million, Bremen boasted shipyards and a steelworks to supply all of Germany's aviation industry. The port was also the terminus for foodstuffs and raw material, which were trans-shipped from the city to the rest of the Third Reich, which covered most of Western, Central, and Eastern Europe at the time. By bombing Bremen "back into the Stone Age," to use a phrase from a future war, the pilot was performing crucial war work. And again, without losing a single one of his men.

Lay was being a bit *blasé* when he pooh-poohed the danger of the Bremen raid and dead wrong—at least according to a United Press wire story—that Jimmy's group didn't encounter any resistance during the attack. The UP story, which was picked up by the *L.A. Times,* led with a phrase that must have made Stewart cringe more than all those flak attacks during the mission: "Capt. James Stewart, *film star,* led a squadron of Liberator heavy bombers over Bremen yesterday in a heavy attack by the U.S. 8th Air Force on that port. His squadron battled its way through the *heaviest anti-aircraft and fighter opposition ever encountered* over Germany's second largest port to hammer Bremen yesterday." At night, when it was safer, the British continued the annihilation of the port city, the *Times* added.

Although strangely it didn't mention the American attack, the Nazi news service *(D.N.B.)* in an incredible display of *chutzpah* scolded the British "bombers [for dropping] high explosives and incendiary bombs that inflicted considerable damage to property and loss of life to the German civilian population." This from the same government that would flood its own subways filled with refugees from air raids to prevent the invading Allies from using the underground as a transport route!

In the dangerous universe of bombing Germany into oblivion, Jimmy's luck couldn't hold out for long, and it didn't. His third mission tested Jimmy's mettle. The mission over Ludwigshafen also proved that Jimmy was a good Scotch-Irishman, stubborn, and not a good "German," blindly obeying orders. Although he was eventually decorated for his third mission, Jimmy actually disobeyed orders in order to do the right thing—save his men. Despite an act of insubordination, Stewart not only received a commendation, he got a "fan letter" from his commanding officer. Hollywood pursued the reluctant star all the way into enemy territory.

Jimmy's worst subject in flight school had been navigation. It was college algebra come back to haunt him all over again. Ironically, despite his lack of navigational "talent," it was navigation that saved him and his men from certain death during their mission over Ludwigshafen.

After the squadron had been airborne for a while, Jimmy discovered to his horror that the planes flying ahead of him were 30 degrees off course. When he radioed this crucial information to his commanding officer, unnamed in the *Post* article but one who should have been called "Wrong Way Corrigan," the officer in effect told Jimmy to shut up and stay in formation.

Jimmy now faced two alternatives, both awful and neither close to any moral or physical dilemma he had ever faced on screen or even in civilian life. He could disobey a direct order, put his wing back on the correct course, and at least ensure his own men's safety because they would have the protection of the accompanying American fighters, flying "bodyguards" for the bombers. That would save Jimmy's men but leave "Wrong Way Corrigan's" wing alone and easy prey for German fighters, according to Lay, since it would be separated from its fighters' protection. Lay writes, "Wandering even a mile or two often meant that instead of coming home without a flak hole, you arrived all shot up and minus six or seven crews."

It was truly a case of pick your poison: Jimmy's other choice was equally toxic. Obey Wrong Way's orders, miss the target altogether, and expose his men to the same German fighters that would pounce on Wrong Way's gang.

Jimmy's decision can only be attributed to temporary insanity. For a while, he decided to be a good "German" and follow Wrong Way into certain death. On cue, the Luftwaffe materialized out of the clouds. German fighers annihilated Wrong Way's plane and the rest of his wing immediately.

Jimmy was shocked into making the right decision and fled the area before the Luftwaffe could turn his group into plummeting hamburger.

"Jimmy brought all his boys safely back to England," Lay wrote.

Wrong Way was never identified in the article, which was written in December of 1945. America wanted heroes. It didn't want a journalist, even a uniformed one, naming names and embarrassing the surviving family members in one of the most widely read magazines in America. The oxymoron "friendly fire" hadn't even been coined yet.

Jimmy, on the other hand, was singled out for praise, even though his behavior in the air had wavered between Teutonic and commonsensical. The Ludwigshafen incident occurred in the first week of 1944. The successful landing in Normandy was still only a glimmer in the minds of FDR and Ike. Stalin couldn't even visualize Hitler's fiery *Gotterdammerung* in a bunker below downtown Berlin. The outcome of the war was in no way assured at the time. America needed a hero. And the brass, in honoring Jimmy, was not going to quibble about his Pavlovian response to stupid orders.

A few days after the unnecessary deaths over Ludwigshafen,

Jimmy's boss, Col. Robert Terrill, received what amounted to a fan letter from Col. Milton W. Arnold, who had flown on the same mission. Arnold praised Capt. Stewart's "good judgment" in maintaining excellent group formation, yet making every attempt to hold his position in the combat wing formation . . ."

If I have decoded the above bureaucrat-ese correctly, the starstruck Colonel Arnold is praising Jimmy for following Wrong Way Corrigan to what should have been certain death. If Arnold wanted to praise Jimmy for his real heroics that day, it should have been for ditching Wrong Way and saving his own men, although that would have meant putting in writing that an officer had messed up big time and caused the loss of his entire wing. (In the 1970s, as a civilian, I worked for a major military contractor which employed many retired noncoms. I learned from these men a pathetic acronym, "CYA," which is common usage throughout the military-industrial complex. CYA stands not for Christian Youth of America but "Cover Your Ass." Colonel Arnold's fulsome praise of Stewart is a creepy example of "CYA" in all its gutless wonder. Corrigan's incompetence was buried in a blizzard of well-deserved praise for the Army's most famous flyboy. Jimmy had (finally) made the right decision. Corrigan had literally disappeared in the clouds above Ludwigshafen.)

In January 1944, when Jimmy was promoted to major, his behavior during the Ludwigshafen run was cited as one of the reasons for his promotion. Lay wrote that he "was promoted in part because even while following lethally inaccurate orders, he had saved his group from annihilation." The letter of promotion went on: "He had served notice he possessed the cardinal virtue of the soldier. Persuade your leader of his mistake, if you can, but follow him right or wrong."

A month later, the newly minted major flew the first of two missions over Brunswick. The first time, he got the awful taste of "just following" orders out of his mouth when he unilaterally aborted the mission in mid-air because of lousy weather conditions. Shortly after Stewart had ordered his wing to return to base, headquarters radioed him the exact same orders for the exact same reason. This time he hadn't blindly followed orders, he did the right thing on his own.

His second cruise over Brunswick earned him the ultra prestigious Distinguished Flying Cross. The commendation said in part: "Major James Maitland Stewart, 0-433210, Army Air Forces, United States Army. For extraordinary achievement . . . on bombing mission over Germany (Brunswick) 20 Feb. 44 . . . The courage, leadership and skillful airmanship displayed by Major Stewart were in large measure responsible for success of this mission."

Jimmy never let such encomia go to his head. He always kept a sense of self-parody about himself. The logo on the cockpit of his B-24 suggested just how little he was impressed with himself. It said, "Nine Yanks and a Jerk." Since Jimmy had painted it himself, everyone knew the identity of the jerk he was referring to.

By now, Major Stewart was becoming famous throughout the Army, and it had nothing to do with romancing Rita Hayworth before the hostilities began.

Gen. James Doolittle, commander of the 8th Air Corps, had impressed on a subordinate, General Hodges, that the annihilation of Brunswick was particularly important for reasons which Lay didn't bother to go into. General Hodges asked his subordinate, General Timberlake, the name of the officer in charge of the Brunswick offensive. "Stewart," Timberlake said. Hodges was relieved. "I've got so I don't worry much when Stewart's leading. We always have a pretty good day."

Jimmy's performances over Brunswick lived up to Doolittle's expectations. He received the Distinguished Flying Cross for leading the February 20th air raid. In a rare newspaper quote, Jimmy said about the medal, "I guess I'd best send it home. I'm mighty proud of it." Jimmy would have cut out his tongue before adding what he was probably thinking. "Dad can put the medal right next to the Oscar in the store window."

Jimmy's reputation for responsibility had as much to do with his courage as it did with his old-fashioned work ethic. Whether it was showing up in a small town in Alabama for the local premiere of *Ziegfeld Girl* and giving interviews to the local paper or cramming for the next day's air raid over Nazi Germany, Jimmy was the Protestant Ethic incarnate.

Reading between the lines, you suspect that the *Saturday Evening Post* actually sent Colonel Lay to Stewart's base for an interview. As with all interview requests during the duration, Stewart politely turned down his superior officer. (One wonders why Lay didn't just order him to spill his guts.)

Undeterred, the budding journalist apparently followed Jimmy around the base, recording his impressions for the article. One incident Lay observed exemplifies how Stewart's obsession with work saved lives.

In February 1944, Lay spotted Jimmy eating alone in the mess hall, which was nearly empty because "thirteen crews had failed to return from the day's mission to Gotha." Jimmy didn't touch his food. His appetite had been destroyed by the fact that the next day he would be leading *his* group over the very same route to Gotha which had resulted in the death of 13 crews earlier that day.

No wonder Jimmy had no appetite, but he didn't let fear and depression immobilize him. Realizing he'd never be able to get any sleep because of the next day's nightmare, he stayed up all night inhaling maps of the flight plan and the orders that emerged non-stop from the teletype machine.

Jimmy's obsessiveness paid off. After memorizing the maps, he knew Gotha's layout better than the city's local Chamber of Commerce.

The following afternoon, he showed up at mess with a voracious appetite—and every single member of his group. Jimmy's all-night cramming resulted in not a single loss of life in contrast to the previous day's carnage.

Although Jimmy's wartime career sounded like a movie, there were times when he wished his mistakes could end up on the cutting room floor the way his film miscues did.

Not to mince words, Jimmy completely screwed up the day he *tried* to bomb Troyes, France. Due to his old bugaboo, navigational error, in addition to misunderstood radio orders, Stewart missed the entire city! Colonel Lay failed to say where the bombs actually landed. Troyes had been targeted by the

Allies because of the city's major tire manufacturing plant, plus many lesser factories. The historic capital of Champagne, its Municipal Library (founded 1651) also housed one of world's greatest collections of illuminated medieval manuscripts, spirited there from Paris during the church-bashing hysteria of the French Revolution. Although it's a preposterous fantasy, one would like to think that Jimmy was just being a super-competent bomber when he completely missed this treasure trove of Medieval art.

Jimmy's screw-up was not star-like, but his reaction was pure Hollywood. After every mission, fair or foul, it seems there would be a critique of everyone's performance. During this day's particular Maoist orgy of self-criticism, Jimmy took all the blame for messing up. Lay wrote, "No mission that Stewart ever flew did more to win the respect of his colleagues than the *one* mission in which he missed the target and refused to alibi out of it." Talk about *déjà vu* all over again. Like his early films, Jimmy didn't get the girl, but he got the glory. That scene alone makes you wonder, "Where's a good screenwriter when you need one?" Ironically, there was one right on the premises. After the war, as we've noted, Lay became a journalist and a film scenarist.

In fact, Colonel Lay was there to record some of Jimmy's best performances—or at least his most crucial in terms of saving lives. Shy and reticent most of the time, when Jimmy was given the assignment to lead briefings on bombing raids, he turned into a figure of Shakespearean gravitas. He would ignore his Hollywood roots when it came to special treatment, signing autographs or giving interviews, but when the lives of the men under his command were at stake, Jimmy was ready to do *Mr. Smith Rides Again to the Shop Around the Corner in The Mortal Storm*.

Although their lives literally depended on the critical information he was disseminating, it was still easy to get bored silly absorbing the minutiae of bombing stats. It was Jimmy's self-imposed job to make these lectures as riveting as Senator Smith's filibuster, but without distracting theatrics. If it would have helped, he probably would have swabbed that toxic mercury solution on his throat to keep his audience razor sharp and receptive.

Lay writes, "He used all his tricks as an actor to get and keep the attention of the men he was lecturing on the boring but critical minutiae of the flight plan. He talked clearly." None of the mumbling or aw-shucksing he employed when a screen role called for such shtick. "A professional showman, he knew how to rivet the attention of every man in the room and hold it."

But Jimmy was no ham. He didn't engage in theatrics when men's lives were at stake. In fact, while other officers turned into virtual Hamlets during their briefings before D-Day, Stewart gave three briefings before the Normandy invasion with "unemotional matter-of-factness." He wisely realized this was not the climactic filibuster speech in *Mr. Smith*. This was an historic occasion that would result in the deaths of 50,000 American servicemen.

After D-Day, Jimmy was promoted to lieutenant colonel and received an Oak Leaf Cluster. The next month he made it to full colonel and was named chief of staff of the 2nd Combat Bomb Wing, second in command to General Ted Timberlake. This position almost always went to a West Point Graduate or at least a regular Air Corps officer, many of whom were available for the job, Lay writes. Jimmy, a *reserve* officer, got the prestigious position for one reason alone, as Timberlake explained. He gave the job to the one-time song and dance man from Princeton instead of to a fellow alum from his alma mater, West Point, because "Stewart was the best man available," the general told the *Saturday Evening Post*.

Jimmy, however, wasn't Superman—he never played the role on screen or during the war. He was a mere mortal who screwed up just like everybody else did. Navigation was Jimmy's worst subject in flight school, and he was equally maladroit on the ground in a jeep. In a legendary trip between headquarters and Tibenham field, a mere five-mile distance, he got lost and ended up in Birmingham—200 miles away! Jimmy could pinpoint a munitions factory from 28,000 feet, but he could miss an entire city at sea level. Fortunately, he had been commissioned as a pilot, not a navigator, or the war might have gone the other way.

More seriously, during a routine visit to a flying field, he once crash landed a cub plane. Stewart was having trouble landing the lightweight craft in a 25-mile-an-hour wind, so he turned it over and crashed it upside down. Lay reported that the ground crew that pulled him from the totalled aircraft was furious, but he adds, Jimmy "was lucky that day, but it wasn't dumb luck that Stewart flew 19 (actually 20) combat missions without injury to himself or to any member of the crews who occupied his airplane." So he demolished a little military hardware and took the long way—via Birmingham—to flight headquarters. When it came to his men, they were treated like Fabergé eggs, not expendable demolition derby contestants.

Lay was actually understated in his praise. He was trying hard to be an objective journalist and to hide the pride he and everyone who came in contact with Jimmy during the war years felt.

Jimmy's commanding officer felt no such restraint. General Timberlake's successor as Jimmy's boss was Colonel Milton W. Arnold. At the end of a 1,000-word letter of commendation reprinted in full in the *Post* article, Arnold sounds as gushy as any fan who ever asked the movie star to autograph an 8×10 glossy: ". . . I desire to take this opportunity to commend you for an outstanding performance of duty. It has been a sincere pleasure to serve with you *and to be associated with you.* (Signed) Milton W. Arnold, Colonel, Air Corps, Commanding."

That letter was dated May 8, 1945, VE Day. Two days later, Jimmy was promoted to wing commander. Lay insisted it was a nominal honor since all Jimmy had to do was supervise the transportation of war-weary veterans back home. But the position called for him to be promoted to brigadier general. Despite Timberlake and Arnold's enthusiasm, this promotion inexplicably never came with his new duties.

Twelve years later the omission would come back to haunt Jimmy and humiliate him in national headlines.

Chapter 20
Flight from Fear

In researching this biography, I examined thousands of magazine and newspaper clippings and rarely found an exception to "Stewart's Law." It was a simple doctrine Jimmy adhered to for the rest of his life after mustering out of the Army Air Corps. The Oscar-winning movie star refused to discuss Hollywood (or give interviews) during the war. Back in Hollywood after VE Day, the World War II hero just as adamantly declined to discuss his wartime heroism. Pressed on the subject, the most he would say was "the war was just something everyone did."

Jimmy was better at keeping a "secret" than many CIA agents, who occasionally become best-selling blabbermouths once their careers with "The Company" are over and they can star in their own one-man shows, murderously revealing the names of double agents.

The only major exception I ever found to "Stewart's Law" was hidden away in the archives of the Academy of Motion Picture Arts & Sciences Library in Beverly Hills. Amid stacks and stacks of manila envelopes stuffed with interviews the accommodating star had given over the past half century, I came across a photocopy of a 500-word article for a New York-based magazine called *Guideposts*. The religious but nondenominational monthly describes itself as a "first person true life narrative designed to show people from all walks of life how to overcome difficulties through faith and positive attitudes. It's a practice guide to successsful living, whose pages are written by people from all walks of life." The brief two-page piece, published in October 1981, contained a detailed account of Jimmy's state of mind the night before a bombing raid.

The shocker was that the by-line belongs to none other than Jimmy Stewart himself—"as told to Richard H. Schneider, Guideposts Senior Editor." After snubbing both the *New York* and *L.A. Times* and every wire service in America—not to mention his superior officer, Colonel Lay—Jimmy had finally come clean to some obscure little magazine, giving a *first-person account!*

Jimmy remained a staunch Presbyterian all his life, and the fact that *Guideposts* was a religious magazine offers a clue as to why Jimmy after a 30-year silence, had finally discussed a subject that from the tenor of the article suggests was still excruciating to relive.

Jim McDermott, *Guideposts'* current senior editor, finally got Jimmy to spill his guts. The interviewer, Richard Schneider, still on staff, "is a very personable, understated, understanding man. People have a way of opening up to him. He's so ingenuous and kind himself," McDermott told me over the phone. Jimmy apparently had come face-to-face with his alter ego and told all to his *doppelganger,* the personable Schneider.

But a much more likely explanation for this sudden revelation is hinted at in the headline: "Flight From Fear." While generals and colonels might gush about his heroics and even the "pleasure" of his company (in the middle of 50-million war dead), Jimmy was not the type to toot his own horn—or tout his outstanding military record.

But with typical self-deprecation, he *was* at long last willing to describe in a magazine article how scared he was during the entire time he was playing the most "fictional" role of his career—a *fearless* bomber pilot!

Any critic who ever carped that Jimmy was always "playing himself" should read the *Guideposts* article. (You can find it at the Academy library in Beverly Hills in the Jimmy Stewart manila envelope marked "1980–1989 magazine articles.") As the article suggests, throughout the war, Jimmy did a "stretch" that makes Meryl Streep's Auschwitz survivor in *Sophie's Choice* seem easy.

Jimmy wasn't acting macho or engaging in bravado for the sake of his image when he gave the performance of his life as a fearless aviator. A 1952 issue of the Los Angeles *Times Magazine* summed up the phenomenon succinctly. "The strange fact about Mr. Stewart is he was more of a hero than the movies ever dared make him."

He had already played too many geeky losers on screen to start worrying about competing with John Wayne. He did, however, have the crucial concern that if his near-paralyzing fear became visible to the men under his command, their paralysis would lead to disaster.

Jimmy's anxiety attack gained momentum one night when he counted B-24 bombers returning from a raid over Germany. He knew that 12 had left the base, and with a sinking feeling he counted their return—which stopped at 11. One of the planes had been shot down. The men had either died in a flame-out or parachuted into captivity in a POW camp.

Added to the dispiriting count was another sickening realization. The next morning, as squadron commander with the U.S. 8th Air Force, Jimmy would lead his men to perhaps the same fate. The target was deep inside Germany. Due to the distance and fuel-tank capacity of fighters of the day, these "flying bodyguards" could only accompany Jimmy's bomber squadron part of the way. For the rest of the trip they would be on their own over the Third Reich, which resisted fiercely with its own fighters and flak.

The night was freezing as Jimmy poked the coal in a little iron stove in his hut. He could have saved himself the effort. He was so terrified perspiration formed on his forehead as he imagined the worst-case scenario the next day.

Jimmy had a duty to perform, and fear would keep him from performing it, so he practically ordered himself not to be afraid. And Jimmy always followed orders. "Fear is an insidious and deadly thing," he wrote in 1981 with the descriptive immediacy of an event taking place as he wrote about it. "It can warp judgment, freeze reflexes, breed mistakes.

"Worse, it's *contagious*. I knew my own fear, if not checked, could infect my crew members. And I could feel it growing within me."

The anxious evening Jimmy described took place some time in 1943 or 1944, an era when people didn't go running to a psychotherapist at the slighest twinge of *tsuris* or melancholy. It's a safe bet that Jimmy, the "most nearly normal of any of the Hollywood stars" in Louella's phrase, never burrowed into a psychiatrist's couch. Yet, he intuitively coped with his fears in a way that's straight out of a pop psychology best-seller today.

To calm himself, he compiled a worst-case scenario. "I began writing out a list of emergencies and how I would handle them. Everything I could think of. If our ship is mortally hit, I will try to get the crew out before I bail out—provided it doesn't blow up first." Jimmy even rehearsed in his mind how he would deal with interrogators if he fell into the hands of the Gestapo. "If I'm shot down and captured, I will reveal nothing but my name, rank, and serial number." Jimmy continued to write down all the awful possibilities of the next day's flight.

Then, after using a tool straight out of a self-help book that will probably be featured on a talk show some day, Jimmy did something very old-fashioned.

He prayed.

His grandfather had fought in the Civil War, his dad in both the Spanish-American and First World Wars. When he asked him about his wartime experiences, his father, with the same lack of machismo his son would cop to in a magazine article years later, admitted that he too had been terrified. But then his father suggested something you're not likely to hear on *Oprah*—or at least not on *Geraldo*. "Just remember that you can't handle fear all by yourself, son. Give it to God; He'll carry it for you," Jimmy remembered his father telling him when, just before he left for England, Alexander Stewart gave him a copy of the 91st Psalm.

As he wrestled with his anxiety attack on the cot in his hut, Jimmy took out the Psalm and reread it for the umpteenth time:

". . . I will say of the Lord, He is my refuge and my fortress . . . His truth shall be thy shield and buckler. Thou shalt not be afraid for the terror by night; nor for the arrow that flieth by day . . . For He shall give His angels charge over thee, to keep thee in all thy ways. They shall bear thee up in their hands, lest thou dash thy foot against a stone . . .

"They shall bear thee up in their hands. What a promise for an airman!" Jimmy wrote with still-tangible gratitude for this particular variety of religious experience.

"I read those comforting words . . . Then I relinquished to the Lord my fears for the coming day. I placed in His hands the squadron I would be leading . . .

"I had done all I could. I had faced each fear and handed it over to God. And now, no matter what might happen, I knew that He would be with me. In this world or the next."

The simplicity and sufficiency of Jimmy's faith may explain why he never discussed—except in a religious magazine—his wartime experiences and how his religious beliefs had been literally life-saving. Not necessarily through divine intervention, although Jimmy clearly felt they were.

On a purely practical or psychological level, Jimmy's faith had helped him fake fearlessness and stopped him from communicating his fear to his men. The last thing Major Stewart needed was a bomber crew quaking in their regulation Army boots along with their quaking commander.

Is it any wonder that Jimmy remained a staunch Presbyterian through much of his nearly 90 years on the planet?

Chapter 21
Public Relationships

Jimmy took a proactive approach to helping his men combat their fear instead of just hiding his own. Happily for his crews, he was a much more accomplished pianist than accordion player. (The 8th Air Corps might have been the first military unit in U.S. history to mutiny if Jimmy had tried his Falmouth tearoom set on the combat-weary aviators.) Jimmy was no ordinary pilot, syndicated columnist Vincent X. Flaherty wrote. "His outfit was attacked by Germany fighter planes, shot up by anti-aircraft fire. Many buddies died. After a violent mission, Jimmy played the piano for his pals just to settle them down, even though he was just as stressed out as they were."

Poor Flaherty. He must have had to steal his wire service stories from the *Stars and Stripes* and secondhand quotes from Stewart's crewmates. Because Jimmy never talked to Flaherty, an embarrassing fact the award-winning journalist owned up to. Not only the wire services, but the Army itself flew Flaherty overseas to get the scoop on Stewart. The intrepid reporter even followed Jimmy to Paris for some unexplained military mission. Finally, Flaherty filed his last non-story on Stewart: "But that was one assignment I never fulfilled. He didn't want himself played up as the hero."

Gen. Jimmy Doolittle, a legend himself, told the columnist that Jimmy was "the greatest morale factor" in his command.

Whatever the frustrated press felt about their Garboesque quarry, Jimmy's men, not just the brass, adored him. Flaherty, resorting to interviews with acquaintances again, wrote, "Stewart has already made a big hit with the men he will lead into aerial battle. A member of the squadron said, 'He is plenty OK, but for a movie actor he sure is publicity shy, and he takes his present job a lot more seriously than he ever did acting in front of cameras at $3,000 a week.' "

Typically, when a star refuses to talk to the press, journalists, denied the opportunity to do their job, understandably get ticked off and retaliate by printing unflattering stories, usually relying on "unnamed sources," who one frequently suspects is the ticked-off reporter himself.

Jimmy's uncooperativeness went beyond shyness, however, and seemed tinged with atypical anger. The man who showed up for the opening of an envelope if L.B. commanded him to treated wartime PR as though it were practically giving aid and comfort to the enemy, when it was designed, however tastelessly, to do just the opposite—whip up public morale on the homefront.

Years later, the *Saturday Evening Post,* during an extensive interview with the now-accessible superstar, speculated on the source of such bitterness from a normally accommodating fellow. "During his early days in the army, Air Force *(sic)* PR officers tried to hitch their publicity wagons to his stardom, *and it had eaten into his soul.*"

The press during the war years, especially during our last *popular* war, didn't have the luxury of excoriating uncooperative stars, especially those in uniform, who were putting their lives on the line every morning when they flew off into the wild blue yonder.

As with all the other stories filed on Jimmy during the war, it's obvious in an AP dispatch of Feb. 16, 1944, that the luckless reporter never got a chance to talk to his subject. But that didn't stop the journalist from presenting an ultra-flattering portrait of the uncooperative airman.

"A U.S. BOMBER BASE IN ENGLAND, FEB. 16. (AP) He is Major James Stewart, in peacetime one of Hollywood's leading actors. But around the brightly burning little belly stoves of Nissen huts, in mud and damp English cold of this Liberator base, where Jimmy commands a squadron, a lot of the time you'd hardly know he was around. When he walks into the intelligence office and reads a magazine for an hour in front of the stove, no one pays any attention to him." (Except, obviously, the poor wire service reporter who had so much time on his hands he could devote an entire hour to watching Jimmy read a magazine!)

The reporter (un-bylined) was at least allowed close enough to Jimmy to eavesdrop if not actually participate in the conversations.

The men, the journalist wrote, joked about the shortage of hair tonic. "Stewart, feeling the stubble on his jaw, said, 'I find I'm having less and less use for my after-shave lotion.'" That is the one and only quote (and an indirect one at that) that Jimmy ever "released to the press" visiting the bomber base.

Considering his touchiness on the issue, his colleagues never referred to Stewart "as an actor," the AP story said. "They say he is a 'real soldier.' That's about the highest compliment at their command.

"Little things have won him the above reputation. When his group left base in Sioux City, Iowa, Stewart said, 'Let's clean this place up.' He set the pace himself by grabbing a broom and going to work on the litter."

With understatement worthy of Miss Manners, the reporter ended his dispatch: "Stewart dislikes receiving attention because of his movie career. He wants his crews to get credit for their dangerous work and shuns the spotlight himself."

In August of 1944, the *L.A. Times* sent Arthur Bartlett to the English airbase to get an exclusive with the movie star turned war hero. By now, Jimmy's exploits in the air and on the ground had surpassed his prewar fame as an Oscar-winning movie star.

Subtlety was not part of Bartlett's repertoire, surprising in a reporter for a major daily. By then, he must have known from previous press reports like Flaherty's and the AP story above that if there was one thing Jimmy avoided more than the press it was discussion of his prewar career.

The *Times* reporter showed up at the base's press office and fatuously asked for "Jimmy Stewart, the movie star." That would be like going into a men's social club in Little Italy and requesting an interview with "John Gotti, the well-known gangster."

Like most publicists, in and out of uniform, the base's flack wasn't taking any flak from the press, not even if he was from Jimmy's hometown newspaper. The press liaison officer frowned and said to Bartlett, "Don't call him a movie star," as though the reporter had uttered a profanity. "That's prewar talk. The man you want is *Major* Stewart, our group operations officer."

That was indeed the man Bartlett wanted, but there wasn't a snowball's chance in Saudi Arabia he was going to get his man. Like poor Flaherty before him, Bartlett ended up spying on Stewart, observing him without ever getting an interview until his last day on the base.

Finally, the state of affairs dawned on the reporter. At least it gave him some kind of story to file for the fans back home. Bartlett wrote in the Aug. 28, 1944, issue of the paper's *This Week* magazine, "If you insist on thinking of him as an ex-star, put the emphasis on the 'ex.' For Jimmy Stewart, movie star, stopped existing—except in the persistent minds of a few million fans—when James M. Stewart went into the Army."

Besides modesty, there also may have been a practical reason for Jimmy to dump his Hollywood baggage. Another reporter referred to Jimmy's prewar status as a "handicap." A movie star, unlike other soldiers, couldn't complain about anything from K-rations to drafty dormitories. "If Stewart griped, he'd be likely met with the chorus, 'What? Too tough for the big Hollywood movie star?' " the *Saturday Evening Post* speculated.

Bartlett wasn't good at getting his man, but he was excellent at "reading" his subject. Jimmy apparently didn't object as

Bartlett stared and wrote long picture essays on the defrocked movie star.

"He had that not-too-deceptive air of casualness which marks most flyers who have faced death on mission after mission and know they are going to keep on doing it.

"But in addition there was the austerity of a mature senior officer who knows that other men—men he is talking with, eating with and living with—are going to die following his orders." Jimmy was only 36 when Bartlett filed his story, but the reporter—a keen observer if not a good PR person—was already describing his subject as "mature" and "senior." As for Bartlett's other observation that Jimmy knew men were going to die following his orders, he was dead wrong. None of the men who flew with Jimmy died. He was famous for bringing his crew back intact.

Like Flaherty, Bartlett was reduced to interviewing Jimmy's crewmates, who were eager to be quoted in a newspaper their relatives might read back home. Everybody was a ham, it seems, except Jimmy.

"Usually," Bartlett quoted a fellow officer, "he doesn't talk much. If we're talking shop in mess he will tune in with a word or two, but he doesn't pay much attention to just plain chatter." Jimmy felt he had the weight of the world on his shoulders—or more precisely, the lives of his men in his hands—and small talk was just too small, to waste his limited mental energy on. His press shyness may in part have been caused by the same thing—putting up with brainless questions about career and starlets when he knew that tomorrow he might make a mistake that would lead to the death of a plane-load of 20-year-olds with their entire lives ahead of them.

Finally, Bartlett got his man. Jimmy's innate politeness must have at least overcome his disdain for publicity. But even when he did grant Bartlett a few minutes of his time, he made it clear he was there to talk about the war, not MGM or its starlets.

"I don't mean to be temperamental about this publicity stuff," he finally said to Bartlett. "If there's anything I can tell you *about the job we're doing on this base,* I'll be glad to do it. We're flying missions in support of the invasion troops.

Right now that's all I have time to think about, and all I want to think about." Now, he implied, was not the time to ask him about Harlow's kissability or the corrosive liquid that lent reality to his filibuster speech. Bartlett, the reporter who originally asked to speak to "Jimmy Stewart, the movie star," finally got the message.

Bartlett also reported that Jimmy's attitude toward the paparazzi changed, briefly. "He had been very sour about a previous request to have his picture taken. Anyway, a photographer fearfully approached and asked if he could take his picture when they pinned the Distinguished Flying Cross on him." Although his modesty must have cringed at the request, "Jimmy had a change of heart and relented. 'Sure, I'll be proud to have that picture taken.'" Maybe he planned to get a copy to send home for Dad's hardware store memorabilia collection.

Bartlett's final take on Stewart before returning stateside summed up the amazing accomplishments of the man who had managed to totally leave behind the Hollywood hoopla in the mud of an unnamed English airfield. "While I was at the base," Bartlett wrote in his last dispatch, "my whole impression of him was of a man who had completely lived down his past. The fact that it was a brilliant past makes that something of a feat."

Although Jimmy successfully avoided most interviews, he couldn't avoid a direct order. He was Lt./Capt/Maj./Col. James Stewart first, Garbo second. On several occasions he was ordered to make documentary films, playing "Jimmy Stewart, Academy Award-winning Star," to boost enlistment and war bond drives. Flaherty correctly surmised that Jimmy had been ordered to lend his name and prestige to the documentaries. It was probably the closest Jimmy ever came to insubordination. Where was his agent, Leland Hayward, when he needed him to get him out of a "picture"?

An AP headline, datelined London, captured Stewart's discomfort perfectly: "Capt. James Stewart Upset by News Parley." The story from Dec. 2, 1943, mentioned that he even flubbed his lines while making a newsreel and the scene had to be reshot.

The AP story, blithely unaware of just how much Jimmy hated the whole "press parley," reported, "Captain James Stewart has been away from the floodlight and cameras so long he got jitters at a press conference today and an entire newsreel had to be reshot. He apologized after flubbing the prepared newsreel script. 'I said when I entered the Army as a private that I was proud to be here and was going to do my best as a soldier of the U.S. Army. Now I have my own outfit and I can say that we are going to do our best as soldiers of the U.S. Army.' " If the U.S. Information Agency wanted vapid vacuousness, Captain Stewart was happy to oblige with an appropriate quote.

Then he began to stumble through the script: "I'm afraid I'm a little bit out of practice at this business of appearing before the camera. I remember three years ago . . ." The reporter said Jimmy suddenly got stage fright and in the middle of the sentence had to stop. It required three takes before the newsreel camera got what it needed.

The accompanying AP photo is a semiotician's gold mine. Jimmy's body language speaks volumes more than his brief newsreel propaganda speech. The normally sprawling, lanky actor is practically imploding into himself to avoid physical contact with the women reporters (three of them) who share a single wing-backed chair with him. It looks like Marlene in the Winnebago all over again. The women's body language speaks volumes as well. Just as Jimmy tries to take up as little room as possible on the crowded chair, the women are leaning forward to the point of sexual harassment.

During the ensuing interview, one of the female reporters asked if he had ever been to England before. Forgetful perhaps, or just annoyed, Jimmy said he couldn't remember. The AP story said, "Leaning forward until she almost fell off" the chair, another woman reporter demonstrated her knowledge of Stewart trivia by answering the question for him. "It was in '39," she "breathed," to use AP's verb.

If Jimmy had mutinied right then and there, refusing to continue the interview, not a single court martial in the armed forces would have convicted him.

That was his first, but unfortunately not his last, encounter with horny news hens, as *Variety* called female journalists in those pre-Fredian days.

Jimmy's second press outing was even more demeaning than the first, if that was possible. In the same month he was interviewed in an overcrowded armchair, Jimmy was trotted out once again for the delectation of the press. The even stranger headline this time, in the *New York Tribune*, made him sound like a prize stallion, which no doubt was the image that popped into the minds of some of the women journalists at the non-event; perhaps a male editor had composed the headline with telepunchwriter firmly in cheek: "Capt. James Stewart *Exhibited* to Press."

The story led with "Capt. James Stewart of Hollywood was introduced to the London press the other day at the Eighth Air Force headquarters . . ." In the very next sentence, the reporter mentions inexplicably that "roast beef and sherries were served." Inexplicable until one recalls that wartime shortages made the one-time British staple of roast beef as rare as well-done chateaubriand. Stewart's presence must have made the occasion especially important to serve such a delicacy.

Food, however, was probably not on the mind of yet another woman reporter who said, "Oh, Captain, you do look sunburned." Was she suggesting he was sitting around the pool at the Beverly Hills Hotel while the rest of the world went up in flames? Close. Jimmy squirmed, stuck out his lower lip and said that someone "fresh from Florida is apt to look sunburned." The dizzy news report failed to explain the Florida reference. Presumably, Stewart had been Stateside for an aviation or navigation course in Florida, not sunning himself in Brentwood. Noticing Jimmy's increasing discomfort at this press conference from hell, Col. John Hay Whitney of the 8th Air Force, the base's in-house publicist, rose and cleared his throat. "It is my pleasure, ladies and gentlemen, to present to you Captain Stewart. I understand there is some question about the basis of his being in this country. Captain Stewart is a qualified flying officer and is now a qualified combat pilot. He is not here by courtesy of anybody except the United States

Army Air Force and his own determination.'' The Army flack was referring to the 200 hours of flying time Jimmy had logged at his own expense prior to enlistment. Whitney then sat down, the *Tribune* said, and ''Stewart squirmed again and crossed his legs.''

This was Jimmy's second and last taste of PR hoopla for the duration. After the mothering newshens and moronic question and answer session, is it any wonder that he refused all further interviews, even with legitimate journalists who were not starstruck.

Wisely, the military never again pressured Jimmy to do another press conference, which seems problematic when you consider how relentlessly other stars, male and female, were used to hustle the war effort. It's easy to suspect that Jimmy merely made another one of his famous phone calls to old school friends now in high places in Washington to put an end once and for all to any more star mistreatment.

With or without help from pals in D.C., he did refuse to pose for a WAC recruiting poster. Based on other star poseurs, you can imagine how the army flacks, as horny as their Hollywood counterparts, would have used tacky cheesecake pinups surrounding Stewart to lure women into the WACs. Lucky Jim was never *ordered* to pose for that poster.

The only other exception to Stewart's Law was a few lines in an extensive interview the actor gave to animal activist Cleveland Amory for *Parade* magazine in 1984. It had been nearly 40 years since a newshen had breathed on him, and Jimmy may have finally put the memory out of his mind. More likely, Amory, a best-selling author who writes intimate ''biographies'' of his cats, must have bonded with Stewart, a major animal lover. Somehow, Amory got Jimmy to open up just a bit. Mostly, Jimmy stuck to statistics that depersonalized a traumatic subject. ''Sometimes we had more than 1,200 bombers in those raids,'' Jimmy recalled, with awe still audible in his voice. ''Each B-24 would carry more than two tons of bombs and we had to fly awful close to each other.''

The subject of payloads emboldened Amory to ask an exceedingly tacky question of the then 76-year-old actor in the privacy of his living room. "Did you ever think of all those civilians you were dropping bombs on?" Amory inquired.

Still courtly in the face of such crassness, Jimmy kept his cool and replied, "I thought about them, but I also thought about the Germans who had been dropping bombs on civilians for all those years on those other countries, like Yugoslavia." Jimmy may have been thinking of the Luftwaffe flying at rooftop level over Belgrade, a picture postcard city wtih no anti-aircraft guns. With no responding flak to prevent them, the merciless Germans could drop bombs inches away from civilians drinking their *ersatz* morning coffee.

And to his credit, although he probably swore to his dying day that it had been a mistake and not intentional, Jimmy failed to drop a single bomb on Troyes, France—and its municipal library filled with priceless illuminated manuscripts from the Middle Ages.

(There's an AP wirephoto dated July 1944 which shows General Martial Valin, chief of staff of the Free French Air Corps, pinning France's highest honor on Jimmy, the *Croix de Guerre* with palms. Decades later he would win another decoration from France, the Victoire—for acting, not for failing to bomb irreplaceable manuscripts. The French bigwig actually came to Jimmy's base to confer the honor rather than summoning him to Free French HQ in London. (Paris wouldn't be liberated for another month.) One wonders if the general was actually grateful to Jimmy for *failing* in his mission to bomb his native land's Troyes with its irreplaceable art treasures.)

Ignoring Amory's impertinence, Jimmy opened up a bit and hinted at how he and his men coped with death on a daily basis. Jimmy said the men never discussed the odds of dying. "Never, but we all prayed a lot. I didn't pray for myself. I just prayed I wouldn't make a mistake."

It's no surprise that Jimmy's lifelong work ethic didn't desert him during the war. When his tour of duty in England was over, the war wasn't, so he volunteered to stay on. In retrospect, and even more so at the time, that decision was unadulterated bravery verging on the suicidal. A cynic would say he was plain nuts. You don't have to be a student of the science of chance and probability to know that every time Jimmy flew another mission, statistically his chances of crashing and burning increased.

By 1944, Stewart was a squadron commander in charge of 15 bombers and 150 men. Typically, squadron commanders took turns going on raids. Not Jimmy. As one AP dispatch reported, "Stewart would go on every raid if they'd let him, greatly increasing his chances of dying." Then the reporter mentioned a fact that sounded more scary than heroic, compulsive rather than commonsensical. "He goes to bed at 2 A.M., gets up at 4:30 A.M. for a briefing." One hopes that that sleep schedule only applied to his non-flying days. Who would want to be led into battle by someone with only two-and-a-half hours' sleep?

His work ethic exhibited itself in other, less lethal, although even more exhausting, ways. His promotion to Major included the task of working out the tactics for each bomber mission assigned to his group. He spent all day and night examining maps to find the best and safest routes possible for his men. After staying up all night with his maps, he gave pre-dawn briefings. Almost like a character in a Jimmy Stewart movie, he answered every single question his nervous interrogators posed. An eyewitness recalled that one terrified youth kept asking the same question with only slight variations again and again. It was clearly the boy's way of assuring himself that he had covered all the bases. Jimmy demonstrated the patience of Job by answering the same question over and over until the youngster finally calmed down. Jimmy was an even better armchair psychotherapist than he was piano player when it came to putting stressed-out soldiers at ease.

After the interminable questions of the briefings, he saw his men fly off as the sun rose. Only then did he allow himself the luxury of a two-hour nap. Soon though, he was back on the field, searching the sky, looking for his men to return. When some of the planes that had left in the morning didn't come back, Jimmy remained in his open jeep, almost willing them to return even though he knew they wouldn't. Streaks of gray began to appear in his jet black hair. This stress and workaholism took their toll on his most sensitive feature—his weight. But for once Jimmy could ignore the tyranny of the scales. He was already in. MGM in a moment of madness might be able to fire him if he became too thin for leading man roles, but the Army was stuck with him. During this period of mapping, napping, and briefings, his weight plummeted to a scary, all-time low of 132 pounds. Amid the daily terror, Jimmy must have smiled secretly, thinking he could tell his old tormentor, MGM's Don Loomis, to go bench-press himself. Plus, Jimmy never had to go near another brandy-banana milkshake in his life if he didn't want to. And considering his workload, alcohol was probably off limits to this Calvinist for the duration, despite a prewar reputation as a star with a hollow leg.

In a January 10, 1944, AP story chirpily headlined, "Jimmy Stewart Eludes Nazis and Publicity Equally Well." The female reporter, Collie Small, commented that Jimmy was beginning to look as though he were auditioning for *The Thin Man.* And like every other Hollywood reporter, she also complained that he was turning into the Garbo of aviators: "If Captain Jimmy Stewart, film actor turned Liberator pilot, is as hard to catch in the air as he is on the ground, he doesn't have to worry about Nazi fighters. Many optimistic war correspondents have braved mud and the commanding officer at this base in their pursuit of the elusive Jimmy. But not one so far has even come within sight of him." Small must not have had Bartlett, Flaherty, or Lay's snout for sniffing out the truffle of movie stars. She did discover one thing, "It is possible to report that Stewart is getting dangerously thin. A wingmate said, 'If you think he is skinny in the movies, you ought to see him now.'"

Bartlett, the *Times* reporter, admitted that the thought had crossed his suspicious journalist's mind that Jimmy had been promoted to briefings officer to keep him safely on the ground and away from flying the not-so-friendly skies. The reporter immediately confessed he was wrong for two reasons.

"If the idea ever occurred to you—as I confess it had to me—that he was promoted because the Army wanted to protect a famous movie star from the constant risk of combat flying, *forget it.* He was given the job because when Lt. Col. Ramsay

Potts was appointed to the command of a Liberator [bomber] base, he wanted the best operations chief he could find—and he picked Stewart.''

The colonel's optimism was not misplaced. Jimmy was as big a star as an operations officer as he was in Hollywood. "In two months,'' Bartlett proudly reported in an era when the press was much more partisan, "the base led its division in bombing efficiency.''

As for the cynical canard that the Army was keeping its Oscar-winner out of harm's way, Barlett added, "Even though the operations officer wasn't required to, after his promotion to the position he insisted on continuing to fly on missions.''

Jimmy had originally turned down the promotion, but it was for modesty's sake, not to stop from being grounded for briefings. He was refusing promotion to major, he explained, "until my junior officers get promoted from lieutenant,'' friends quoted him as saying. On January 27, 1944, his juniors must have finally received their promotions because on that day Jimmy exchanged his captain's bars for the golden oak leaves of major.

That was no doubt one of the many reasons his subordinates were so fiercely loyal to their boss. When GIs from another base cynically suggested his promotion had more to do with promoting morale than performance, a fight almost broke out when his men came to his defense.

Hard work alone, not to mention his famous competence, would have justified his promotion. When a fellow officer saw him hard at work at 2 A.M., poring over a map of the next day's mission, he said, "You're working pretty late.'' Jimmy dismissed the compliment. "Oh, lots of them work late around here.''

Even an obsessive like Stewart got leave time, but Jimmy never seemed to leave the base. The famous prewar night-clubber who lost his pants at the Trocadero and discovered a little girl named Judy Garland singing her heart out there, never set foot inside one of London's swanky clubs.

The boulevardier was simply too bushed. That didn't stop his compatriots. Movies and books have been written about the

American soldiers' influence on British society during the war. The male Brits did not appreciate their American counterparts even though they were saving their country from certain invasion by the Nazis. The popular putdown described the Yanks as "overpaid, oversexed, and over there." British women adored the GIs, and not merely because the strong American dollar *vis à vis* the British pound made virtually every Yank seem rich. And it wasn't the nylons or the chocolate bars either. Most of the British males of fighting age were stationed in North Africa or Southeast Asia. The Americans were on site and ready to party hearty. But what most attracted the English women to the GIs was their gentleness relative to their rough British counterparts, especially among the working classes. More than one British GI bride would confide in her diary and to friends that the Americans seemed to lack the machismo and crudity that characterized British men of certain social strata.

Jimmy Stewart's prewar screen persona of accessible Everyman embodied exactly what kept English ladies swooning for the men Over There. Unfortunately for his British movie fans, these women would never get a live taste of that choice morsel on screen. As Collie Small reported with disappointment in her AP dispatch, "He avoids social gatherings except at the Officer's Club, where he is the group's favorite pianist."

Chapter 22
Post-World War II Blues

Jimmy returned home a war hero. He was promoted to full colonel in April 1945. He was overseas 21 months, during which time he flew 20 missions. He won six battle stars. He also picked up four medals: the distinguished Flying Cross with two Oak Leaf Clusters, the Air Medal, the Three-Oak-Leaf Cluster, and of course the *Croix de Guerre* from an art-loving French general. Mentioning modesty and Jimmy Stewart in the same sentence has almost become redundant by now, but here goes. He *modestly* pooh-poohed all this "fruit salad" by saying, "It was wartime. Price controls and medal inflation . . ."

But all he wanted to do was return to acting. Strangely, everyone wanted to celebrate his wartime heroics, while people in power seemed intent on not letting him get back to he work he loved.

A huge New York welcome had been planned for Jimmy, which he promptly refused. Instead, he rented a car and drove from New York to the family's home in Indiana, south of Pittsburgh.

A *Collier's* magazine writer understood the psychology of his decision perfectly. There's something grotesque about celebrating carnage and destruction, even if the cause of celebration is surviving those horrible things. "He vetoed all coming home parties and celebrations, like most guys who have been in the war long and deeply enough. He had had enough of it and wanted to forget it . . . fast."

Jimmy could avoid a ticker-tape parade, but Stateside he couldn't avoid the press anymore. Reluctantly, he posed for a cover story in the September 24, 1945, issue of *Life* magazine, still in his colonel's uniform—he hadn't been officially demobilized yet. The cover shows him nattily dressed in military togs with a belltower in the background topped with a huge "Welcome Jim" sign on top. This was the first and almost the last time Jimmy would do any postwar publicity related to his wartime experiences.

Jimmy certainly wasn't showing off. He was still officially an officer in the Army Air Corps, and he had to wear his uniform.

The headline for the story said: "*Life* comes home with Jimmy Stewart."

Too polite to avoid the press as he had in Europe, Jimmy was photographed by *Life* signing autographs on Indiana's Main Street for a mob of bobby-soxers who didn't think the distinguished, gray-haired 35-year-old war hero was too old for them at all. While Jimmy had no trouble giving the cold shoulder to journalists in England from major publications back home, back home he reverted to his movie star philosophy that fans were not "customers," they were "partners." And like customers, "the partners were always right." Besides, he didn't have to worry about risking his men's life the next day with a bombing raid over Pittsburgh.

The huge *Life* photo spread spoke volumes of Alexander's pride in Jimmy's accomplishments on screen and in the air. The store was a veritable shrine to his son. The now iconic Oscar in the store window (under a glass dome to protect it) was topped with an American flag. In case any shopper missed it, there was also a spotlight riveted on the statuette.

Jimmy may have reverted to accommodating movie star, but he hadn't turned into an egomaniac. When the Chamber of Commerce proposed an official party welcoming him home, he flatly refused. Autographs were tolerable and even part of his job description, but a miniature ticker tape parade down Philadelphia Street was almost as nightmarish as flying 30 degrees off course en route to Ludwigshafen.

While he was willing to do movie star duty, *Life* approvingly noted he didn't act like one. A photo showed him leaning back in a chair in his father's hardware store, schmoozing with friends from 20 years past. You almost expected Dad to show up and tell his laggard son to get to work and wait on customers. *Life* also dutifully reported that Jimmy slept late, played the piano, and in the afternoon went fishing. Another photo captured him driving a ''one-horse shay'' through the Pennsylvania snow. Without comment, it also said his eccentric father planned to give the sleigh to Jimmy's agent, Leland Hayward, and Hayward's wife Margaret Sullavan, for their children to ride . . . in Hayward's hometown, Beverly Hills.

An unidentified magazine clip from the period claimed Stewart's background was ''as typically American as his appearance.'' This fatuous assertion was somewhat undercut by the *Life* photo of the Stewart mansion on Vinegar Hill. ''This is the house where Jimmy Stewart grew up,'' the caption reads. The huge neo-colonial would have looked right at home on Camden Drive.

Another photo looks like a still from his next film, *It's a Wonderful Life*. The scene in the dining room looks as though someone stole the soundstage furniture for the Stewart's Indiana home, including the maid serving the family. The photo caption reads: ''Jimmy helps clear away table after family finishes dinner. The Stewarts have a cook, but Jimmy's sisters served the food.'' The caption doesn't explain why Jimmy and not the maid is bussing tables. The photographer probably told the obliging star to.

Hinting at the horrors of 20 bombing missions over Germany and the loss of close friends, the *Life* story concludes, ''With his boyish face a little leaner, hair a little gray, eyes a little *tighter,* Jimmy Stewart came back home recently after four years of war.'' And from hell, the magazine might have added, if it hadn't been so relentlessly upbeat.

The next press report finds Jimmy returning to Southern California. The headline in the October 3, 1945, edition of the *L.A. Examiner* spoke volumes without realizing it: "Jimmy Stewart Longs For Role."

A photo shows him stepping off the Santa Fe Chief in Pasadena. Still in uniform, his chest has enough medals to decorate a Christmas tree.

Work, which would be denied him for a while, was paramount in his mind. The first thing he said as he exited the train was, "I want to get out [of the Army] as soon as possible. *I want to get back to making some pictures.*"

Jimmy was already worrying about his film career. And as his experiences would prove, with good reason. But even the first apostle of the Protestant Ethic wanted some R&R. "But first, I'll take a rest—you know stretch my legs, read a good book, and stuff like that."

Amid the puffy press questions at the train station, someone indelicately hinted at his recent trauma overseas. Jimmy took the tactless question in stride. "Where did you get the gray hair, Jimmy?" a reporter asked. With understatement that would soon turn to stony silence about his wartime experiences, Jimmy simply said, "It got pretty rough overseas at times."

But before Jimmy was allowed to suffer Post-Traumatic Stress Disorder or bombing flashbacks, even before he got off the train, the moronic press of the day said "This is a bad question, Jimmy, but is there any sweet little thing you've come home to?" Jimmy didn't miss a beat. "No. That is, not yet. But you're right—it's a bad question."

Then, without prompting, he repeated his earlier wish. "I want to start making pictures as soon as possible."

While there was no "sweet little thing" waiting for Jimmy at the Pasadena station, his best friend was. Henry Fonda had been demobilized only a week before Jimmy's return. He mustered out after Naval service in the Pacific theater of war as a lieutenant junior grade. Jimmy had entered the Army Air Corps a buck private, and two years later left with a colonel's oak cluster pinned to his shoulder pads. What *had* Fonda been doing in the war all this time?

No doubt, Jimmy was merely delighted to see his best buddy after two years of separation and didn't ask any embarrassing questions about underachievement in the Navy.

The war hero's welcome Jimmy received was not mirrored in the welcome he received from the film industry. When he told the *L.A. Examiner,* ". . . first I'll take a rest, read a good book, stuff like that," he hadn't planned on such a long period of enforced R&R.

Jimmy was joking, but there was a hint of the problems he would encounter when he tried to rejoin the "workforce" in his answer to a question posed by columnist Sidney Skolsky, who inquired about his postwar plans.

Jimmy cracked, "Oh, I'm going back to pictures. At least I hope so. Maybe as Mickey Rooney's . . . *grandfather.*" At 37, Jimmy was joking that he was over-the-hill enough to play the twenty-five-year old Rooney's gramps, but the power brokers in Hollywood didn't get the joke. Some of these moguls with hearts of zinc were ready to accept as fact that Jimmy was over the hill, and if a grandfather part did happen to come along, well, maybe they'd give Jimmy's agent a call.

Or as *Collier's* magazine summed up the feeling of studio executives, "It was obvious to the wise men of Hollywood that Stewart was going to be a neurotic case or hopelessly stuffed shirt, or both. In any event, he would be washed up as an actor for good."

Chapter 23

Thanks for the Memories, Now How About a Job?

To say post-World War II Hollywood was not kind to Jimmy Stewart is like saying Richard Nixon didn't get a hero's welcome when he showed up at post-Watergate Republican fundraisers.

While MGM trumpeted the return of its No. 1 star's first film after the war with the adline: "Gable's Back! And Garson's Got Him," the same studio which had tried to turn Jimmy into a draft dodger because of his commercial value to the company didn't even renew Stewart's contract. This after putting out a big press release when he enlisted that MGM was generously waiving his contract for the duration of the war!

The former movie star found himself an unemployed war hero. "My contract had run out and nobody remembers you," he told *Parade* magazine almost 40 years later, the recollection still irking him. He and Henry Fonda found themselves reverting to their starving actor days in New York. (This time, they weren't starving literally—except for work.) As they had in Central Park in what seemed like a different universe, the two ex-stars built and flew box-kites and assembled model airplanes. Jimmy who had only recently flown the real thing in a trail of destruction over Europe was now consigned to gluing together little plastic models of his Liberator bombers.

"People felt downright sorry for Jimmy Stewart when he came shambling back from war, gray-haired and tired-looking, to seek his old job at the studio," the *Los Angeles Times'* magazine *This Week* said.

This was a man who had just won an Oscar when he took off for World War II and was one of the highest paid stars in Hollywood. Polls consistently showed he was *the* most popular actor in the industry among fans. Directors loved working with this most egoless of stars, evidenced by the fact that he had made numerous films with the same directors.

When he left the Army at 37, he realized, "I'd been a flyer almost as long as I'd been a movie actor. Who could tell whether I was an unemployed actor or an unemployed flyer?" Either description was a case of pick your poison: there weren't many jobs for aviators now that the war was over. As for being an unemployed actor, the phenomenon is so common it's practically one word—*unemployedactor*. Today's equivalent for Hollywood wannabes is actor/model/waiter/whatever.

After half a decade in the movies and two Oscar nominations on his résumé, Stewart must have been shocked to find himself in this Lotusland limbo. Jimmy didn't entirely blame an industry with the attention span of a gnat for his current postwar unemployment blues. He had been out of the limelight for four years, and he was out of shape as an actor. "You get rusty in this business just like any other one. And boy, I was. Memorizing parts—Hell! I couldn't even remember my hat size!"

Jimmy wasn't engaging in self-pity with revelations like those. In 1946, it's not an exaggeration to say that James Stewart's career was down the tubes.

Historical proof lies in a headline from the normally restrained *New York Times,* which sent a reporter to interview Jimmy. The headline said pointedly, "The Rise and *Fall* of Jimmy Stewart." This about a man who had managed to stay airborne during 20 bombing missions over Germany.

Even more cruelly, a *Los Angeles Daily News* story said, "When he returned from the war at 33 (*sic*), he found a lot of new screen heroes firmly established around the movie lots. A lot of new movie-goers had never even heard of Jimmy Stewart. People around town began saying that the gangling, unloquacious star was dead, professionally, as the proverbial doornail.''

While Jimmy was overseas, his seven-year contract with MGM had expired, and the studio didn't even offer to renew it. *Collier's* magazine claimed that was Jimmy's idea, because he would make more money as an independent agent. But only if the roles rolled in, the way they automatically had when he was under contract to a studio, sometimes two or three simultaneously.

Perhaps because of a lifelong interest in aviation that began with putting together model planes as a child (and later, sadly, as an unemployed adult), Jimmy had invested wisely in the up and coming industry of aviation. He was out of a job, but he wasn't out of pocket. He wouldn't have to play his accordion on a street corner in Times Square for nickels and dimes—and verbal abuse from best friend Fonda. A British magazine called *PIX* in 1947 said—correctly—that he was rich enough from savings and investments to retire. At the age of 39!

The term ''retirement'' must have sounded like blasphemy to a man whose guiding principle was the Calvinist work ethic.

The inactivity must have tormented the actor/aviator who just wanted to be a working stiff. And he had living proof of just how disastrous a mere four-year absence from the public eye could be. The career trajectory of fellow actor Craig Reynolds must have terrified him, although Jimmy's investments— and at the very worst a job at dad's hardware store—meant he would never hit Reynolds' hellish bottom. Still, Reynolds' story was a cautionary nightmare. The matinee idol had been the No. 3 box-office draw at Warner Brothers, and the first actor to enlist, long before Pearl Harbor, just like another patriotic movie star by the name of James Stewart. Reynolds joined the Marines and fought at Guadalcanal. Wounded, the handsome actor spent months recuperating in a veteran's hospital. Then he returned to Hollywood. It was a classic case of Craig Who? Warners wouldn't take him back. No other studio would have him. Reynolds ended up finding work as an ice man, driving a truck that supplied huge blocks of ice to housewives in the days when modern refrigerators hadn't completely replaced old-fashioned iceboxes. What must have been going through Jimmy's mind when he read of Reynolds's fate in the trades? Lie back and clip coupons from his aviation portfolio? Or go back home? "Selling screws and nails won't be *that* bad . . ."?

If it was any consolation, at least he hadn't been abandoned by everyone, just the studios he had enriched before the war. After the war, MGM might have forgotten the war hero it had locked out of its Culver City gates, but the rest of the nation hadn't.

With his success as an aviator during the war, Jimmy was a latter-day Lindbergh and, like Lindbergh, he was offered the presidency of an airline. Jimmy, the pilot who had helped bomb Germany (but not Troyes' library) back into the Stone Age, said modestly, "I have no business experience for commercial aviation," and turned down the job, which probably would have amounted to window dressing anyway. Lindbergh, with much more flying time than Jimmy (50 missions in the Pacific), didn't have such scruples and accepted an executive position.

There were even better offers, the stuff that washed-up actors' dreams are made of. In 1946, the Democratic Party of Pennsylvania asked—hell, begged—its native son to run for governor.

This is not Hollywood lore. There's documentary proof from Western Union. Thomas P. McHenry, County Commissioner of Philadelphia, wired Stewart, requesting permission to put his hat in the ring. McHenry explained in his telegram "ex-servicemen are forming Jimmy Stewart for Governor Clubs throughout the State."

Jimmy, holed up in his tiny Spartan pad in Brentwood with only a canary for company and model airplane construction for entertainment, was touched by the request, but he turned down the offer with his typical grace and modesty.

"I'm only good at playing make-believe politicians," he explained with a wink at his Oscar nomination for *Mr. Smith*. The *Motion Picture Herald* reported on Feb. 23, 1946, "Stewart said he considered the offer a great honor and deeply appreciated it, but that he desired to continue with his acting career so he had to decline the offer with regret.''

Jimmy also offered this practical reason for his refusal: ''I just don't think I'd make a very good politician. I don't talk fast enough.''

When his acting career resumed so shakily a while later, he may have regretted rejecting the offer to run for governor. The gubernatorial offer wasn't as farfetched as it might seem today. A much less well-known war hero won a seat in Congress the same year the Democrats were begging Jimmy to run. The freshman Congressman was, of course, John Fitzgerald Kennedy. As a beloved movie star (beloved by everybody but MGM, it seems), Jimmy would have been a bigger shoo-in than JFK. A local Pennsylvania newspaper on Feb. 18, 1946, couldn't resist a Capitalist pun to announce Jimmy's decision: ''Mr. Smith Doesn't Go to Harrisburg.'' The story said, ''Stewart yesterday declined with thanks a proposal to submit his name as a candidate for the Democratic nomination for Governor of Pennsylvania at the primary election, May 21.''

Journalism in those days often didn't even pretend to be objective. In an article for the *L.A. Times'* magazine *This Week*, movie editor Louis Berg wrote, ''But if Jimmy Stewart ever should decide he's too gray for Hollywood and really wants to run for Congress, I'll vote for him, and so will millions of other people.'' The *Motion Picture Herald* erroneously reported his reason for rejecting public office: Jimmy had leads in several films.

Not quite.

Jimmy loved acting. He had even referred to it as an infection. ''The acting bug is like all bugs. Their bite can be incurable.'' When his country called on him to fight (actually when he volunteered before being asked), he set aside his film career to do his duty—at the near cost of his life and now, it seemed, at the cost of his beloved career. He didn't owe the U.S. any further service besides paying his taxes, which would be hefty if he ever got back into the movie business.

On the schmooze factor alone, Jimmy would have made a great politician. Years later, campaigning for friends, he wasn't

above a little larceny when appealing to a town's local pride—
and its voters. During an appearance in the state of Pennsylvania, he said, "It's good to be back here for I was born in
Pennsylvania." True enough. But two states over in Indiana,
he really fudged the truth when he claimed during personal
appearances in Terre Haute and Fort Wayne. "It's good to be
back here, for I was born in Indiana." Well, he *was* born in
Indiana, but not the Indiana of the citizens of Terre Haute and
Fort Wayne. Jimmy was inherently a politician *manqué*.

Erskine Johnson of the *Los Angeles Daily News* bluntly
described Jimmy's dilemma: "His major anxiety is to resume
acting where he left off, which—and that's what scares him—
was right at the top. He won the Oscar for best male performance
in 1940, and when he enlisted in 1941, he was at the height of
his glory. His following was tremendous and of both sexes. He
created the Stewart type, a cross between Van Johnson and
Gary Cooper, wholesome, lovable and rough-cut.

"In females he aroused a powerful maternalism, and males
recognized that he didn't need mothering; he was a good guy
who could take care of himself."

While Erskine was brilliantly dissecting the source of Jimmy's allure and his problems reentering the work force where
he left off, the moguls at MGM and elsewhere, whom Jimmy
had always spoken of with respect, weren't interested in analysis of an allure that was four years old—an eternity in the
flavor-of-the-month mentality that dominated Hollywood then
and now.

Unemployment depressed Jimmy. His spartan house
reflected not a dearth of cash but a lack of enthusiasm about
anything. If decor reflects one's state of mind, Jimmy's digs
in Brentwood might have been described as Clinical Depressive
Chic. When Hedda Hopper dropped by for a visit after the war,
she abandoned her usual boosterism and said Jimmy's residence
"had all the homey comfines of a gymnasium locker room!
His father," Hedda added, "had been visiting and left a canary
when he departed, explaining, 'I want you to have *something*
alive in the house.' "

Jimmy's anxiety about being unemployed showed just how

work-obsessed he was. It might make an eye-catching headline to write, "The Decline and Fall of Jimmy Stewart," but the decline was only as steep as an ant hill and the fall as injurious as a stumble onto a feather mattress.

Jimmy returned to the U.S. in September 1945, looking stern on the cover of *Life* magazine. He spent a whopping six months unemployed, an eternity for someone anxiety-ridden about getting back into the industry he loved. Honest Jim was lying through his teeth when he insouciantly told the AP's Bob Thomas, "I guess every guy's got a little bum in him and mine's coming out. I'm enjoying it. There's an art to doing nothing, and it requires planning a day ahead." The true intensity of his anxiety shows up in another quote: "You know this movie business if a funny racket. There are lots of tricks to acting in front of a camera and a guy is liable to forget them in five years."

Like most actors, all of them insecure, he felt every job was his last. "I've always been that way. When I was between pictures, I'd think that I had just made my last film. That no one in his right mind could possibly want me. I was sure that I'd never appear in another movie. I'd also worry about my acting. Let's face it. Nobody ever gets to the point where he can truly say, 'I now know it all.' " Jimmy said that in 1941, right after he won the Best Actor Oscar. If he could feel that insecure about unemployment at the very pinnacle of his career, it's not hard to imagine the near terror he must have felt after a five-year absence from a soundstage.

Friends confirmed the anxiety that lay just beneath his insouciance. An unnamed friend told the *Saturday Evening Post* in 1951, "He is an outstanding worrier. Not working makes him nervous. If he's not working, he thinks he's washed up. After each picture he feels no one will ask him to do another. He fears that the paycheck he's just cashed will be his last." (The date of this article is particularly relevant because by 1951 Jimmy's postwar blues were long over, and he was one of the top box office stars in the world.) But the friend went on, "He even worries about whether or not he should have been an actor. There is enough of the Presbyterian child in him to make him think he should have been something more solidly respectable. But since he is an actor, he worries because he's not a better one.'' Jimmy Stewart was his harshest critic, even harsher than Dad.

But back in 1945–1946 he could have spared himself six months of hand-wringing had he known the phone would ring around Christmas (what a present!), and he'd be reporting to work a little more than a month later.

Chapter 24

It's a Wonderful Friendship

During his six months of involuntary inactivity, Jimmy must have felt a lot of creepy *déjà vu*. He and fellow unemployed actor Henry Fonda found themselves once again holding on to the end of a string with tissue paper attached to the other end. Except instead of Central Park near their down-market railroad apartment, they were killing time in one of L.A.'s pricier neighborhoods, on Brentwood's grassy median strip that is still used by joggers today. Fonda had married his second wife, New York socialite Frances Brokaw, but Jimmy was a frequent guest whom Mrs. Fonda was considerably less smitten with than his legion of bobby-soxer fans.

The demanding socialite didn't like sharing her husband with his best friend. Once, when Jimmy showed up at their door, Mrs. Fonda said, angrily tapping her foot, "If you're looking for Hank, he isn't here. He's out flying his kite."

When the two men weren't flying kites, Jimmy could be found in the Fondas' basement, fiddling with a model train or playing the piano with four fingers and singing. Although during the war Jimmy's piano playing had calmed the nerves of frazzled flyboys, Mrs. Fonda recalled that his playing merely frazzled her nerves. "And he sings worse than he plays," she said. Mrs. Fonda got a break from these unsolicited concerts at least one night a week when her husband, Jimmy, Burgess Meredith, and Benny Goodman resurrected their New York gathering, called the Thursday Night Beer Club. And happily for Mrs. Fonda, club meetings were not held in the Fonda basement.

During the war, after Jimmy's seven-year contract with MGM had expired, his then agent, Leland Hayward, told him not to re-sign, to wait for an offer to do a specific film.

"I sat around and waited for the phone to ring. My roommate Hank Fonda did, too. We built and flew kites together," Jimmy recalled. (Fonda was estranged from his wife by then. Must have been all that kite-flying.)

Hayward was being kind. No one wanted to re-sign Stewart. But perhaps without knowing it, he had wisely advised Jimmy not to seek indentured servitude for another seven years, if any executive had been willing to so enslave him.

While Jimmy and Fonda were perfecting the Zen art of kite building and flying, the phone finally did ring. It was for Jimmy, and the man on the other end was his favorite director, Frank Capra, the man who had guided and tortured him through his breakthrough film, *Mr. Smith.*

Capra invited Jimmy over to his house to tell him the outline of a film the director was making as the first project for his new independent company, Liberty Productions. It silently speaks volumes of exactly where Jimmy's career was at this time. Prewar, post-*Philadelphia Story* Oscar, Capra would not have summoned one of the biggest box office draws in Hollywood to his house like some electrician called to fix a blown fuse.

But Col. James Stewart, medaled hero of 20 successful bombing missions over Nazi Germany, was now an out-of-work actor who had nothing better to do than go fly a kite. Capra didn't even have the courtesy to suggest a neutral, face-saving meeting place like Musso & Frank's, the Morton's of its day.

Although he certainly was entitled to, Jimmy didn't stand on rank, literally, since Capra left the services a captain. In fact, the only emotion Jimmy felt after this imperious phone call was gratitude.

"That's why I thank Frank Capra in my prayers every day. He just out of the blue called me up and said, 'I got an idea for a story.' "

Stewart described the plotline that everyone who ever celebrated Christmas in front of a television set knows by heart.

"We were neighbors. [Capra said,] 'I have an idea. There

is this small town. You're a man out in the world. Your father owns a small bank *[sic]*, you work for him. He dies. You have many troubles. Things go wrong. You can't take it anymore. You go out to kill yourself. While you're on the bridge, an angel falls from heaven into the water. You jump in to save him. He has no wings. He tells you he has to earn them.' "

OK, so it wasn't a high concept storyline like "shark terrorizes resort community," and Capra apologized for his inelegant description of the plot. "I'm not telling this story well." Jimmy said, "Frank, when do we start? I *love* the story."

Jimmy may have been engaging in a little bit of revisionist history when he recounted that story in 1984. An earlier quote has him expressing his faith in Capra while implying his doubt about the low concept of the film: "Frank, if you want to make a movie about a fella who wants to commit suicide and an angel with no wings, I'm your boy."

When Jimmy was under contract to MGM, his scripts were chosen for him, including those little monsters that had the congenital klutz warbling and limping to the beat of a big band. When he became his own "story editor," his taste was impeccable, as evidenced by the very first film he chose on his own, a little classic called *It's a Wonderful Life*. As usual, Jimmy was self-effacing about his talent in this department. "The disadvantages in being your own boss is deciding yourself what scripts to make. Then if the picture isn't good, you think, 'What a fool I am not to let somebody else take responsibility. On the other hand when you are on weekly salary at a big studio, you have to take the stories (including musicals) chosen for you."

As history shows, Jimmy was off-base when it came to criticizing his film aesthetic. While he did appear in the occasional gobbler, he also *chose* to star in some of Alfred Hitchcock's, Anthony Mann's, and of course Capra's greatest films.

Jimmy's six-month ordeal of inactivity and kite-flying was over. The workaholic could go back to work and indulge his obsession, acting.

Little did he know, the ordeal was just about to begin.

Chapter 25

Don't Argue With Me, It's a Wonderful Film

When movies began to talk in the late 1920s, most of them were based on hit plays or best-sellers. There was an exodus from East to West of poorly paid geniuses like Dorothy Parker and F. Scott Fitzgerald, brilliant writers who were put to work at enormous salaries of $3,000 a week to adapt junk from Broadway and pulp fiction. Parker and Fitzgerald took to drink in their gilded cages. William Faulkner politely asked L.B. Mayer if it was OK if he wrote at home. Even the monumentally ignorant Mayer knew the colossus that Faulkner was and gave his blessing to the unusual work arrangement at a studio where all the other writers literally punched a time clock. But the next time Mayer tried to get the author of *The Sound and the Fury* on the phone, he was told the writer was at home ... his summer home in Pascagoula, Mississippi.

It's a Wonderful Life was unique in that it was not inspired by the theater or the publishing world. Writer Philip Van Doren sent out Christmas cards in 1945 containing a very short story called ''The Greatest Gift.'' Capra bought the story (the card, actually) for the first project of his new indie prod, as the trades call them. In retrospect, Capra must have been delighted that he was on Van Doren's mailing list because he would later say

"The Greatest Gift" was the "story he had been looking for all his life."

During and after the film was made, Capra would sometimes probably wish that he had never found it.

When he fell in love with the Christmas card, Capra didn't know what a mixed blessing this literary love affair would turn out to be. After securing the rights, he handed the card over to two Hollywood veterans, the husband and wife writing team of Albert Hackett and Frances Goodrich, the latter a Pulitzer Prize-winning playwright. They cranked out one of the best screen yarns ever told in a mere three weeks.

If only the making of the film had been as smooth and quick as writing it.

The set of *It's a Wonderful Life* was not so . . . wonderful. Its two principals were suffering something akin to Post-Traumatic Stress Disorder. Their low-level anxiety communicated itself to the rest of the cast and crew. Jimmy should have known what he was in for. *It's a Wonderful Life* was not his first return to acting after the war.

Desperate for a break from kite-flying and model airplane building, Jimmy had agreed to the downscale job of doing a one-shot radio appearance. He didn't even have to memorize any lines, just read from a script, which was a radio recreation of his huge prewar hit, *Destry Rides Again*. After risking his life during 20 bombing missions over Germany, Jimmy found standing in front of a microphone and a radio studio audience terrifying. Eyewitnesses recalled that his hands were shaking so badly while holding the script, the fluttering pages could be seen from the control room.

This was the world Jimmy had chosen to return to.

Frank Capra should have had an easier time of it. Although he too took time out from Hollywood during the war, he stayed in his chosen profession, making a series of documentaries, *Why We Fight,* that became instant classics. (One in fact was too classic—or true to life—for the propaganda tastes of the U.S. government. Capra's friend John Huston made a documentary on soldiers suffering battle fatigue—today we call it Post-Traumatic Stress Disorder—and it was a little too cinema *verité.*

The film was quietly suppressed until recently when it finally aired on Public Television.)

Although Capra kept "in shape" making movies during the war while Jimmy didn't exactly perfect Method acting inhaling pure oxygen at 30,000 feet, both men were scared to death. And they communicated their fear to everyone else.

Stewart and Capra worried that thay had lost their know-how during the war. "There are two million dollars invested in this picture," Jimmy told the Washington *Star*. "I just can't let Frank Capra down." A reporter for the *Star* mentioned that the two principals' "mutual anxiety made the set an unpleasant place."

If there was anything Jimmy feared more than fear of acting itself, it was using his heroic war record to sell movie tickets! He would become positively garrulous about any movie he was asked to promote, and he would go to the opening of a supermarket or an eyelid if it helped sell tickets, one reporter joked, but he kept mum about the war.

And he didn't have to worry about using his war hero status for promotional purposes. Answerable to no studio boss, Jimmy had a clause written into his contract for *It's a Wonderful Life* "forbidding exploitation of his war fame." The *L.A. Daily News's* Erskine Johnson wrote, "Jimmy still has the morbid horror of seeming to trade on his war record. When he signed to make *It's a Wonderful Life*, he had a clause inserted in his contract forbidding exploitation of his war fame."

His then agent, Leland Hayward, was shocked by this unique act of self-effacement. In 1951 the *Saturday Evening Post* described the agent's amazement, which also included a lot of admiration. "Never in all his bargaining days had he [Hayward] been asked to insert a clause in an actor's contract which remotely resembled the one demanded by the thin, gawky man slouched on the far side of his desk." Stewart explained to Hayward that while he trusted Frank Capra with his life—and his throat—he wanted the no war-hero-clause in black and white. So Hayward put it in writing. A clause in Jimmy's contract for his favorite film stipulates: "In all advertising and publicity issued by the Corporation, or under its control, the

Corporation will not mention or cause to be mentioned the part taken by the artist in World War II as an officer in the U.S. Army.''

The publicity people and the press weren't the only ones kept in the dark about the war. Even his future family was kept out of the loop. More than half a century later, his daughter Kelly would tell me, ''He never talked about the war, even when we asked him.''

Without his cooperation, newspaper accounts of his wartime missions had made him one of the most popular men in America. Whenever he appeared on radio programs, the primitive equivalent of today's Nielsens ratings, showed the listening audience skyrocketing. Jimmy also had it written into his radio appearance contracts that his war record was a *verboten* topic of discussion. As far as he was concerned, the most traumatic upheaval of the 20th century never took place.

Or else he felt a radio or press interview to promote a movie was not an appropriate venue to bring up 50 million war dead.

It was the new ''war'' he was about to wage that had him almost as scared as he was on his first air raid over Bremen.

The night before shooting began, Jimmy recalled admitting to himself, ''The truth is I'm scared as hell.'' So he called the production company and asked what scene was first up the next morning. He was told page 33. During the war, Jimmy had learned, if not to conquer his fears, at least to control them through overpreparation, memorizing a flight plan until he could have flown the mission blindfolded.

The same work ethic didn't quite work in the crazy world of filmmaking. True to form, Jimmy stayed up all night, memorizing page 33 until he could recite it in his sleep—which he didn't get to do since he was so anxious. By dawn he knew his lines and everyone else's on page 33. If an all-nighter could get him safely to and from the airspace above Nazi Germany, the same study habits could lick his stage fright.

Frank Capra didn't coddle his actors. In fact, he could be downright inconsiderate. Bright and early, Jimmy showed up on the soundstage, ready to act the hell out of page 33.

''Jimmy,'' Capra said nonchalantly, ''I meant to call you

last night to tell you our first scene starts on page *31*, not 33. Ready?''

Capra was fortunate that Jimmy's father had long ago taught his son not to shoot mad dogs—no matter how much they tick you off. Jimmy was a trouper and they shot page 31, prepared or not. Terrified or not.

He was fortunate enough to find a mentor on the set who helped him regain his self-confidence. Ironically, it was the actor who played the unredeemably evil villain of the piece, Lionel Barrymore's Mr. Potter, the banker who initiates George Bailey's suicidal ideation.

Off screen, Barrymore was the antithesis of the greedy banker. He was more like Jimmy's personal on-the-set therapist. Jimmy had mused out loud to cast and crew that he feared his five-year absence from Hollywood had made him forget how to act. When Barrymore learned of Jimmy's insecurity, he came rushing over to hold his hand, so to speak. ''Forget about this being away for five years,'' Barrymore told him, sounding like the fatherly judge in the first of the Andy Hardy series instead of evil banker Potter. ''Don't you realize you're moving millions of people, shaping their lives? What other profession has that kind of power? Acting is a noble profession. Now just do what you're doing. You're doing fine. Now keep up and don't go moping around here,'' Barrymore almost scolded him. Jimmy repeated that pep talk verbatim 50 years later and said simply, ''I'll always be grateful to him for that.''

Barrymore's performance kept Jimmy humble too. ''Once in a while, I get to thinking I'm not so bad. In fact, I begin to think I'm pretty darn good. Then I go charging into a scene with Barrymore [and] get my ears pinned back, the scene stolen right out of my hand. Then I wonder if, in arguing that I'll be a whiz of an actor by eighty [Barrymore was only 68 in 1946], I'm giving myself enough time.''

Actually, Jimmy wasn't giving himself enough credit. In contrast to Jimmy's multi-layered performance of a man racked by self-doubt, anger, and feelings of utter failure, Barrymore turned in a one-note performance as an arch-capitalist whose only motivation was greed. Maybe it was the script's fault that

Barrymore's character remained so one-dimensional, but the venerable actor never, in Jimmy's words, "pinned his ears back" with a performance superior to Jimmy's.

Despite the anxiety of returning to his old profession, the old pro became his old professional self again. "Things eased up later on. It took me a few weeks to get over this business of trying too hard." Jimmy did the psychological equivalent of slapping himself in the face and shouting, "Snap out of it." A visitor to the set did note, however, that the mutual anxiety of the director, who had sunk all his own money into the film, and the star, who realized this was possibly his last and only chance at a comeback, made the set "an unpleasant place."

(You couldn't studdy too hard for a bombing mission. You could, however, be overprepared for a movie scene. "I could see the strain in the daily rushes," Jimmy later said of his early earnestness. But even that presumed fault enriched a film about a man at the breaking point.)

Despite the fact that *It's a Wonderful Life* is a Christmas classic with an ending so happy I cry every time I watch it, it's also a film about bankruptcy, misappropriation of funds, grand theft, clinical depression, and suicidal thoughts. The "strain" that Jimmy could see in the rushes was appropriate for a movie filled with so many themes of distress.

Film historian Paul Hendrickson felt he saw a lot more than "strain" on Jimmy's face. Hendrickson came up with the ingenious idea of watching the movie during a non-holiday period. Let's face it, *The Texas Chainsaw Massacre* could be a feel good movie on Christmas Eve with enough spiked egg nog and Christmas carols playing in the background. Without the sappiness of the holiday mood, however, Hendrickson was struck by what a near-psychotic creature George Baily is for most of the movie.

It's a Wonderful Life is basically the story of a secular saint, a man who spends his entire life deferring his own dreams and desires to make others' come true. His reward for a lifetime of good deeds is a betrayal so cruel he finds himself facing 20 years in the slammer for a crime—embezzlement—he didn't commit. Bailey makes what many other depressives would consider the only choice—to kill himself. God sends an incompetent angel named Clarence to earth to stop George by showing him what life in his hometown would be like if he hadn't existed. Life in Bedford Falls is hell without George's generosity over the years. He comes to realize just how important and significant his life has been. So what if he ends up in the state pen for a crime he didn't commit? George Bailey chooses life while the film ends with the entire cast singing "Auld Lang Syne."

But before divine intervention in the form of Clarence changes Bailey's mind, we see a man in full mental crisis. Hendrickson writes, "I found myself a little startled. Because this time I seemed to be seeing primarily not my all-time favorite character's goodness—it was there, of course—but the crazed, terror-eyed, sweat-soaked, suicidal self underneath, a self saved in the nick, as we all know, by a corny angel named Clarence. What hit me more than anything was George Bailey's anger, the potential for violence seething just beneath his selfless surface." It was a grown-up 10-year-old, armed with a gun, trying to decide whether or not to shoot a puppy that deserved to die.

Jimmy Stewart: "crazed, terror-eyed, sweat-soaked, suicidal." And other critics had the chutzpah to say the actor was always playing himself. Let's hope not in this case.

The intensity of Jimmy's performance may also have owed a lot to his own psychological history. In several incidents in *It's a Wonderful Life,* George Bailey first gives up his plans to go to college, then to go on a trip around the world, and finally cancels his honeymoon, so a) his kid brother can go to college, b) fulfill *his* career dreams, and c) the citizens of Bedford Falls won't lose their homes if the Bailey family's savings and loan goes under.

In a classically constructed but totally improvised scene, George and his bride (Donna Reed) are on their way to a honeymoon in the South Seas. George will finally get to fulfill two dreams at once: get out of provincial, boring Bedford Falls and realize his lifelong fantasy of traveling to exotic places—with his beautiful bride for company!

But before leaving for the train depot in a taxi, he notices a mob outside the Bailey thrift. There's a run on the bank, and the depositors are demanding their money. Poor George just happens to have a huge wad of cash in his hands meant for the honeymoon. The money earmarked for the South Seas ends up in the pockets of the depositors, stopping the run on the savings and loan.

Although the scene was beautifully constructed thematically and dramatically, the writers can't take credit for the dialogue. Jimmy was forced to make it all up!

Frank Capra could be a torquemada when it meant servicing a film or a performance. If Hitchcock hadn't allegedly said it first, Capra might have compared his actors to cows.

The script called for Jimmy, who had by now overcome his postwar stage fright and was letter perfect, to make a long, impassioned speech to the depositors, begging them not to withdraw their money. Capra wanted Jimmy to really work to get the depositors to change their minds. In the middle of Jimmy's carefully rehearsed speech, Capra set off a fire alarm. All the extras in the bank lobby set ran away from Jimmy to the windows, looking for fire. According to the *Washington Star,* "Jimmy through sheer force of his *improvised* oratory, made the extras return to the set so he could finish his speech. The cameras caught [Jimmy's improvisation] in the outtakes," which were incorporated into the final cut.

The *Star* added that Capra was "ruthless with his star. He'd throw Jimmy into a scene and say, 'Make up your own dialogue as you go along. Just say whatever seems natural, the first thing that comes to your head.' " This to a man who stayed up all night before the first day of filming in order to make sure he had memorized the script perfectly. Thank God Capra wasn't his co-pilot on any of those bombing raids over Germany. Imagine "winging" a flight plan.

Jimmy was a real trouper—or a real masochist—because he never complained about Capra's abuse, indeed praising the director's leadership and inspiration.

"We did 104 scenes in *It's a Wonderful Life,* and most of us would have done 104 more and liked it, for Frank always knows where he's going and what he's doing,'' Jimmy told Louella Parsons a year after he made the film.

The following scene in the movie was much less dramatic than the run on the savings and loan (and there weren't any little sadistic surprises from the director), but the sequence must have had enormous autobiographical resonance for the actor. With a few details changed, Jimmy could have been reenacting a scene from his own psychodrama after graduating from Princeton. In the film, the thrift's board of directors is willing to keep the concern going, but only if George Bailey agrees to stay in Bedford Falls and manage the mismanaged concern. Poor George, once again, was just on his way out of town to begin his world travels. It's a case of the lady or the tiger, except poor George knows exactly who's behind which door. Stay in Bedford Falls and make cheap loans available to first-time homebuyers. (This was right after the war, when thousands of returning vets were encountering the same experience.) Or gratify his own needs and personal aspirations and get the hell out of town.

George Bailey, the secular saint, puts his personal dreams on hold—permanently, it turns out—for the greater good of his fellow citizens and his brother.

In real life, Jimmy Stewart did just the opposite. The dice weren't nearly so loaded in his own situation as they were in the movie, but Jimmy did show himself to be a proto-representative of the Me Generation in 1932—forty-some years before the term was coined.

After graduating from Princeton, instead of returning to the Stewart equivalent of the Bailey thrift, Jimmy in effect said, ''Thanks, Dad, for putting me through college. Now I'm going to go conquer Broadway and Hollywood instead of helping you sell nuts and bolts.''

Jimmy chose self-fulfillment over self-sacrifice. In his defense, the hardware store was nowhere near the financial mess the Bailey Savings and Loan was. In fact, the store had made the Stewarts one of the richest families in town. Still, as he recalled in the *Collier's* first-person account quoted earlier, Jimmy's father gave up *his* dream of world adventure to please his father, the first James. Jimmy instead chose to *shtup* every other starlet in Hollywood.

Throughout his nearly ninety years on the planet, James Maitland Stewart was renowned for his acts of kindness and philanthropy. Hospital wings and gorilla enclosures were named after him. He must have felt some guilt when he left Pennsylvania behind and took off for Cape Cod, Broadway, and Culver City.

George Bailey and *It's a Wonderful Life* in a small, symbolic way allowed him to expiate his "sin of omission" and do the right thing, if only on acetate.

The intensity of Jimmy's performance communicated itself to Academy voters, and he received this third best actor Oscar nomination. Capra's sadism paid off and he was nominated for best director. The film was nominated for best picture and a few technical awards. Surprisingly, it was ignored for best original screenplay, even though *It's a Wonderful Life* is inarguably one of the best stories ever plotted.

It's a Wonderful Life was shut out at the Oscar ceremonies by *The Best Years of Our Lives,* which picked up seven awards. The latter film's sweep shouldn't have been a surprise. The sappy drama recounts the experiences of three GI's returning home and adjusting to civilian life. Things are bumpy for a while, but eventually all three men realize the American dream. Even the poor vet who returns from the war with hooks instead of hands ends up with his adoring, adorable childhood sweetheart. (And the actor, a total amateur named Harold Russell, a real-life veteran and double amputee, won an Oscar for his first and only screen performance. Years later, strapped for cash, Russell would scandalize the Academy by being the first recipient to sell his statuette.) The movie's biggest crisis involves whether or not Dana Andrews will get a good job after the war.

As the syrupy title suggests, *The Best Years of Our Lives* was a feel-good movie for a country that was feeling great after winning the war and becoming the most powerful nation in the world. *It's a Wonderful Life,* despite *its* sappy title and inevitable happy ending, took people places where they didn't want to go: bankruptcy, depression, despair, suicide.

And one place people definitely didn't want to go was a theater showing *It's a Wonderful Life.*

Despite its Oscar nominations and Jimmy's heartfelt performance, the film lost half a million dollars and bankrupted Capra's production company before it even got off the ground. It was Liberty Productions' first and last production. Jimmy, who had only a small piece of Liberty and a huge piece of Westside real estate, could remain philosophical about the failure of the film and his good friend's film company. "I don't think it was the type of story people wanted right after the war," Jimmy said. "They wanted a war-related story or pure slapstick Jerry Lewis type of comedy. Our movie just got lost."

In fact, in choosing the film, Jimmy had failed to follow his own advice. During his first visit home in 1945, he told *Life* magazine he didn't want to make war pictures. "The country's had enough of them. I want to be in a comedy." Instead, he chose—actually it was the only thing offered him—a film about suicidal depression and the redemptive qualities of human kindness.

There's an old saying that bank robbers and movie stars have one thing in common: the public loves to build them up just to see them fall.

Howard McClay of the *Los Angeles Daily News* seemed to be enjoying Jimmy's fall when he gleefully wrote, "What [Stewart] hoped would be his big comeback film, *It's a Wonderful Life,* did little to give him his second wind."

Erskine Johnson, from the same newspaper, had always been a big booster of Stewart, so his criticism was kinder but almost as pessimistic as his colleague's at the *Daily News.* "They say Jimmy Stewart is a forgotten man. I'd like to argue about it, but the box office data on the last Stewart picture, *It's a Wonderful Life,* makes that 'forgotten' business hold water. It was a good picture, it had comedy, hometownness *[sic],* good entertainment, and lots of good supporting players around Jimmy."

And it lost half a million bucks.

The movie was considered such a loser that in 1973 when its copyright expired, no one bothered to renew it, and the film became public domain—and round-the-clock programming on local TV stations because it was free.

Finally, its classic status was recognized when it finally received the large audience it deserved. In the period between Thanksgiving and Christmas, it seemed impossible to channel-surf without running into Jimmy Stewart helping an overweight angel earn his wings.

I know of at least one other case where the film had an even more powerful impact on an individual. Every Christmas Eve, I watch *It's a Wonderful Life* and weep, usually whenever Jimmy does something saintly and self-sacrificing. (It was one of the unexpected fringe benefits of researching this book that I learned the off-screen Jimmy was virtually George's identical twin.) And I am not alone in my sappy appreciation of this golden sap. When Presidential aide Robert McFarlane confessed various crimes at Congressional hearings during the Iran-Contra scandal in 1987, he also confessed that watching *It's a Wonderful Life* persuaded him not to commit suicide. He didn't have an angel, just Jimmy's angelic performance.

In 1994, NBC idiotically bought exclusive rights to the film and aired it only once during the holidays. By then, everyone had seen the movie so many times it ended up in the basement of the prime time Nielsens.

After the commercial failure of the film, Jimmy's new no-nonsense agent, Lew Wasserman, the Mike Ovitz of his day, told his client bluntly, "Sorry, Jimmy, they've forgotten you. You'll have to start all over again."

Then there were the journalists who apparently never read *Variety* but merely cranked out psychotically upbeat stories at an editor's behest, regardless of the facts. How else do you explain this evaluation of Jimmy's career at the time? In Britain's *PIX* magazine, Bill Miller, who apparently had been vacationing on Venus during the failure of *It's a Wonderful Life,* filed this "account" of Jimmy's career right after World War II. "Jimmy didn't find getting back to the screen very difficult. Not only had his fans been faithful, they loved him. If they found him a little older, a bit more grim and saddened looking in his first postwar movie, *It's a Wonderful Life,* it agreed with their own mood." *PIX* magazine in the late 1940s sounds a lot like another British glossy today called *Hello!,* which manages to find an upbeat angle in every story about the Royal family, even when discussing the Princess.

It's a Wonderful Life's grim subject matter did *not* reflect the public's mood. America was one big happy camper after winning the war. The campers wanted bread and circuses, not castor oil and tragedies. The most powerful, richest nation on earth wanted froth, not pop Freud. And Jimmy, who still believed the fans were partners, felt a fiduciary responsibility to give them exactly what they wanted. Or what he thought they wanted.

His next film was 1947's *Magic Town,* a comedy so compulsively frothy it could serve as an Alka-Seltzer substitute. Although directed by the great William Wellman, the film was so "Capraesque," according to film historian Dennis John Hall, the plot was practically a parody of one of Capra's feel good prewar films, but without the substance. Like so much other Capra-corn, *Magic Town* takes place in a small town that represents a gold mine to a statistician (Stewart) because the inhabitants exactly reflect the rest of America's tastes in everything from soap to politics. Jimmy's Everyman travels to Everytown, here called Grandview, to find out why the citizens are a demographer's dream. What little conflcit there is in the film comes from the editor of the local newspaper, played by Jane Wyman, who wants to shake her readers out of their bourgeois complacency. In the process, however, she will ruin Jimmy's demographic gold mine if the people of Grandview start having independent—and statistically atypical—ideas and tastes. Stewart's fling with Wyman seems tacked on for no other reason than that you have to have romance in a romantic comedy.

While the public did indeed want froth, it wanted good, entertaining froth. *Magic Town* was stale, recycled Capra fizz that had gone flat. The RKO fim, like the studio's previous release, *It's a Wonderful Life,* failed commercially. MGM was beginning to look savvy rather than cruel in not renewing its prewar star's contract.

But 1947 wasn't a total calamity for Stewart. His alma mater awarded him an honorary Master of Arts degree. You can't help but feel that Princeton was being just a bit snooty, since a star of Jimmy's magnitude, not to mention his war record, should have received an honorary *doctorate*. The award read, "James Maitland Stewart, a graduate of Princeton who whether in his chosen profession or in the grave business of war, has demonstrated ability, modesty, leadership and above all integrity, in a way which has warmed our hearts and stirred our pride in his achievements." Years later, both Pennsylvania and Indiana Universities made amends of sorts by awarding Jimmy honorary doctorates.

The Princeton honor was especially sweet for Stewart since his father, a very active Princeton alumnus, ran all over town bragging about his son, "the M.A." Princeton's acknowledgment of his son impressed him more than Jimmy's Oscar nominations or box office success. And Jimmy loved getting Alexander's usually stingy approval.

The summer of 1947 also represented one of the few pleasant periods in his career immediately after the war. The moviegoing audiences apparently didn't appreciate him or patronize his films, so Jimmy tried an even tougher audience—Broadway—and succeeded marvelously.

Harvey was a Pulitzer-Prize-winning comedy about an alcoholic who hallucinates he has a best friend, the title character, a nine-foot tall rabit only the dipsomaniac protagonist, Elwood P. Dowd, can see. Frank Fay, the Broadway veteran who originated the role, wanted some time off, and Jimmy courageously agreed to step into a part already made famous by someone else, thus risking unflattering comparisons. Theater critics have and still are notoriously cruel to movie stars who attempt to "stretch" and go slumming (fiscally at least) in the theater. Poor Jessica Lange's Blanche DuBois was barbecued by the critics a few years ago, yet when she reprised *A Streetcar Named Desire* as a three-hour TV movie, her beautifully modulated performance won her an Emmy.

Jimmy, luckily, wasn't barbecue meat for the critics when he essayed Elwood P. Dowd. Brooks Atkinson, the omnipotent critic for *The New York Times*, which then as now could make or break a play, didn't exactly, damn Jimmy with faint praise, but he paid him at worst a left-handed, condescending compliment when he wrote, "Although the structure of Mr. Stewart's performance is much weaker than Mr. Fay's, his honesty as a human being gives the climax of the play warmth and emotion. In every way that counts, Mr. Stewart is thoroughly admirable." It almost sounds as though Atkinson were reviewing Jimmy's offstage personality rather than his onstage performance. Theater-goers were much more enthusiastic, and the entire run of the play with Jimmy in the lead was sold out.

Shortly before he left L.A. for Broadway, his friends played an unfunny joke on Jimmy by sending him one rabbit every hour. By the time they were through, Jimmy found himself the unwilling owner of 20 rabbits! (An animal lover who turned his backyard into a feeding station for the neighborhood squirrels and who shared his Brentwood bachelor pad with 10 stray cats, three dogs, and Henry Fonda after the war, Jimmy didn't turn the bunnies over to the pound for euthanization. He found a home for them at a chicken farm down the road run by his housekeeper's daughter.) At a going-away dinner, Henry Fonda played a much funnier joke on his best friend. All the other guests were served steak, but Jimmy's dinner arrived on a covered plate. Underneath was yet another live rabbit. Jimmy asked his friends to give up on the rabbit jokes, and Fonda, treating Jimmy like the hallucinating character he would soon play on Broadway, responded, "What rabbit? Are you seeing things?"

His Broadway triumph was a short-lived pleasure. Back in Hollywood, Jimmy's next choice of film suggests a man grasping at straws, desperately trying to figure out what the public wanted. It didn't want despair, it didn't want carbonated water with no bubbles, so he tried something in between called *Call Northside 777*. It was a drama with a serious theme shot in a documentary style. The great Italian directors like Rossellini and Visconti had recently introduced this ultra-realistic style of moviemaking and appropriately dubbed it *neorealisma* (which the French would shortly expropriate as their own and call *cinema verité*).

The drama was shot on location, including scenes at Joliet's Stateville Prison, to recreate the real-life story of a youth wrongly convicted of murder and locked away for 11 years.

Stewart is an investigative journalist whose reportage frees the innocent young man.

Artistically, Jimmy was lucky he was a free agent who could work for a studio, Twentieth Century Fox, that was willing to take risks with innovative filmmaking. Unlike other studio chiefs who probably couldn't even spell *neorealisma,* much less agree to put money behind such an uncommercial style of filmmaking, Fox's Darryl Zanuck was a maverick. He, like Jimmy, was obviously familiar enough with the exciting new European genre to want to participate in an American version of it.

Unfortunately *Call Northside 777* proved that while most moguls were aesthetic ignorami, they knew what the public wanted, and it didn't want *neowhatchamacallit* in general, or *Call Northside 777* in particular. In 1948 film was what is known as a *succes d'estime,* which means the critics loved it and the public hated it. The *London Daily Mail* esteemed it as "a most satisfying thriller, generously streaked with class." The *Washington Star,* which recognized *neorealisma* when it saw it, called it, "absorbing, exciting, *realistic.*"

Fox committed a major no-no while publicizing the film. Although every contract since *It's a Wonderful Life* expressly forbade using World War II to promote Stewart's films, Fox's inhouse newsletter, *20th Century Fox News,* ran this paragraph, which Jimmy must not have read or it never would have seen the light of day. Despite its less than altruistic intentions, the newsletter entry provides a literally unique look at Jimmy's postwar psychological makeup.

"There's no getting away from the fact that war did something to Jimmy. He's more serious than he used to be. He smiles less frequently. The social whirl of Hollywood seems to appeal to him less and less. Jimmy saw a lot of the sad side of life overseas . . . very, very often, there's a faraway look in his eyes. He's more introspective than ever before. What he saw seems to have left a marked impression on him. Twenty missions over Germany as a B-24 squadron commander have brought out gray hairs in spots."

This must have been a very nervous time for Stewart. Fortunately he had all those successful financial investments so he never had to worry about becoming an iceman like Craig Reynolds rather one day reviving *The Iceman Cometh* on Broadway. A friend at the time said, ". . . don't fool yourself. Jimmy knows what the score is. He's smart about money and he has good investments, real estate and so on."

Jimmy was frugal, a good Calvinist, even though he could have afforded to live the life of Riley or Bob Hope. A friend said that despite his wealth, Jimmy had "stashed away ample funds to care for [his family] if the movie gushers ever run dry." The friend mentioned that Stewart sat on the "board of directors of two western airlines, owned a few oil wells and a sizable chunk of real estate in West L.A." in 1948, long before the real estate boom of the 1970s made land on the West Side more valuable than any oil that might be found underneath it. His one indulgence: a charter plane company, which Jimmy confessed in a fit of Calvinist guilt "gives me planes to fly if I want one, even though it doesn't make that much money."

Yet another acquaintance suspected he was as wealthy as another movie star who had invested his film chips wisely, Bob Hope, "only Jimmy didn't hire a press agent to make sure everybody knew how rich and smart he was about money."

Jimmy's next film, *A Miracle Can Happen* (also known as *On Our Merry Own),* was a case of good/bad news. The good news was he got to work for the first time with his closest friend, Henry Fonda. The bad news was that the comedy again reflected Jimmy's desperate attempt to put his finger on the public's pulse. Fonda and Stewart play musicians in a big band. The two men had only one scene, basically cameos, in the episodic comedy, which also had several directors, credited and uncredited. The film is only interesting because you can feel the real-life friendship between the two stars. It's the only convincing thing in the film, which flopped.

Jimmy's next fim was—as Claude Rains says to Humphrey Bogart at the end of *Casablanca*—the "beginning of a beautiful relationship." *Rope* (1948) marked the start of what was to be the most aesthetically successful collaboration in his career, working with Alfred Hitchcock. The box office failure of the film was not indicative of the huge financial and critical encomia they would enjoy in the three films they made together during the next decade.

It's hard to guess why Jimmy agreed to appear in *Rope*, since his role was not much more than a cameo. (And Fonda wasn't his co-star.) Maybe he just wanted to work with Hitchcock, who was already considered one of the greatest directors of all time—and his career wasn't even half over. Or less likely, perhaps Jimmy just needed a job, and he hoped Hitchcock, whose previous films had been mostly moneymakers, would jump-start his stalled career.

Rope was an amazingly experimental film—not to mention a financial risk—even for a no-name distributor like Transatlantic seeking to make a name for itself. Hitchcock used the bizarre conceit of shooting the entire film in one take with no cuts! In fact, the only cut in the film occurred when the camera magazine ran out of film and had to be reloaded. Hitchcock preserved the illusion of no edits by cutting away to the dark interior of a briefcase during the reloading of the camera. If only the tedious storyline had been as ingenious. Two brilliant young psychopaths, vaguely patterned after Leopold and Loeb, decided to put their Nietzschean *übermensch* philosophy to practical use by murdering an "inferior" acquaintance. Jimmy has a supporting role as the philosophy professor whose former students misinterpret his theories to justify their crime. Jimmy turns amateur sleuth and solves the murder. The film was mildly intriguing for two other reasons besides its unusual cinematography. Released only a few years after the war, the students' philosophy is the same Nietzschean rhetoric Hitler used to justify his Final Solution. And, unheard of at the time, the two students (Farley Granger, John Dall), it's suggested, homosexual lovers.

Jimmy never regretted his participation in the failed experiment and found the actual shooting of the film so fascinating he only half-jokingly suggested to Hitchcock that they set up bleachers around the soundstage and charge an audience five bucks a head to watch them shoot.

Jimmy only had one certifiable hit during the late 1940s, and his choice of subject matter again shows how willing he was to take a risk with iffy stories. In 1949 *The Stratton Story* was, in *Variety-ese,* a bio-pic about a real life big league baseball player, Monty Stratton, who despite the loss of his leg, returns to the diamond with the love and encouragement of his wife (June Allyson).

MGM financed the film, grudgingly. Fortunately for the studio, Jimmy didn't hold a grudge against his former employer for its cavalier postwar treatment of him. In fact, he flat-out lied to Louella Parsons when she asked why he hadn't returned to MGM after the War. Instead of angrily revealing that the studio had dumped him, he diplomatically replied, "Oh, I like to pick my own stories. Of course, I don't deny it's a good idea to have a studio in back of you. They handle all your problems, but I'm very friendly with MGM or else I wouldn't be making the Monty *Stratton Story* for them."

It was amazing the film got made anywhere. Stewart was turning into the 1940s version of the 1930s Katharine Hepburn, box office toxin. Even more importantly, Louis B. Mayer, displaying a rare delicacy, hated the script because he found it too "depressing." Mayer allegedly shouted at the luckless producer who brought the script to him, "How do you think people will feel when this man with one leg goes to bat and hits a single and can't run to first base? How will all the pregnant women in the audience feel watching such a disgusting thing?" Today, with the existence of politically delicate terms like "physically challenged," it's hard to imagine a time when people felt a handicap was unwatchable on the big screen.

Somehow, somebody changed the mogul's mind, and the movie got made. The film was a huge commercial hit, and Mayer said he wept—probably over the box office receipts and not over the sentimental plot.

The Stratton Story was Jimmy's only oasis during his years in the box-office wilderness—the late 1940s. While some men—and women—might seek to anesthetize themselves during a difficult period with booze, it seems Jimmy picked promiscuity as his drug of choice.

A cautious, still Victorian press could only hint at what what we know from latter-day tell-all autobiographies (Shelley Winters, Evelyn Keyes, Mickey Rooney) was basically Sodom by the Sea. (Actually, more Gommorah than Sodom, since there were a lot more unfaithful husbands like Gary Cooper than switch-hitters like Errol Flynn or gays like Tyrone Power and Montgomery Clift in the movie colony.) Fading stars like Flynn and John Barrymore drank themselves into stupors to forget their box-office grosses. Chaplin had a yen for underage girls and even married one when she passed jail-bait age.

The war may have changed Jimmy's taste in women. Pre-war, he had whirlwind courtships with classy actresses like Olivia de Havilland and Ginger Rogers. After the war, his taste tended toward what the French call *nostalgie de la boue* and what in those days were known as "party or B-girls," euphemisms for prostitute.

Characteristically, Jimmy avoided public scandal by taking these "dates" to out-of-the-way restaurants with only a small group of friends, unfashionable spots that would never be discovered by the paparazzi. Officially, he insisted he was a "good boy." His argument, however, wasn't very persuasive: "I don't have time to fool around," he told a reporter. "Often, I have to work on Sundays. Now, I ask you, how can ardent love thrive under such conditions?" Such a busy schedule didn't rule out quickies in a backlot Winnebago or late-night rendezvous. (Shooting rarely lasted all night because of the cost of overtime.)

A "party girl" who caught Jimmy's attention, although not in the way you might think, was Barbara Carroll. The starlet attended what was supposed to be a stag party, i.e. a men's only gathering, at Cary Grant's. The self-censoring press described it as a "boisterous midget-ridden stag party with guests sipping champagne from the slippers of glamorous women, some of whom secured admission on the basis of their impressive measurements." In the days when people didn't have "enquiring minds," what the circumspect journalists declined to report was that no wives were invited, but there was plenty of single women and married men in attendance.

Thirty-six years after the event, Carroll could be more upfront. She noticed that many of the male guests were A-list movie stars. The women she didn't recognize from fan magazines or anywhere else. "I've been to some Scale-10 parties," she told Jhan Robbins in *Everybody's Man,* "but this was Scale-11.'' Faking naïveté, Carroll asked the host why an unknown actress like herself had been invited to such a stellar gathering. Grant refused to play along with her feigned innocence. He said bluntly, ''Because you're 34-24-34.''

Midgets at the party lent a bawdy, Medieval court flavor to the goings-on. *Life* magazine innocently sent a photographer to what probably turned into an orgy. A caption in the magazine describes a photo of one of the G-rated events. ''Jimmy meets two midgets who popped out of a serving dish at the party.''

Restaurateur Mike Romanoff (the Wolfgang Puck of his day, a British immigrant who claimed to be a member of Russia's imperial family despite his strong Cockney accent) catered the affair. The place was so full of gardenias, Carroll eerily felt as though she were at Forest Lawn instead of a stag party. ''Pink champagne was actually poured into the ladies' slippers. I remember Jimmy saying [prudently], 'Thank God, there aren't too many open-toed shoes.' '' Even at an orgy, Jimmy's puritanical waste-not-want-not ethic was at work.

Carroll's memoir is chiefly memorable because it suggested that Jimmy might be a card-carrying member of this landlocked Club Med, but he was still a gentleman. He may have been a slut, but he was a discreet slut.

In fact, Jimmy came to Carroll's rescue when ''one of the guests got roaring drunk and started making passes at the women. I was one of them,'' Carroll said. ''Jimmy saw what was happening and quickly put a stop to it. I don't know what he said, but it sure worked. I watched him as he walked the man to the door and practically tossed him out. I was very grateful and tried to thank him, but was drowned out by the music.'' Jimmy Stewart was a proto-feminist who didn't believe in sexual harassment.

Jimmy was being his usual gentlemanly self—and discreet. There may have been another reason for his discretion. This stag party was actually a bachelor's party to celebrate the ''retirement'' of a man who for the past 15 years had been regularly described in the press as ''Hollywood's most eligible bachelor.''

The town's most popular single guy had finally been hooked.

Chapter 26
Gloria, Get Your Gun

In 1949, Jimmy Stewart was 41 and unmarried. Almost every interview from the time he became a star included the inevitable question, "Why aren't you married?"

His agent dryly noted that at his age, most of his colleagues were already "working on their third or fourth wife." That comment answered the question on every journalist's notepad more succinctly than Jimmy did in a 1947 interview in *Collier's*.

"It soon became apparent he hated to talk about himself," Barbara Heggie wrote in an article entitled "Penrod in Hollywood." "But when he got on a topic close to his heart, he could talk well and with keen collegiate wit. His ruling interest seemed to be aviation and his ruling worry, marriage." The reporter noticed that the actor became depressed when she brought up the subject. Ironically, it wasn't loneliness but the inconvenience of bachelorhood that distressed him. "All his friends are married and Jimmy can't drop in without disturbing married couples." If he wanted to go fly a kite, he had to do it by himself.

Jimmy gave a profound explanation for his bachelorhood, when he told *Collier's*, "I don't want to marry one of these actresses and have it last a month. And if I find some nice girl and bring her out here, what would Hollywood do to her? I'm not so conceited that I think I can buck what a lot of other guys haven't been able to buck." And in a rare allusion to you know what, he said, "From what I see in Hollywood, maybe war's easier."

So when Jimmy at age 41 finally decided to settle down it was with neither an actress (too divorce-prone) nor some shy, innocent, small town girl who would have been overwhelmed by the sophistication of the movie colony and her husband's stardom.

He met the future Mrs. Stewart at a party hosted by Gary Cooper and his wife, Rocky. Besides her full-time job as a Hollywood wife, Rocky Cooper moonlighted as a matchmaker. (Her husband was engaged in a tortured, guilt-ridden affair with a co-star at the time, so maybe Mrs. Cooper consoled herself by making other people's love lives happier than her own.) Whatever her motivation, Rocky had been trying forever to match up her best friend, Gloria McLean, and her husband's colleague, Jimmy.

Rocky finally got the two together at a dinner party she had planned for exactly that purpose. Mrs. Cooper seated them next to each other. She was an inspired yenta because Gloria fit Jimmy's bill brilliantly. She was perfectly at home in Hollywood, where she had grown up, the daughter of MGM's chief legal counsel, Edgar Hatrick. She had no interest in acting, which meant there was no aspiring starlet agenda when she laughed at all Jimmy's jokes during dinner at the Coopers'. Years later, Gloria would explain the reason for the longevity of their marriage. She genuinely thought her husband was hysterical. She was absolutely right about humor being the union's salvation but not just because her husband kept her entertained. He also used it to defuse potential spats. Gloria was notorious for her outspokenness, which during one interview bordered on rude, and Jimmy didn't hesitate to tell her so, although in an amusing way that prevented a marital squall.

As usual, during the interview with the *L.A. Times,* Jimmy stammered and stuttered. Gloria finally said, "Oh, that sounds like somebody doing an *imitation* of Jimmy Stewart." Jimmy was not a milquetoast and replied, "Gloria, that's unkind." But he smiled when he reproved his wife. She pressed on, "But, Jimmy, they invented fire and the wheel during pauses that long." Stewart's riposte: "Well, it wasn't a total loss then." Gloria giggled, and Jimmy kept the marriage working.

Gloria was definitely not a fortune hunter. She was, however, divorce-prone, one of the reasons Jimmy had given for not taking an actress to the altar. When they met, she had been divorced from her husband, Ned McLean, for less than a year after a five-year marriage that had produced two sons, Ronald and Michael. Her ex-husband had settled a comfortable sum on her and their sons. He could afford to. He was a high-level executive at the Hearst publishing empire. Ten years later, Gloria and her ex would be named co-trustees of a huge fortune their sons had inherited. Ned's mother, the late Evalyn Walsh McLean, had been a Washington hostess, an heiress and one-time owner of the Hope diamond—the world's largest—which led Gloria to joke that her husband came along with the jewel's famous curse.

Despite the fact that Jimmy was the most eligible bachelor in Hollywood, Gloria was gun-shy about remarrying. And as a Hollywood princess at the court of L.B. Mayer, she was totally unimpressed with her dining companion's star status. A friend, columnist John Swope, inaccurately claimed Stewart never trusted anyone in the film industry. Swope said, "He never found anyone before Gloria who could separate him from his film image," which must have required surgical skill on Gloria's part, since the man and the image were practically inseparable.

Also at dinner on that historic evening were Ronald Reagan; Ann Sothern; Leland Hayward, Jimmy's ex-agent; and Hayward's gorgeous wife Slim. Gloria recalled that she and Jimmy didn't talk all that much, although she did notice that the mention of her two preschool sons didn't seem to scare him off. The only time during their brief first encounter when he seemed to light up was when she revealed that they shared a mutual passion, conservation.

Although Gloria was even more conflicted about marriage

than Jimmy, she later explained nonchalantly, "It wasn't that hard to fall in love with Jimmy. After all, he was *always* my favorite actor."

But she concealed her secret admiration better than any professional actress ever could. After dinner, the party adjourned to Ciro's, where Gloria remembered Nat King Cole performed that night. When Jimmy drove her home, he demonstrated his impeccable manners by not inviting himself in for a nightcap— or whatever. As he later said, "I could tell right off that she was a thoroughbred."

Their first "real date" was non-glamorous, no-nonsense, and must have endeared Jimmy to Gloria: They played golf. And Gloria beat him. "This was 1949," she recalled years later, when feminism had entered the national consciousness, "way before women began burning their bras, much less displaying athletic abilities superior to men." Then she hinted at what really attracted her to Jimmy, and it wasn't the fact that he was her favorite actor. "He didn't mind," she said with amazement, that she had beat him!

Jimmy's non-macho acceptance of Gloria's golfing superiority clinched her attraction to her future husband. It was Gloria's German shepherd that made him realize he *must* love this woman if he was willing to put up with her hound from hell.

After Jimmy drove her home from his humiliation on the links, Gloria took the initiative and invited him in for a drink— or whatever. He was, after all her favorite actor. Jimmy declined, but for once it wasn't because he was a gentleman who didn't do it on the first date.

He was terrified by the Cerberus on her doorstep, growling like a victim of hydrophobia. "Only as I drove away did I realize how smitten I was by Gloria. I wanted to see her again, but I knew I would have to win that dog over because Gloria was obviously devoted to it," Jimmy recalled.

To woo Gloria, he had to woo her dog too. Jimmy went about schmoozing both with typical thoroughness. He would show up for a date with a steak from Chasen's under his arm as a peace offering for the German shepherd. The dog was no gourmet and continued to growl at him. He tried talking baby talk to him, patting him, praising him. "It was terrible, humiliating, but I finally got to be friends and was free to court Gloria.

"It took me a year to get her to say yes." He didn't say how many chateaubriands from Chasen's it took to get the German shepherd to agree to the union.

The real reason it took so long to land Gloria probably didn't have anything to do with dogs or even her fear of marriage after her disastrous, short-lived first one.

Despite his reputation as Hollywood's most eligible bachelor, Jimmy could be quite dense when it came to showing, as they said in those days, a girl a good time.

He apparently didn't mind in the least that Gloria always beat him at golf because their first half dozen "dates" took place on the links. Finally, the outspoken divorcée said to Jimmy, "You know, I eat too." Jimmy immediately invited her to her German shepherd's favorite restaurant.

In 1985, he would say of Chasen's, which had devolved into the Spago of Generation Geritol, "And we're still going there." Gloria's dog had probably died of gout or arteriosclerosis before its time.

Jimmy's actual proposal was as no-nonsense and no frills as he was. And he gave his fiancée an engagement *compact* instead of a ring! Gloria recalled the less than Cyrano-esque manner in which he asked her to share his life with him. "I was at his house on his birthday. The phone rang. He answered it, and after he hung up, he said, 'Will you marry me?' 'What?' I asked. 'Will you marry me?' 'Oh yes,' I said."

Her divorce barely a year old, Gloria admitted she was reluctant to take the plunge again so soon. This was definitely not a star-struck woman. Yet Jimmy seemed so right despite her disillusionment about marriage in general, she didn't hesitate when he asked. "I wasn't anxious for marriage with anybody when we first met, but when he asked me I wasn't stuck for an answer."

Anything but a publicity hound, Jimmy still felt obliged enough to his studio's publicity machine (he was working for MGM at the time) that less than 24 hours after Gloria accepted, he called the newspapers. The next day, the *L.A. Examiner* quoted the ecstatic groom-to-be: "I pitched the big question to her last night, and to my surprise she said 'yes.' I'm as happy as a kid!"

Just as Jimmy's selection of films during this period showed a certain daring, his choice of a wife was no less unconventional.

Today, it's hard to imagine an era when a divorced woman was also considered a scarlet one. That is not an exaggeration. A king gave up his throne 13 years earlier simply because he wanted to marry a divorcée. Until the 1970s, a divorced man or woman was not allowed admission to the Queen of England's tent at Ascot. The rule even extended to a prime minister, who was kept out of the royal enclosure because the woman accompanying him was his second wife.

It isn't an exaggeration to say Jimmy was supremely open-minded in choosing Gloria, a divorcée with two sons.

In 1949, the Wallis Warfield Simpson syndrome still prevailed. The headline on the front page of the *L.A. Times*, May 23, 1949, used Gloria's marital status as the chief identifying factor: "Jimmy Stewart to Wed *Divorcée* Gloria McLean."

Fortunately for Jimmy, he wasn't Roman Catholic, and his Presbyterian faith was even less puritanical than the *Times's* headline writer. A tiny squib in the July 24 edition reported, "A committee on marriage and divorce of the Presbytery of L.A. after reviewing the facts, ruled that a Presbyterian minister would not be *guilty* of any impropriety in officiating at the ceremony." The article explained that the amazingly loose rules of the Church okayed her remarriage because her divorce from her first husband took place "more than a year ago."

His choice of life partner also showed Jimmy was no cradle robber. Although one journalist described Gloria as looking like a "well-scrubbed debutante," at 31 she might have been considered slightly over the hill in an era when men still expected their first wife, at least, to be a nubile virgin. Still, Jimmy wasn't exactly slumming when it came to his bride's physical attributes. *Voque* gave its professional imprimatur when it called her "refreshingly handsome, with large green eyes, clearly marked brows and loosely combed, bright brown hair. She looks in casual clothes the way most people hope they will look in casual clothes."

An AP wirephoto of the time shows a remarkably thin woman in an age of zaftig beauties like Monroe and Mansfield. Gloria looks her age. Her finest feature is a delicately chiseled nose. Broad-schouldered and wasp-waisted, she isn't spectacularly beautiful, but she is in a phrase popular at the time, noticeably "stacked."

Producer Jerry Wald's widow, Connie, described Mrs. Stewart at the time of their marriage: "Gloria is a show-stopper, big eyes, glorious figure, fabulous features. It's a fabulous marriage." Gloria was glorious, his and her friends both agreed.

The wedding itself, however, like the engagement compact, was very understated. Only 18 guests attended the August 9, 1949, ceremony. The guest list showed that Jimmy tended to hold on to friends for years. They included his first mentor in Hollywood, Spencer Tracy, who first worked with him in 1935; Billy Grady, also circa 1935; the David Nivens; the George Murphys; Ann Sothern; Mrs. Van Johnson; Dorothy McGuire; columnist John Swope; Harry Crocker from the bank of the same name; restaurateur Mike Romanoff; and producer Joe DeBona. The absence of Hollywood royalty at the wedding suggests gossip columnist Swope may have been only slightly exaggerating when he said Jimmy didn't trust anybody in Hollywood.

Jimmy's father as usual stole the show by passing around the collection plate at half-time. He strong-armed the small party of 18 into coughing up $400 to buy badly needed new pews for the church, he later boasted to his new daughter-in-law. Gloria's reaction to this pious extortion was not recorded.

The bride walked down the aisle of the Brentwood Presbyterian Church on the arm of her brother-in-law, New York manufacturer Greg Drady. The matron of honor was her sister, Ruth Drady. Jimmy's best man was his original benfactor at MGM, Billy Grady. (Both Gloria's parents were too ill to attend. Both Jimmy's parents showed.) When the vows were exchanged, a newspaper reporter noted that Jimmy's "I do" was "barely audible." He later explained, "I got a frog in my throat."

Maybe he was gagging on the thought of abandoning 41 years of unwedded bliss and becoming the instant father of two preschoolers. Gloria, in contrast, said, " 'I do' loudly." Their wedding bands were plain gold and inscribed simply "Gloria and Jimmy" plus the date. The bride wore what a reporter described as a "cocktail length" gray satin dress with gray satin shoes, a white flowered hat, white orchid, and carried a white prayer book. Jimmy, the newspaper noted, "arrived in a blue suit and a somewhat bewildered look." Interestingly, he didn't wear a tuxedo for this exceedingly non-glam affair, which lasted only 20 minutes and was followed by a small reception at the Beverly Hills home of publicist Jack Bolton and his wife.

In a gesture worthy of the self-sacrificing George Bailey, Jimmy actually postponed their Hawaiian honeymoon for three days because he had promised to be parade marshal of the National Soap Box Derby. Not exactly an A-list event. But a promise was a promise, and he had apparently agreed to host the derby before he had promised to love, honor, and cherish Gloria.

The *L.A. Mirror*, tongue in typewriter, reported on Aug. 8, "An enduring U.S. institution collapses at 5 P.M. tomorrow before the altar of the Brentwood Presbyterian Church, 730 S. Bundy Dr." The address conveniently alerted his fans to the wedding's whereabouts, but in a rare show of restraint, perhaps respect, they massed quietly outside the church without causing the usual celebrity circus. Maybe the bobby-soxers were so sedate because they were in mourning. The *L.A. Mirror* said, "Those on the outside acted as if the hero of *Mr. Smith Goes to Washington* had announced his plans to leave for Moscow."

A sad historical footnote to the best year of Jimmy Stewart's life: while Jimmy's long life of marital bliss was just beginning, his best friend's second marriage had crashed and burned. Later that year, Henry Fonda announced he was divorcing his second wife, the woman who had resented her husband's close friendship and kite-flying with Jimmy. After the announcement, Mrs. Fonda, mother of Jane, suffered a nervous breakdown and was committed to a mental institution, where she committed suicide a year later.

On a happier note, the ditzy Louella Parsons for once got it right when she wrote, ''Yes, I think Mr. and Mrs. James Stewart are going to be happy. Jimmy always said that when he married it would be for keeps, and I have known Gloria since she was a little girl, and I can't help but say I think they are so right for each other.''

Jimmy and Gloria would be ''right for each other'' for the next 44 years.

Chapter 27

The Comeback Kid Also Hallucinates

Marriage must have agreed with Stewart, or maybe it was just a coincidence that the end of his bachelor days coincided with the resurrection of his career. And he got even richer, astronomically richer, to boot.

Henry Fonda got it all wrong when he predicted right after the war, "When Jim stops pretending to be so young, he'll become an artist." During the 1950s, Jimmy did indeed meta-morphose from movie star to one of the great actors of his generation, but it had nothing to do with faking youthfulness, which Jimmy never did. But his meteoric rise may have had something to do with the simple fact that practice (by then 15 years of it) had finally made perfect. Whatever the reason, Jimmy, like a fine wine, just got better with age.

The film that banished Jimmy's box office blues was a West-ern, *Winchester '73*, part of a two-picture deal his agent, Lew Wasserman, negotiated with Universal-International. The other was the film adaptation of his Broadway triumph, *Harvey*, a classic today, ignored by movie-goers in 1950. Academy voters, however, begged to differ, and the shaggy rabbit story won Jimmy his fourth Oscar nomination. Ironically, it was *Harvey,* an ultimate moneypit, that made *Winchester '73*, a gold mine, possible. Jimmy described the Hollywood adaptation of his Broadway role and its movie sibling: "When they sold [*Harvey*] to the movies I had sort of an inside track on that. There'd also been a Western kicking around town for several years. Nobody'd make it. Nobody liked it. So they tacked it onto the deal with *Harvey*, which seemed like a sure thing after its Pulitzer Prize-winning run on Broadway."

For Jimmy, the Western was also a tactical decision, a preemptive strike against involuntary early retirement from a profession he loved. He didn't mention art or a desire to stretch his acting muscles when he explained why he picked *Winchester '73*. "It was survival. When I came back from the War, I made a couple of pictures which were no great shakes at all at the box office." For once, he wasn't being modest. "It became very obvious that the kind of comedies I'd done before weren't what people wanted anymore. I didn't want to go out to pasture that early in life," the hardest working man in show business explained. He also joked that he liked the easy "commute" on Westerns, since locations were usually only an hour's drive from Los Angeles to the desert.

Winchester '73 was a huge gamble that paid off. It was such a big risk because the Western genre was a big stretch for Jimmy.

Although *Destry Rides Again* was, strictly speaking, his first Western and proved he could succeed in that format, it was such a send-up of the genre that there was no guarantee he would enjoy similar success in a classic Western that didn't feature a catfight or an unarmed, pacifist gunslinger. In *Destry* Jimmy didn't even believe in carrying a gun, a big contrast to the fetishistic significance he and everyone else in *Winchester '73* bestow on the title shotgun. Also Jimmy hadn't straddled a horse on camera for more than a decade. Would movie audiences accept their urban hero as a tumbleweed tyro?

Winchester '73 was virgin territory, terra incognita, for Jimmy, and he would have to prove he could do serious sagebrush. When the camera in the first scene pans to Jimmy astride a horse, he looks as though he's in period drag, perhaps an investment banker by day, a Rhinestone cowboy who two-steps at an urban country-western bar at night. At 42, he was still too boyishly preppy despite what film scholar Dennis Hall calls his ''rugged maturity'' at the time. In the opening scene Jimmy looked about as rugged as Mickey Rooney.

The Western era also didn't suit Jimmy, who had an indelibly 20th century face. Today, you can easily believe someone like Robert Duvall might have lived in the 19th century. Sylvester Stallone, on the other hand, would be hilarious as a cowpoke even if he lost his Philly accent. If he wore a gunbelt, you'd expect to see an Uzi in the holster.

Yet Jimmy was such a good actor that by the end of the film, having survived a small massacre of Indians, a rifle-whipping by his brother, and a shoot-out with the same, he not only looks as though he's aged, he looks genuinely grizzled. In the short space of only 82 minutes, Jimmy had stretched into his role. Not only had he morphed into his cowboy persona, his face looked as though it belonged in the 19th century. Eventually he would come to own the genre almost as proprietarily as John Wayne already did.

The Western was a huge commercial hit because of its ingenious plot and superb direction by Anthony Mann, who would collaborate on four more Westerns with Jimmy. Stewart plays a gunslinger with near supernatural marksmanship and a Lieutenant Gerard-like obsession to get his man. Unlike Lieutenant Gerard, however, Jimmy literally wants to kill the guy. It's the movie's brilliant conceit—and probably why it cleaned up at the box office—not to let the audience in on the reason for Jimmy's murderous monomania until the last five minutes of the film. It's hard to think of another movie that conceals a major plot point—as opposed to a surprise ending—from its audience for so long.

The title of the 1950 film refers to a perfectly made Winchester rifle, model year 1873, that is coveted by everyone in the film with a fanaticism that's near fetishistic. It may be the first film where brand name recognition is a major plot point.

Rock Hudson fans will find the film noteworthy because it marked their idol's third screen appearance, however inauspicious. Hudson at 6'4", bare-chested and buffed, looks risible as the tallest Indian ever to roam the Old West. His monosyllabic utterances recall Mark Twain's comment on James Fenimore Cooper's depiction of Native Americans: ''A cigar store Indian is more lifelike.'' The screenwriter couldn't resist further handicapping the character with the double entendre name of Young Bull.

Winchester '73 was Jimmy's comeback film, but it has far greater historical significance than that. The hit marked the beginning of the end of the studio system. And the beginning of star salary inflation that would end with Arnold Schwarzenegger making $25 million for six weeks work on the fourth installment of *Batman.* (Plus a large cut of all the *Batman* toys.) It all had to do with a phenomenon called profit participation. And Jimmy Stewart initiated it.

Winchester '73 was a gamble for two reasons: Jimmy astride a horse was an iffy proposition, but an even bigger gamble was the way in which he agreed to be remunerated for eating dust over the three-month shoot.

The idea was actually hatched by his super-savvy super-agent, Lew Wasserman, whose 10 percent of Jimmy's earnings among others made Wasserman's talent agency rich enough eight years later to buy the studio, Universal-International, where the agent had negotiated the deal for the Western. But it was Jimmy who took the huge financial risk. To keep the budget down at the cash-strapped studio, Jimmy agreed to work for practically nothing. Instead, he would take a fifty percent cut of the profits—if there were any. This is why the agreement was a big gamble, and the odds weren't in his favor, considering the box-office performance of all but one of his late 1940s films. If the film flopped, Jimmy wouldn't get a dime beyond union scale, a fraction of his usual salary. If it hit, he would earn considerably more than his usual take.

Winchester '73 was one of the top 10 moneymakers of 1950, and Jimmy's gamble ended up looking in hindsight like a sucker bet. And 1950 also marked the first time in his career he made the list of the top 10 box-office stars of the year. Near the end of the decade he would top the list!

UPI columnist Aline Mosby approvingly noted Jimmy's

business acumen. Although monstrously rich by now, he was mercifully not *nouveau riche*. Literally. Both sides of his family were old money. He would simply add to the family's generation-spanning wealth, big time. Mosby wrote, "While many film stars gain recognition by salary strikes and a show of wealth, Jimmy Stewart has quietly become one of Hollywood's *few* millionaires with his own 'share-the-profit plan.' " Like the war, his wealth was something Jimmy didn't feel comfortable talking about, even with family members. His daughter Kelly told me, "Dad has never discussed money."

His former agent, Leland Hayward, testified to how unpretentious Jimmy was about his wealth. He cared so little about money he had an annoying habit of never having any of the stuff on him. During a trip to New York, Hayward remembered serving as Jimmy's unwilling ATM machine. Hayward paid for all the taxis, restaurant tabs, the hat-check girls. When Jimmy had to make a phone call he even borrowed the change from Hayward. Exasperated, Hayward finally exploded after Jimmy asked for money to buy a newspaper. "Don't you ever carry money?"

Hayward immediately regretted his show of pique. Jimmy looked stricken after the scolding. "I could see that I really upset him. He looked real unhappy and reached into his pocket. Out came a dried up, shriveled banana. I burst out laughing."

Unlike a lot of rich people who got rich by hoarding their money, Jimmy was not cheap, merely absent-minded. Hayward recalled, "The next day, he sent me a gift—a hand-tooled leather wallet that obviously had cost him 20 times the money I'd spent on him.

"How could anyone possibly be angry with such a guy?"

Just how little money mattered to Jimmy is indicated by an incident that occured decades later. In Jimmy's case, it is possible to literally put a price on what a promise was worth to him—four million dollars. In 1987, PBS contacted Stewart personally and asked him to collaborate on a book and TV special about his life. As everyone who follows the right-wing Congressional attacks on public funding of the arts knows,

PBS is dirt poor and didn't offer Jimmy much money for his participation. Jimmy said yes immediately.

When his manager, Herman Citron, heard about the un-deal, he was apoplectic. The agent was in the middle of negotiating a similar book and network special for a whopping $4 million. Jimmy lamely explained that he didn't realize the PBS special was about him. He thought it was about the Golden Years of Hollywood, and he would merely be one of many talking heads on the documentary. "I . . . I . . . I . . . didn't realize they were talking about my story when they spoke to me," he said, apologizing for his gaffe. Citron volunteered to get Jimmy out of his deal with PBS, which after all was based on a handshake rather than a contract.

Suddenly, Jimmy stopped being apologetic and said firmly, "No, you won't. As long as they think I agreed to that—and I have to admit I wasn't listening too closely (he was practically stone deaf by this time), well, you'd better forget the commercial end of it. I said I'd do it, and I will." True to his word, Jimmy was the centerpiece of the March 1987 PBS documentary, "James Stewart: A Wonderful Life."

If virtue is its own reward, Jimmy got more than he bargained for. Although the multimillionaire was out $4 million, which he didn't need anyway, the documentary won an Emmy nomination for Outstanding Informational Special. Considering his oil wells and barony on the pricey West Side of L.A., the Emmy probably meant more to him than the $4 million.

We don't know exactly why Jimmy's agent in the 1950s, Lew Wasserman, chose the actor out of all his star-studded stable to bestow this mitzvah of profit participation on, but it's easy to guess. The hard-boiled mover and shaker adored his client. A friend of Wasserman's said, "Judging by the service he gives Stewart, you'd think Jimmy was his only client." Wasserman proved that assessment wasn't hype when he said, "Sometimes I wish he *were* [my only client]. "He's strictly a two-way-street guy. He gives as well as takes. When he asks, 'Have you got time to see me?,' it's not an act."

(For the record, Wasserman was also fond of Fonda, because he soon negotiated a similar deal for Jimmy's best friend.)

Wasserman's innovative negotiating didn't impress everyone, and it helped fully drag from the closet an anti-Semitism that was always poking its head out. Three years before Jimmy's landmark deal, *Gentleman's Agreement* won the Best Picture Oscar for exposing what everybody already knew. Anti-Semitism was alive and sick in America in 1947. Four years later, the WASPish and atypically waspish *Saturday Evening Post* would show that things hadn't changed all that much. In a 1951 article on Jimmy by Pete Martin, the lead paragraph unabashedly compared his Jewish agent to the villain of Shakespeare's anti-Semitic masterpiece, *The Merchant of Venice*. While the article stopped short of actually calling Wasserman Mr. Shylock, it compared the Venetian businessman's famous bargain to Wasserman's modus operandi. "Louis *[sic]* Wasserman . . . is a driver of hard bargains. The pounds of flesh plus blood that he has exacted for his clients have left many a movie director and producer whimpering into their hand-painted neckties . . ." (For those who don't know the plot of *The Merchant of Venice*, the Jewish title character lends money to the Christian hero with the proviso that if he doesn't repay the debt, the creditor is to be repaid literally with a pound of his debtor's flesh.)

Jimmy preferred to put a Protestant Ethic spin on profit participation instead of making classical, anti-Semitic allusions to Elizabethan plays. "I find myself working harder, trying to do a better job. When a guy has a share in what he's doing, it makes all the difference in the world." Jimmy as usual was downplaying his conscientiousness. When he was a wage slave at MGM before the war, he worked just as hard and promoted as enthusiastically every movie he made for the studio.

And it wasn't merely money that made him such a big booster of profit participation. A genuine lover of the medium that had made him rich and beloved, he honestly believed that the new system, because it rewarded its star for a job well done, would result in "a better picture nine times out of ten. And the only reason I didn't say all the time is that I like to be conservative," he told the *L.A. Daily News*.

He reiterated his boosterism with a caveat to UPI when he

said, "If a picture is good, we both make money, if it isn't, we lose. It's a gamble." So why didn't a classic like *Harvey* make money? Jimmy was ready with an answer. The rights to the Pulitzer Prize-winner cost $1 million and ate up all the profits, the studio's and Jimmy's. "Basically, I acted in that one for free. The budget was just too big for that type of picture." He wasn't complaining. He loved Elwood P. Dowd so much he would reprise the role on TV, Broadway and London's West End in the 1970s with even greater critical and financial success than his original 1947 stage appearance.

Wasserman, a full-service agent, also figured out a way to let Jimmy and other clients donate less of their newfound riches to Uncle Sam. He spread out the star's take on an individual movie over several years. Wasserman may have had his eye on the tax man when he explained exactly how rich *Winchester '73* made Jimmy. In its first year of release, the star collected a handsome but not Croesus-like $150,000. Then spread out over the life of the film, Jimmy banked another $350,000. Universal, on the other hand, flat out said Jimmy's take was a whopping $2.5 million, and in its press release the studio didn't sound happy about Jimmy's windfall. Profit participation had created a precedential bandwagon that other stars would climb all over.

Universal, then the schlockmeister of Hollywood, was the only studio willing to accept Wasserman's offer. It hoped some of Jimmy's class would rub off on it. And the financially troubled studio got him almost for free. Little could the studio guess that far from being free, Jimmy would cost it $2.5 million.

Jimmy mentioned that every other studio, including his old home MGM, had turned the deal down flat. And no wonder. Wasserman's terms, which only Universal was desperate enough to accept, stipulated that Jimmy would collect between 37 and 50 percent of the picture's profit "after everything is paid, including publicity and exploitation." Current studio heads must be glad Wasserman is one of them (or was one until he was unceremoniously down-sized) because his terms would be ruinous today when movies like *Batman* gross more than half a billion dollars worldwide.

More than the money, Jimmy simply loved the genre. In fact, after making *Winchester '73*, but before its release proved what a personal gold mine it would be, he had already decided that his next film would also take place in the Old West. "There was a Western scheduled for production out at Twentieth Century Fox called *Broken Arrow*, and I wanted to try it. Everybody thought I was out of my mind. I remember [studio chief] Daryl Zanuck saying, 'Gee, you can't do this, Jimmy. You're a comedian!' " Zanuck's comment showed an atypical conservatism since he had approved *Call Northside 777*, Jimmy's disastrous attempt at *neorealisma*, American-style. Or maybe he simply proved that Louis B. Mayer wasn't the only Yahoo Mogul in town. Hadn't Zanuck seen *It's a Wonderful Life* or *Mr. Smith* or . . . ?

Instead of saying, "Daryl, you moron, don't you know I won two Oscar nominations for drama?" Jimmy politely agreed to disagree with his temporary boss. "I thought maybe he was right, too. But I went ahead and did it."

Broken Arrow didn't do the kind of land rush business its predecessor did, but it represented an even greater risk thematically. Twenty years before Brando boycotted the Oscars and sent a Vegas showgirl in Hiawatha drag to pick up his Academy Award, *Broken Arrow* may have been the first Western that not only declined to use Indians merely for target practice but actually portrayed Native Americans as three-dimensional characters with a justifiable beef against the White Man.

The film also explored the then-taboo subject of miscegenation, which wouldn't be seen on screen again until 1967 when Sidney Poitier came to dinner at Kate and Spence's.

Stewart plays an Army scout who tries to broker a peace treaty between his government and the Apaches, led by Cochise (Jeff Chandler), who is portrayed as humane and charismatic instead of the usual Red Man with a fetish for Caucasian males' hairpieces. During negotiations, which tragically fail, Stewart falls in love with *and marries* an Indian woman (Debra Paget).

Jimmy's personal life flourished as happily as his professional efforts. And when it came to production, he was equally prolific off screen.

Chapter 28
And Babies Make Four

In 1949, shortly before he got married, Jimmy showed that this move was no different from any other important step in his life. It was made after much thought and deliberation. "I'm not going into this thing lightly. After all, I'm getting a wife—and two sons."

Marriage seems to have transformed him thoroughly. After returning from an atypically self-indulgent three-month honeymoon in Hawaii, Jimmy temporarily moved into Gloria's Coldwater Canyon home in Beverly Hills. They soon found a relatively modest Tudor-style home with a mere eight rooms in another section of town. Still the armchair architect, Jimmy described the exterior of the then 32-year-old pile as "Mediterranean Ugly." A maid at the time said neither Gloria nor Jimmy ever treated her like a servant. "He treats everyone very nice in the house," she said. The household staff was miniscule by Hollywood-rich standards. The Stewarts never had more than two servants even though the family would soon balloon to six.

Friends claimed Jimmy became talkative, extroverted, almost gabby after slipping on the wedding ring. "He spouts whole paragraphs at a time now. Time was when Jimmy was as monosyllabic as a talking dog," one friend said. His father, famous for withholding approval, gave Gloria unconditional credit for transforming his boy. "A yes girl would never have got this fellow Stewart," referring as he typically did to his son by his last name. "He needed a girl who could make him heel. Also he's too quiet. Gloria has brought him out a lot," he confided to Jimmy's good friend and best man, Billy Grady.

A closet Warren Beatty during his bachelor days, Jimmy became Mr. Monogamy. During their 44-year marriage, not even a hint of infidelity ever attached itself to Jimmy. Everyman became Everyhusband. Jimmy attacked marriage with the same industry he applied to all the other "tasks" in his life, whether it was figuring out descriptive geometry at Princeton or memorizing a bomber flight plan. Nightclubs became forbidden territory for the former boulevardier. As he told Hedda Hopper in 1951, "Nightclubs are like the measles. I've had them both, and once is enough." Three years later his satisfaction with married life had grown even stronger. He told the *L.A. Examiner*, "I used to enjoy being a bachelor. I never stayed home. I found excuses to go places, do things. Home was strictly for eating and sleeping. But now that I'm married I'd rather be home than any place in the world. Because I've got a swell wife, Gloria . . ."

Gloria felt supremely secure about her husband's fidelity. She said, "My husband is much too normal to be an actor. He shuns nightclubs and likes nothing better than to spend an evening at home."

In rare censorious mode, Jimmy made it clear that he didn't approve of husbands who strayed. In a comment filled with euphemisms that nevertheless revealed exactly what he really meant, Jimmy said, "Know Frank [Sinatra] a little. Like him. But I can't say his lifestyle is my lifestyle. I have no real feeling about it." Obviously he did.

A seemingly confirmed bachelor, once Jimmy made up his mind, he was willing to upend his cozy single life and become a husband and instant dad. Little did he know that in less than two years, his family would instantly double.

Jimmy and Gloria got a wonderful early Christmas present

on December 19, 1950, when her obstetrician told them she was not only pregnant, but there would be two little bundles of joy. Gloria called Louella Parsons and said, "It's the best Christmas present either of us could have."

Jimmy didn't object to having his family double overnight, or in nine months. "Getting a big family right away was fine with me. When I go in for anything, I like to get it over with."

In the days before amniocentesis and ultrasound, the sex of the twins was anybody's guess. Jimmy didn't care what sex they were, but he did hope they would be identical. (They weren't. Later Gloria tried to explain to a friend the difference between identical and fraternal twins. The dim acquaintance just couldn't get it, and Gloria was beginning to get a bit frustrated when Jimmy defused the situation by punning, "Golly, I always thought [the twins] were *nocturnal*." As a magazine noted at the time, "Gloria loved him most of all for his humor.") Gloria's wish list included one of each, a boy and a girl. As in all family matters, Jimmy's dad had to put his two cents in. He was so sure of the embryos' sex, he went around telling friends, "When the two boys are born . . ."

With typical thoughtfulness and foresight, Jimmy had it written into his next contract that he could leave the set when his wife gave birth. This might have led to a comic situation. The film was *The Greatest Show on Earth*, and Jimmy played a clown who spends the entire movie hiding his criminal identity in full clown makeup and costume. You can imagine Jimmy, looking like a literal Bozo, rushing to the maternity ward when he got the word.

But there would be nothing comical about Gloria's delivery, since it almost killed her.

Twin girls were born prematurely and by Caesarean section on May 7, 1951. Unnamed when their births were reported in the press, one infant weighed 6 pounds, 6 ounces; the other, 5 pounds, 12 ounces. The obstetrician, Dr. Leon Krohn, would soon be proved disastrously wrong when he told the *L.A. Times*, "Mom and twins doing well." Jimmy was his usual tight-lipped self despite his delight. All he could bring himself to say was, "They're beautiful!"

A few days after the birth, Gloria did not return home from the hospital as expected. Instead, she stayed at Cedars of Lebanon because of what the press at first called a "minor complication." The complication was complicated enough to require surgery. The escape clause in Jimmy's contract came in handy. He shut down production on Cecil B. DeMille's all-star circus movie so he could hold Gloria's hand during what he was assured by the doctors was minor surgery for an "intestinal complication."

A week after giving birth, the *L.A. Times* headlined a story, "Jimmy Stewart's Wife Gravely Ill After Operation." The report listed her in "critical condition" after undergoing "major surgery, her third operation in a week." She spent two hours on the operating table. Louella Parsons reported after the second surgery, "Gloria is a very sick girl." During the ordeal, Jimmy never left his wife once, Parsons noted approvingly.

Gloria was actually near death. The situation's seriousness was underscored by the fact that her mother and sister *flew* to Los Angeles from New York. In those days, flying cross-country was a primitive ordeal, and most people chose to take a luxury, non-stop express train, the Super Chief, which could cross the continent in a mere three days. Gloria's mom and sister apparently felt they didn't have three days.

Jimmy had planned to return to location shooting in Washington, D.C., on Saturday night, the night his wife had her third operation. He cancelled the trip.

Three weeks later Gloria was still not only hospital-bound, but the press was again describing her as "dangerously ill." The *L.A. Times* said she was listed in "critical condition." It reported that Jimmy tried to cheer himself up by cooing over the twin girls, who despite their premature birth, were completely healthy.

While Jimmy was camped out at Cedars, a nurse on his floor broke her foot. Jimmy set his anxiety aside and took the time to send flowers to the injured woman.

The notoriously autocratic director, De Mille, who liked to show up on the set in an equestrian outfit that included a riding crop, wanted to know when Jimmy would show up for shooting since the shutdown was costing the production millions. Jimmy coldly replied, per Parsons' report, that "he will not leave Gloria until her doctors can assure him definitely that she is entirely out of danger."

Despite her serious condition, Gloria managed to come up with names for the twins, Kelly and Judy. The naming of the girls merited a separate story in the *Times.* By May 19, doctors said she was "definitely out of danger and improving," which gave Jimmy the assurance he required to return to D.C. to get into his clown costume and calm down the by now hysterical director of the Bible's biggest hits.

The press of the day never fully explained what Gloria's problem was except to call it an "intestinal complication." Whatever it was, it required her to remain in the hospital until July 12, almost three months after giving birth. And she was released "as a convalescent," Louella reported. The designation was not surprising since only a week earlier she had had her fourth and mercifully final surgery, which Parsons said was "expected to clear up all complications." Louella was being cautious in her prognosis. Gloria never had another sick day in her life. She also never got pregnant again.

Jimmy's superstar status extended to his wife, whose postnatal complications made the front pages of newspapers around the world. The hospital was so inundated with flowers, for the sake of safety it finally had to refuse delivery of any more floral get-wells. During the 10 days in which she was reported near death, the hospital received the largest volume of mail ever sent a patient. Both the post offices in Hollywood and Beverly Hills were swamped with letters addressed to Mrs. James Stewart. The concern, like the newspaper attention, was worldwide. Holy water and religious medals arrived from Europe via air mail.

In six months the trauma of four surgeries was forgotten amid the joy of the twins' christening on Dec. 23. It was reported that the 7 month-old duo "screamed throughout the ceremony at Community Presbyterian Church in Beverly Hills." Jimmy's parents came to town just for the baptism. In Alexander's eyes, his granddaughters could do no wrong. "The girls yelled through the whole thing, which is supposed to be good, I guess,'' he said. Like royalty, the twins had more than one pair of godparents. They were Mrs. Ray Milland; Mrs. Peggy Bolton (wife of Jimmy's future agent John); Guy Gadbois, Jimmy's business manager; and the man who had single-handedly turned his new goddaughters into instant heiresses, Lew Wasserman.

Fatherhood was as close a fit as any of Jimmy's autobiographical movie roles. He *was* George Bailey—with more money.

A magazine at the time—more with amazement than approval in those unliberated days—mentioned that when the nurse had the day off, Jimmy relieved his convalescing wife of diaper duty by doing the dirty deed himself.

Besides occasionally playing Mr. Mom, Jimmy was a hands-on dad. In a first person account in the *L.A. Examiner* in 1954, he mentioned he and his two stepsons spent six months building a fort in the back yard. Jimmy was more than an armchair architect. "Equipped with timbers and gun-holes, it became a great meeting place for the entire neighborhood.'' Jimmy also took the boys "hunting,'' but like Tom Destry and the 10-year-old Jimmy who couldn't bring himself to shoot a killer dog, their hunting expeditions were bloodless affairs. "The boys and I often go hunting in the Brentwood hills.'' He immediately added, "Ronnie and Michael hunt with cap guns.''

Jimmy was such a wonderful dad he made Robert Young seem like a male Joan Crawford. Money had so little value to him (maybe because he had so much of it), he didn't give any of his children an allowance. The implication, of course, was they got whatever they wanted. "We don't have the children on allowances. They are taught the value of money and are not treated like salesmen on an expense account.'' His children somehow managed to learn the value of money, or at least the value of hard work. Unlike so many other Hollywood brats who sponge off their celebrity mom or dad for life, Jimmy's now middle-aged kids are all overachievers. Stepson Michael, who has a master's degree in economics from Claremont College, is an investment banker in San Francisco. Daughter Kelly earned a doctorate from Cambridge in zoology, and studied the endangered mountain gorillas in Africa with naturalist Dian Fossey. Today, Dr. Kelly Stewart Harcourt is an author and college professor, and was kind enough to take time to answer 58 questions I faxed her. Judy is happy to be a homemaker for her two children and husband, a venture capitalist. Stepson Ronald's tragic story will be told later.

As the allowance issue suggests, Jimmy was a pushover although he gamely claimed in the article that he was a gentle disciplinarian. "Our discipline system is just as straightforward. We've found a good smack in the right place is the most effective punishment ... Timing on punishment is of great importance. It should occur immediately at the time of the crime ... the children know our word is law. I hope they have respect for our decisions. If they don't, they accept them without question."

Both Gloria and daughter Kelly felt Jimmy was imagining things. Kelly told me, "There was no spanking in our family. It was far worse to have Dad look at us and say, 'Your mother and I are *very* disappointed in you.' "

Gloria seems not to have picked up the slack and was as easygoing as Jimmy about child-rearing. She suggested just how little Jimmy cracked the whip when recounting an incident at an ultra-exclusive hotel restaurant in Nairobi during a safari to Kenya. "One of the twins dropped something under the table and couldn't find it. Suddenly all three of us [Gloria and the twins] were under the table looking for it. Then we heard Jimmy speaking in a voice we'd never heard before. 'All right all of you!' he barked. 'Come right up here this instant! I never ever want to see such behavior in a public place again.' "

All three miscreants found Jimmy's sudden transformation into *Daddy Dearest* hilarious rather than Crawfordesque. Gloria recalled, "We almost died trying not to giggle. I felt about 12. The whole thing surprised us so much because really he had never done a thing like that before.

"The funny thing is he *thinks* he was strict. I'm sure he'll tell you that. Because his father really *was* strict, and he always wanted to be just like his father. Actually, he was anything but," she told *Parade* magazine in 1984.

Just how delusional Jimmy was about his authoritarianism is suggested by a visit a reporter from *Parade* magazine made to the house in 1984. All Jimmy's children had left home and run away to graduate school years ago, and Jimmy lovingly referred to his two Golden Retrievers, Beau and Simba, as "the children." More like Children of the Damned, as the reporter, Cleveland Amory, eventually realized. A famous animal activist, Amory noticed that during the interview the dogs locked outside kept hurling themselves at the glass doors leading out of the living room to the backyard. He begged his accommodating host, "Why don't you let them in for just a while?" Jimmy explained that the pair had just graduated from obedience school, and it was part of their post-graduate training not to be rewarded for bad behavior like attacking plate glass. But Jimmy as usual treated this tribune of his fans like royalty and immediately acceded to his guest's request—and was immediately proved correct. One dog jumped on Amory, knocking over both him and the couch he was sitting on, while licking and pawing its victim. The other dog did exactly the the same thing to Jimmy. Amory was transformed from an animal activist who wrote best-sellers about his love affair with his pet cats into a slaughterhouse enthusiast. The curmudgeonly author asked Jimmy angrily, "What exactly did these dogs learn in so-called obedience school?" Amory described them in the article as "the worst behaved dogs in the world." Jimmy wasn't nearly as ticked off as the professional animal lover. In fact, he acted like a proud father. "I really don't know what they learned, but I'll tell you one thing. They had great word-of-mouth at the school. The guy who runs it told me that *everybody* loved 'em. Thought they were the nicest dogs in the world." Like father like sons.

Jimmy's child-rearing habits, whatever his professed beliefs, were the antithesis of his father's, which held that withholding approval would result in excellence. Jimmy on the other hand acted like a one-member fan club for all his children. Daughter Kelly recalled in 1996, "Mom and Dad were both very encouraging when any of us did well in school."

You get the feeling he would have been proud of his kids

if they had all been D students. During a visit from Hedda Hopper in 1951, he asked Gloria to get the girls so the columnist could write about them in her widely read column. Before Gloria materialized with the 7-month-old babies, Jimmy just couldn't wait and whipped out baby pictures, forcing her, in Hopper's words, to "ooh and aah interminably over them." And perhaps to make sure the kids got "good press," he then attempted to charm the powerful gossip by whipping out another photograph, of Jimmy and Hopper starring in the Broadway play, *Divided by Three*.

When Hopper finally got to meet their royal highnesses, she proved a bit prophetic in describing their divergent futures. "Kelly is the serious one, she hardly ever smiles. Judy is the comic; always laughing and making faces. Judy and Kelly do not look alike. In fact, they don't even look like sisters, let alone twins." The photos accompanying the story bore out Hopper's analysis. In fact, it seemed that each twin had inherited one parent's looks and sensibilities. The boisterous Judy, noticeably the prettier of the two, looked and acted like her beautiful, extroverted mom. (She would be content, like her mother, to be a happy homemaker.) Kelly, shy and reticent like dad, also inherited his braininess. (Kelly would matriculate at Stanford and go on to do postgraduate work at Cambridge, then make her way in the world as a scholarly expert on gorillas.)

Although her husband was the professional, Gloria was in charge of entertainment. Jimmy marveled, "Gloria mixes up Little Red Riding Hood, Bo Peep, Hansel and Gretel, Little Miss Muffet and who knows what else, and comes up with the darndest stories I ever heard," Bruno Bettelheim and *The Powers of Enchantment* be damned.

When Jimmy entertained the girls, it seemed as though he was more intent on instilling the work ethic at the earliest possible age. A photo in *Life* magazine when the girls were 4 shows him, like Gloria, reading to the twins, who are crawling all over him. Except he's reading them a screenplay!

Ironically, he would later say—with relief—that none of the four children showed the least interest in following their father into his profession. That may have taken a little of the sting out of any residual guilt he still felt about not following his father into retail.

His stepsons were so unimpressed by Jimmy's star status, they loved to deflate his non-existent ego by telling him point blank that they preferred Randolph Scott Westerns. "Both boys have Davey Crocket uniforms," he told Louella Parsons, who seemed along with her rival Hedda Hopper to have practically set up a branch office in the Stewarts' home. "And I get ambushed by wild frontiersman every day after school. The boys are also movie fans, but they're kind of fickle. For a long time, their favorite cowboy was Randolph Scott. It took me quite a while to break them away."

Although more than a few articles said Jimmy treated his stepsons "as though they were his own and they called him Pop," he was always careful to introduce them as Michael and Ronnie *McLean*.

One wonders why such a devoted stepfather never bothered to adopt the boys. My hypothesis was that their wealthy father, Ned, a Hearst executive, simply refused to let their stepfather rob them of the prestigious family name. Kelly Stewart Harcourt punctured my theory about her half-brothers. Jimmy never even asked to adopt them. "I think Dad felt it was not his place to take my brothers' name away from then and give them another. McLean was their heritage. It had nothing to do with the social prominence of their father."

Hedda, like Louella, camping out at the Stewarts', was bowled over by the exquisite manners of Jimmy's stepsons when she met them in 1950 and they were grade-schoolers. "His sons bowed and shook hands like gentlemen of the old school before going in to dinner." Hedda quoted Jimmy after they left: "Boy, they came off letter perfect. We've been *rehearsing* them all day." You almost suspect Jimmy may not have been exaggerating all that much. The feeding and caring of the press was always one of his most important functions, ancillary to his chief obligation, treating the audience (Hedda and Louella's readers, after all) like partners.

An investigative reporter at heart, Hedda did report that after dinner the boys revealed their true selves by jumping into

Gloria's lap and "demanding" she read them *'Twas the Night Before Christmas*.

Five years later, Louella would report that the twin girls were being brought up just like the boys—to be miniature adults, only even more polite. The twins had a French governess, and the columnist wrote, "They curtsied to everyone."

Proof of just how tight the Stewarts were with their children is indicated by their choice of schooling for the kids. Jimmy spent his high school years away from home in prep school. The children of the rich and especially the superrich are often sent away to boarding school. The McLean-Stewart children were fairly close in age, and the Stewart household must have been a noisy nightmare that would have had W.C. Fields firing up the broiler because he too liked children—well-done. Jimmy didn't follow his father's example. None of the four kids left home until they went away to college.

Gloria sidelined as a Sunday school teacher. Jimmy, who in his bachelor days didn't even know where the local Presbyterian Church was until his father came to visit and dragged him there, suddenly got religion after becoming a father. "The whole family enjoys church, mainly because we all go together," he told the *L.A. Examiner* in 1954. His stepsons sang in the choir, while the twins attended Sunday school, taught by their mother. Kelly remembers that her mother applied her trademark sense of humor to the serious subject of theology: "Mom was a lot of fun as a Sunday school teacher, very easy-going and sympathetic."

The workaholic actor ended up loving his family infinitely more than his work. As he said at the end of the *Examiner* article, "It's wonderful being a father. It's great to hear: 'How's the family?' instead of 'How's your picture?' "

A bizarre and scary incident intruded on this picture-perfect family tableau in the summer of 1952 when the twins were barely a year old. A Los Angeles truck driver and one of the stupidest men on the planet sent Jimmy an extortion note, demanding $1,000 "on threat of injury to the actor and his family," per an FBI report of the time. The clueless kidnapper wannabe actually sent an extortion *postcard* and apparently couldn't find out where Jimmy lived because he mailed it to Jimmy, *care of MGM!*

The FBI arrested Sidney C. Davis, 55, in Carthage, Montana, before he could get anywhere near Beverly Hills and the kids. Jimmy's reaction to this terrifying incident reflected his war-time courage.

He didn't do anything.

No security precautions. No fences or even hedges went up around the house. Jimmy believed in being accessible to his partners. How could he wave to the tour buses while he washed his car if he walled his family in and kept enquiring eyes out?

The 1950s—to paraphrase the title of the film that shut him out of the Oscars for *It's a Wonderful Life*—were the best years of Jimmy Stewart's life.

There's a little gem of a movie made in 1982 that starred Peter O'Toole as an Errol Flynn-like matinee idol who guest-stars on a 1954 variety show similar to Sid Caesar's *Your Show of Shows*. It's called *My Favorite Year*. Jimmy never got around to writing his autobiography. He claimed he wrote even more slowly than he talked. He had planned to keep a diary of his war-time experiences, but after two years he found that he had filled up all of two pages in his journal! If Jimmy *had* written his autobiography, the chapter covering the 1950s would have had to have been titled, "My Favorite Decade."

Chapter 29
His Favorite Decade

Except for a nightmarish run-in with a Congressional committee dominated by a liberal senator from Maine (no wonder he was a lifelong Republican), the '50s were fabulous for Jimmy. His professional and personal life both flourished wondrously. Fatherhood, coming relatively late in life, fit him like an old shoe and kept him perpetually ecstatic. He seemed to be starring in an even schmaltzier version of *Father Knows Best*, only father, instead of being a boring insurance salesman, was a movie star, and mother, unlike Jane Wyatt's frumpy housewife, was a glamorous ex-model and heiress. Jimmy's life was like something out of *Ozzie and Harriet*—if Aaron Spelling or Robin Leach had produced it.

Profesionally, Jimmy simply did the best work of his career during the 1950s. It turned out that 1950 was such a busy year professionally, you wonder how he had time to sire two daughters, much less play Mr. Mom once they arrived and his semi-invalid wife was too weak to care for them on nanny's day off.

The workaholism his father had instilled in him by example rather than persuasion seemed more like brain-washing. In 1950 alone, he made four films. That was the kind of slavery the old studio contract system demanded, yet Jimmy, a free agent, proved to be his own worst taskmaster.

In between *Broken Arrow* and *Harvey* he squeezed in a frothless farce that really wasn't worthy of the superstar he had become. *The Jackpot* made use of the quiz show mania of the 1950s—before the scandals—and cast Jimmy as a big winner on a radio version of *The $64,000 Question*. But instead of cash—and a Congressional hearing into rigged gameshows—he wins icky prizes like a steer carcass and three years' worth of frozen food. Worse, he's forced to pay taxes on these awful gifts, which he can't afford. There's a subplot in which his wife (Barbara Hale) thinks he's fooling around with the artist he's hired to paint his portrait. *The Jackpot* tried to recapture the sophisticated Noel Coward-style comedies of the 1930s, Ginger Rogers' "white telephone" movies, except two decades later people wanted Abbott and Costello and Martin and Lewis' prophetic forerunners of Jim Carrey movies. (Jimmy said he was a big fan of Carrey's too.)

A year later he was starring in an airplane disaster movie, *No Highway in the Sky*, whose ham-handedness would anticipate his embarrassing turn in another aeronautic thriller a quarter century later, *Airport '77*.

A year after that flying turkey, Jimmy proved that when it came to stretching he was practically the elastic comic book superhero, Plastic Man. But Jimmy didn't choose his next film because he wanted to stretch his acting tendons. What he really wanted was to recapture one of the happiest memories of his youth, those smelly, foul-mouthed roustabouts from the circus his father had invited home for dinner, especially the clown who left behind the accordion that was to torment so many future friends and audiences.

While shooting *No Highway* in London, he learned that Cecil B. De Mille was making a movie on the Ringling Bros./Barnum & Bailey circus. Jimmy sent De Mille a wire asking for a part in the film. As the box-office dreadnought he was by then, he could have demanded the swaggering role of the ringmaster, which went to De Mille's in-house Moses, Charlton Heston, a relative unknown.

The director must have thought he was hallucinating when he read Jimmy's simple telegram. "Could I play a clown in your picture?" A dazed De Mille wired back a one-word answer: "Yes."

Jimmy recalled, "I'd never even seen the script."

In a long-distance phone call, De Mille later warned Jimmy, "It's a very small part, and the clown never takes off his makeup." All Jimmy wanted to know was, "Is the role essential to the plot?" De Mille assured him it was. In fact, the clown saves the ringmaster's life at the film's climax. Jimmy said, "It's a deal." It must have been the first handless handshake deal—made during an overseas call from London to Los Angeles.

True to De Mille's promise, Jimmy spent the entire film in clown drag as a doctor who was wanted for the mercy killing of his terminally ill wife.

Henry Koster, the director of *No Highway*, was witness to Jimmy's minimal negotiations for his next film and was amazed at his star's literal self-effacement. "Can you imagine one of the movies' great profiles or lover boys wanting to be in a film in which the audience never sees his face?" Koster asked a *Saturday Evening Post* reporter in 1951. "Jimmy considered it a challenge."

As we have seen by his behavior during Gloria's near-death experience, De Mille was no gentleman and no scholar. (See Edward G. Robinson play an Israelite with a Lower East Side accent in the director's *The Ten Commandments*. Also see Billy Crystal's hilarious impression of it on HBO's *Comic Relief*.) De Mille was an autocrat and an ass. In a 1987 interview with the *New York Times*, Jimmy diplomatically agreed with the reporter that "all directors were demanding" but hinted that De Mille was the Attila the Hun of *auteurs*. With jodphurs, riding boots, and horsewhip, De Mille made Hitchcock's apocryphal claim that actors were cattle seem almost Capraesque by comparison. After the De Mille experience, Jimmy had to give up the mantle he seemed to have inherited from Will Rogers. He had finally met a man he never liked.

For the rest of the decade, Jimmy's industriousness had him

making anywhere from two to four films a year, most of them hits, a few misses.

During the first half of the decade, he tended to stick with his favorite genre, the Western. But another genre intrigued him, the bio-pic. *The Stratton Story* had been his only hit in the late 1940s, and Jimmy loved playing real-life characters so much he spent the next five years looking for another famous person to put on the screen. He finally found a subject with special resonance. Besides loving the music of the Big Band era, he felt a special kinship with the subject of his 1954 bio-pic, *The Glenn Miller Story*. Both Jimmy and Miller did wartime service, Miller and his band entertaining the troops. Unlike Jimmy's scratchless military career, Miller died on a routine flight from London to Paris in 1944 en route to entertain the troops. In some ways, the story was an unlikely choice for Jimmy. His reticence about discussing the war with the press or even his family didn't come from modesty alone. Reminiscing also revived horrific memories of the lost boys.

But he chose to play a man who had experienced a pilot's and Jimmy's worst nightmare—a fatal plane crash.

He attacked the role of the big band leader with his usual industry. It takes years to master Miller's instrument of choice, but Jimmy spent a month and a half during pre-production studying under Joe Yuki so he would at least look realistic playing the trombone. (Robert De Niro, who shares Jimmy's obsession with mastering a role, actually learned to play the saxophone for *New York, New York* in 1977.) Jimmy proved as adept at the trombone as he had been with the accordion. "At first I practiced with the trombone lip open, but after three days of it, my instructor got a piece of cork and plugged it up. He said that at best my music was 'cacophonic.' But then Glenn Miller was no actor!" he told Dennis John Hall in a 1972 interview for *Films & Filming* magazine.

Universal ended up dubbing Jimmy's music. His tutor, Yuki, played off camera providing the musical equivalent of cue cards while on camera Jimmy imitated Yuki's hand movements.

Financially, the studio hoped lightning would strike twice with Jimmy's second bio-pic and even imitated the casting of

The Stratton Story, with June Allyson playing the wife in both films.

His real-life wife made her screen debut (and sole film appearance) as an extra in a nightclub scene. An AP wirephoto showed Jimmy on stage, "lip-synching" his trombone playing, while Gloria danced in the audience with a local theater actor in Denver, where part of the film was shot. In the shot, Gloria is more beautiful than her wedding photo and looks like Grace Kelly's slightly older sister.

Gloria repaid her husband for getting a job by saving his soundtrack. When it came to playing Mama Rose, Gloria could be as big a meddler in her husband's career as his father, although her interference wasn't obnoxious like dad's. Audience response cards after a preview begged the filmmakers to add a trademark Glenn Miller tune which had been inexplicably left off the soundtrack. One card, however, in huge red letters, said, "You don't fool around with a hit." It convinced the studio not to mess with the musical score. Joyce Haber wrote in the *L.A. Times*, "I later learned that Gloria . . . had written that card."

Lightning did strike twice. Directed *by Winchester '73*'s Anthony Mann, *The Glenn Miller Story* made even more money than their first collaboration, which had made Jimmy an instant millionaire. In fact, it was the most commercially successful of the eight films they made together.

The critics panned the movie, but the pain of their barbs must have been healed by the fact, that, per Wasserman's original deal with the studio, he would receive up to 50 percent of this huge hit's take. In three years Wasserman would be chairman of the studio, answerable to stockholders. You wonder if he regretted just how lucrative a deal he had made for his former client.

If the critical barbs did hurt, Jimmy's next film would make the pain go away completely as he starred in one of the very best films of his half century-long career.

Chapter 30

Just Don't Call Him Fatso to His Face

The Glenn Miller Story didn't add any luster to Jimmy's career, but it directly led to his reteaming with the director who would make his best films. Frank Capra may have been Jimmy's personal favorite, and Capra's *It's a Wonderful Life* his favorite film, but two of the films he made with Alfred Hitchcock represented the best work of his life. The first was 1954's *Rear Window*, which was being produced by Paramount. The studio had remained a holdout on Jimmy's profit participation demands until the box office of *The Glenn Miller Story* made him irresistible at any price.

Hitchcock must have found Jimmy irresistible too, but not because of his box office clout or even his demonstrable talent. More than one film critic has hypothesized that the sly director couldn't resist subverting the actor's wholesome Everyman image by having him play in their next three films a voyeur, a sexual compulsive, and a Rambo on a rampage against the kidnappers of his son.

Much has also been made of Jimmy's alleged voyeurism in *Rear Window*, but that's too pathological a term for his character's justifiable curiosity, even if it involves using a telephoto lens to spy on one neighbor in particular. If you thought you saw your neighbor murder his wife, wouldn't you become a Peeping Tom? In fact, today they call it Neighborhood Watch. Jimmy plays a daredevil photographer whose life has come to a boring halt after he breaks his leg getting a great shot of a car crash at a race. He's immobilized in a wheelchair with his leg in a cast, and he has nothing better to do with his time than to watch his neighbors play out little life dramas, their rear windows the proscenium arch. Except one vignette isn't little: Jimmy is certain he sees a salesman (played by TV's Perry Mason, Raymond Burr) kill and dispose of his wife's body in little pieces.

It's a testament to his box office clout that in middle age he could be cast in a role obviously written for a younger man. Early in the movie, his nurse (Thelma Ritter) says in urging him to get married, "You're a reasonably healthy *young* man." And it's testament to his continuing sex appeal that at age 46, it was entirely believeable that his girlfriend, a supernally lovely Grace Kelly, 24 and young enough to be his daughter, kept begging the gun-shy bachelor to marry her. It was, however, inexplicable that he rejects one of the most beautiful women in the world! Kelly is so aggressive that today her character would be called predatory or sexual harassing. The unexamined psychological reasons for his rejection of this unearthly beauty are far more intriguing—and potentially kinky—than his alleged voyeurism. His argument that his career as a globe-trotting news photographer makes him poor husband material *is* unbelievable when any other man in his right mind would be jumping Kelly's bones.

In his next film, he would escape the claustrophobic imprisonment of his apartment and wheelchair in exchange for the wide-open spaces of the Old West in his sixth collaboration with Anthony Mann, *The Far Country* (1955). The boiler-plate plot of a cattle drive that endures grueling obstacles was stale stuff, but one film critic wrote, "The combined skills of Anthony Mann and James Stewart transform a routine Western into a minor classic of the genre."

That same year, Stewart reteamed with Mann on a story that was as close to autobiographical as Jimmy ever got on film.

For the third time, June Allyson plays his sympathetic wife in *Strategic Air Command.* He needs a lot of sympathy when the retired Air Force pilot is dragged back into service to fly a bomber that carries nuclear warheads. At 47, Jimmy was laughably too old to play a dashing young pilot. But if he was a good enough actor to make you believe Grace Kelly had the hots for him, he could just as easily make his flying ace a believable character. It was beginning to seem as though the public would accept him in just about any role, no matter how ill-matched. Fortunately for our memories of him, he wasn't one of those egotistical actors who thought he could tackle Shakespeare, a wise move that Mel Gibson and Keanu Reeves have not heeded. You cringe at the thought of that Pennsylvania drawl impersonating Lear or Richard III. Maybe Petrucchio opposite Kate Hepburn, but God forbid not June Allyson as an infamously *un*sympathetic wife.

1955's *The Man from Laramie* was his last pairing with Anthony Mann, and the plot of revenge for the murder of a family member seems like a calculated attempt to rip off the success of *Winchester '73's* murderous tale of the ultimate sibling rivalry. The sagebrush soap opera is noteworthy for one original element. It was the most violent Western made up to that time and anticipated the later bullet-ridden orgies of Sam Peckinpah and Sergio Leone.

In 1956, Jimmy was back with the master in a remake of the 1934 classic, also directed by Hitchcock, *The Man Who Knew Too Much.* Again, Hitch had a jolly time turning gentle Jimmy into a proto-Charles Bronson, a mild-mannered doctor who turns into an ectomorphic Rambo when his son is kidnapped during a vacation in Morocco.

The climactic scene in London's Albert Hall was as suspenseful as anything Hitchcock ever shot, including pecking birds and knife wielding transvestites. It also showed how willingly Jimmy, the supremely egoless actor, was to subordinate his role for the good of the film. As he chases Doris Day up the stairs of the auditorium, the original script had him chatting up a storm. Hitchcock complained, "You're talking so much I'm unable to enjoy the London Symphony," so the director cut all the dialogue and told Jimmy simply to wave his arms. Another conflicting news story suggests even greater modesty on Jimmy's part. Supposedly it was his idea to dump the dialogue so the music wouldn't have to be turned down for the audience to hear his chattering.

Doris Day was totally out of her depth as his crazed wife. Maybe Hitchcock enjoyed subverting Everywoman's image as much as he did trashing Jimmy's, except Day just wasn't up to the demands of playing a neurasthenic. More likely, the casting was forced on the director by Paramount, since Day was both a box office and pop star at the time. Evidence for this is Hitchcock's unlikely decision to stop the action so Day could sing a few songs to beef up the soundtrack, which included her monster hit, "Que Será, Será." Jimmy accompanied his screen wife on the piano, and he was obviously much better with this instrument than the accordion or trombone, since the studio didn't dub his playing.

The critics generally felt Hitchcock hadn't lived up to the quality of his original. Hitchcock was philosophical about the critiques: "Let's say the first version is the work of a talented amateur and the second was made by a professional," he said. As for Jimmy, he was never in awe of Hitchcock, despite his reputation as one of the three or four greatest directors of all time. In a 1978 interview in the *Village Voice*, he demonstrated an irreverent attitude toward a man the rest of the film community venerated, if not worshipped. "I saw Hitch last week. He's 70, working on a new script. Looks the same. Always had a weight problem."

Jimmy could afford to be irreverent, although he rarely was. *The Man Who Knew Too Much* and his seven previous films since profit participation kicked in netted him a whopping $40 million, an unheard of figure in the days when adult tickets cost 90 cents and a movie that grossed a million was considered an unqualified hit.

Jimmy's next film, another bio-pic about a heroic personality, was an unqualified disaster. Maybe because Jimmy himself was much more heroic that the dubious hero he played in *The Spirit of St. Louis*.

Jimmy couldn't resist playing his childhood hero, but even with his superstar clout he had to fight to get the job. While he could make you believe Grace Kelly lusted after a 46-year-old man, at 48 he was just too long in the tooth to play Lindbergh at 25, the age at which he flew solo across the Atlantic.

Jimmy's idolization of Lindbergh, whose flight he charted in the hardware store window when he was a child, overcame his common sense. His head (and ego) must have been in the clouds when he thought he could play a blond Adonis in his 20s. Both the film's producer, Leland Hayward, and director Billy Wilder had their feet on the ground and summarily rejected the hottest actor in Hollywood, despite the fact that Hayward was one of Jimmy's dearest friends and former agent.

The producer and the director found a curiously passive-agressive way to reject Jimmy. The actor recalled in a 1973 interview for *Films & Filming*: "Both Billy and the producer wanted a younger, unknown actor so they came up with the objection that I was too fat. Now I've been called many things in my time, but never too fat. I was determined to play Lindbergh because he's always been a hero to me, so I went on a really tough diet, and it paid off. After two or three weeks they told me I got the part, but at same time they asked me to *please* stop dieting because I was beginning to look terribly ill; my face was really gaunt and I had black rings under my eyes."

Hayward and Wilder finally gave in *after* Jimmy had stopped lobbying for the role. Jimmy recalled, "I didn't think I had a prayer."

Jimmy had stopped lobbying, but his father, in Hollywood to reprise his role as a male Mama Rose Stewart, was just beginning. In the middle of dinner at his son's home, Alexander whispered to his son, "I'm going to get you this job," and he immediately went into action. Hayward was also at this dinner, and Alexander asked the powerful producer whom he planned to cast as Lindbergh. Hayward mentioned the name of a young unknown. Jimmy recounted the rest of the incident to Jhan Robbins: "Dad acted as if someone had shot him out of a cannon. Smacking his fist on the table, he leaped to his feet and began shouting at Hayward, 'Unknown young actor, indeed!

What's the matter with my boy Jimmy? You've been his best friend for years, now you're deserting him! There's only one man who can play Lindbergh, my son.' ''

Hayward was not intimidated, but Jimmy was mortified. "Of course, I was dying of embarrassment throughout all this commotion. I kept muttering, 'Now, Dad . . .' But he went on ranting and I'll give him credit; he made out a good case for me. My dad never was a quiet man—and he certainly was his noisiest that night.''

The powerful producer was not about to be lectured by an 84-year-old blowhard from the boonies, even if the guy was his good friend's dad. For weeks afterward, Hayward and Wilder refused to consider Jimmy until they invited him to lunch several times and rudely stared at his face the whole time.

They finally gave in after realizing the actor who played Lindbergh would spend most of his time in the cockpit and they needed an experienced actor rather than an unknown, someone who could convey most of his emotions through his face, Robbins wrote.

Perhaps by way of apology for his original rejection, Hayward arranged for the actor and his boyhood idol to have dinner at the producer's home. Both were men of few words, and they didn't talk much during dinner, mostly discussing the technical side of aviation. (Lindbergh worked as a consultant for several airlines; Jimmy owned a few.)

It was fortunate that they were both reticent and didn't get into politics. While Jimmy's boyhood infatuation with America's hero is easy to understand, why he still admired the man at this time is puzzling.

Years after Lindbergh's Death in 1974, correspondence filled with ethnic slurs between him and his wife would reveal that he was a crypto-Nazi—barely crypto. In a widely publicized—and condemned—incident, while visiting Germany in 1938 at the request of the U.S. government to spy on Germany's aviation industry and gauge its might, Lindbergh allowed himself to be decorated by the German government. Newsreels of the day show scenes as shocking as the Duke and Duchess of Windsor's earlier visit to the Third Reich. Clips show some

Nazi functionary pinning a medal on Lindbergh's chest! Jimmy was no anti-Semite. His former agent, Lew Wasserman, had made him one of the richest men in Hollywood, and he seemed to be one of the few people in the business who liked and admired the noxious L.B. Mayer, also Jewish.

The two men's differing *Weltanshauung* went beyond their attitude toward Judaism. Lindbergh had been a notorious isolationist and advocate of appeasement toward Hitler before the war. FDR was not amused and publicly told Lindbergh to shut up. Lindbergh, in a snit, resigned from the Air Force Reserves. FDR got his revenge after the war started by refusing to let Lindbergh return to service. Lindbergh made amends of a sort by flying 50 bomber missions as a civilian advisor in the Pacific theater of war.

Jimmy in constrast volunteered for the Army Air Force Reserves seven months before Pearl Harbor.

In a 1978 interview with Stewart, the *Village Voice* claimed the real reason Hayward and Wilder finally gave in to Jimmy was that they had no other candidates. Every other name actor had passed on the role because they found Lindbergh politically and morally repellent.

For some reason, the nicest man in Hollywood didn't share his colleagues' repugnance. During filming he reiterated his admiration of Lindbergh, which caused problems that had nothing to do with politics. "I worshipped the man for so long. Strangely enough, this makes it very hard for me to play the role. It's just got to be right. So far, from the rushes I've seen, I'm not sure I'm satisfied with myself. Of course being so emotionally involved it's difficult for me to judge."

The movie-going audience wasn't satisfied either and stayed away in droves. The film was a $6 million nightmare, and studio chief Jack Warner complained, "Exhibitors are still moaning about it, and I have never been able to figure out why it flopped." Warner, in fact, had greenlighted the super-expensive project because he thought it would be a blockbuster.

Unfortunately, Warner was unaware of a poll of college students at the time which would have made him realize that by 1957, the hero of 1927 was almost completely forgotten by the most important movie demographic, teenagers. Or maybe the poll just showed that the current decline in SAT scores is not really a new phenomenon.

The survey asked a class of University of California students what Lindbergh was most famous for. One responded that he was the first to fly over the North Pole. Another said he was the first person to fly non-stop around the world. When asked to identify the "Spirit of St. Louis," the name of Lindbergh's plane, one student guessed it was the Santa Fe train. Testament to Jimmy's fame was that another pollee, obviously a subscriber to *Variety*, correctly said it was the title of James Stewart's upcoming film!

The movie's failure can't be entirely blamed on the egregious miscasting of a 47-year-old as a 25-year-old. Good old-fashioned American yahooism was also a culprit.

While *The Spirit of St. Louis* in 1957 was an artistic embarrassment for Jimmy, that same year he would undergo a public humiliation exceedingly more painful. Unlike his film's brief appearance in theaters, this one would go on for more than two years.

Chapter 31

Jimmygate

When it came to talking about his heroic wartime service, the taciturn Jimmy Stewart made "Silent Cal" Coolidge seem like a chatty methamphetamine abuser.

Personally and professionally, 1957 was not a good year for the actor. Besides the embarrassing turn as an over-the-hill Lindbergh, the only other film he made that year, the Western *Night Passage*, also did a belly-flop.

But those screen humiliations were nothing compared to the two-year ordeal he suffered at the hands of a vengeful Senator, a liberal member of the Republican party he loved—as a conservative.

In 1948, Margaret Chase Smith was elected to the U.S. Senate from Maine. She represented that amusing oxymoron, a liberal Republican. To her credit, the pit bull politician was one of the few of her Senate colleagues who had the courage to stand up to the 900-pound gorilla that was Senator Joe McCarthy.

But her treatment of Jimmy Stewart in the Senate and in the press suggests a liberal version of McCarthyism, only directed at one person instead of the thousands the paranoid McCarthy denounced.

L'Affaire Stewart, as it was dubbed in an overexaggerated

comparison to the truly horrific *L'Affaire Dreyfus*, began in August 1957 when President Eisenhower nominated his fellow vet for the rank of brigadier general. Along with the promotion from colonel came the job as the No. 3 man in the Strategic Air Command. (Eisenhower sounds almost Reaganesque, mixing Jimmy's movie role in *Strategic Air Command* with a real-life position. Ironically, both the movie and the job offer proved to be big bombs, literally in the case of the latter assignment.)

Jimmy must have been horrified when Mrs. Smith went to Washington and did her own Zola-esque *j'accuse*. She claimed that the movie star was the beneficiary of the equivalent of celebrity affirmative action. Per Smith, the actor had been accepted over more qualified, lesser known reservists. Worse, he was not even qualified for the assignment for two reasons: he had had only nine days training in the past two years, she claimed. And the No. 3 position would put him in charge of SAC's nuclear bombers. (That's almost as scary as the idea of an Alzheimer's-afflicted President with his hand on the button marked Armageddon.) She made it seem as though Jimmy, whose fetish about not capitalizing on his war record was boiler-plated into his movie contracts, was a vainglorious armchair warrior.

You can understand her concern about letting a Hollywood celebrity have control of the nuclear trigger, but she was simply inaccurate about his lack of training. Long before the flap made front page news, AP reported in 1956 that he had had two weeks' training for each of the past two years. According to Pentagon regulations, that amount of training qualified him for the position, the Associated Press said.

Senator Smith was either uninformed or didn't care. *Newsweek* speculated her persecution of Stewart, like some latter-day Captain Dreyfus, represented a personal vendetta, since her administrative assistant, William C. Lewis, had been denied a similar promotion to brigadier general. More hypocritically, Smith was notorious for being what is called a "double dipper." As a lieutenant colonel in the WAF reserve, she received both a military paycheck and a handsome Senate salary. *Her* qualifications to be a lieutenant colonel were never brought up.

That didn't stop her from denouncing Jimmy's. From the Senate floor, she fired off 100 questions to the Pentagon, demanding that the brass list Jimmy's qualifications.

Col. Beirne Lay could have answered all Smith's questions about whether or not Jimmy was a competent pilot. In his famous 1945 article in the *Saturday Evening Post*, he wrote, "It's a little known fact that the chief obstacles were not German flak, fighters or bad weather. The gravest threat to a successful bombing mission was the inherent difficulty of operations themselves . . . So high were the personal qualifications required for air commanders who led the huge 8th Air Force formations, that success or failure of an air offensive against Europe hinged on the existence of and careful selection of *competent* air commanders. Yet in the spring of 1944 a Hollywood movie star named Jimmy Stewart sat in the lead ship of a procession of more than 1,000 heavy bombers . . . Was Gen. Ted Timberlake crazy? Was Gen. Jimmy Hodges, his air-division commander, impressed with having seen *a lanky actor kiss Lana Turner*? Was Gen. Jimmy Doolittle, head of the 8th Air Force, unaware that an Oscar winner at 23,000 feet with a microphone around his neck was broadcasting 'lines' with a bearing on the lives of 10,000 skilled men and on the destruction of a vital German war plant?"

Lay's implied answer was that nobody could be that star struck or plain crazy to give Jimmy a job in which 10,000 men's lives were at stake.

Less qualified but even more bullish than Colonel Lay was Vincent X. Flaherty, a columnist for the *L.A. Herald Examiner*, who volunteered to clue the Senator in. "It is doubtful if Senator Smith knows much about Col. James Stewart or his brilliant war record, either. If she doesn't, I can fill her in." (Flaherty's defense was particularly generous, since as a war correspondent he had tried to get an interview with Jimmy in Paris. As usual, Jimmy had turned him down flat.)

Suddenly, the idea of a movie star, at least this particular movie star, in the cockpit of a bomber loaded with nuclear-tipped missiles didn't seem like such a crazy idea of Eisenhower's after all.

Senator Smith apparently never read the famous *Post* article. She waged a successful six-month battle which led to a lopsided 12-2 vote of the Senate Armed Services Subcommittee against Jimmy's promotion.

Stewart was, as usual, the living embodiment of Hemingway's grace under pressure. He told the *L.A. Herald Express* after the humiliating vote in the Senate, "I was very honored to receive the *nomination* for this promotion by President Eisenhower and the Air Force," and then, according to the *Express*, "he clammed up."

Actually, in a rare show of public pique he said in another interview, "If the war had lasted a little longer I might have wound up a general." Indeed, his final assignment at the end of the war was seeing GIs safely home from Europe, a position that ordinarily upped a colonel to general. For some reason, maybe because he never asked, Jimmy didn't get the promotion, which was supposed to be almost automatic, according to Colonel Lay.

Mrs. Smith's Lieutenant Gerard like pursuit of Jimmy didn't let up. In 1959, Eisenhower, who must have been a really big fan, again nominated Jimmy for a less demanding position that didn't involve sharp objects or weapons that could end civilization as we know it. Again, Senator Smith blocked the nomination.

Finally, in a victory that was totally pyrrhic, Smith voted for Jimmy when he was nominated to brigadier general as an "information officer." That's bureaucratese for "flack," or press agent for the Air Force. That was exactly the kind of assignment Jimmy had refused during the war when he was intent on active duty against the Gerries.

Even after voting for it, Mrs. Smith couldn't resist one more jab at his eventual job, saying, "That's more like it."

If he hadn't already earned it by then, he deserved the moniker St. Jim when he spoke to Mrs. Smith after the imbroglio. "I talked with Senator Smith on the phone about it, and I understood her reasons," he said without enumerating them. "*She seemed like a very nice person.*"

Daily Variety, usually obsequious to anyone in a position of power or prestige in Hollywood, made this tacky comment about his promotion in the reserves. "If there's another war, Gen. Jimmy Stewart will be a press agent."

Jimmy wasn't one to gloat, but you wonder if he took some guilty pleasure from the ultimate fate of his persecutor. In 1972 Smith was tossed out of the Senate by her own party when her successful challenger in the Republican primary ran on the platform that Smith was too old for the job. (She was 75.) Smith, who had denied employment to Jimmy two times, suddenly found herself downsized, while Jimmy at the time was gainfully employed on a successful TV series.

Three years before Smith's ouster, however, he had voluntarily resigned from the reserves, and in another act that would qualify him for canonization if the Presbyterian faith believed in saints, he donated his entire military pension "in perpetuity." to a scholarship fund that provided special tutoring for new cadets at the U.S. Air Force Academy who were "deficient in math, English, or science skills," but who had the "potential to be great commanders," as *Daily Variety* reported.

The math scholarships stand out like a sore memory. Jimmy must have remembered his own painful wrestling with algebra at Princeton and wanted to help fellow sufferers of quadratic equation syndrome.

Chapter 32

Triumph Among Tribulation

During the two years he spent as Senator Smith's personal whipping boy, there was one major consolation. In the middle of his Congressional nightmare, he made *the* very best film of his career, paired again with his British Buddha, Hitchcock.

Vertigo has characters of such depth that, several of them require—and one gets—psychotherapy. *Vertigo* is also the only Stewart or Hitchcock film to have made the all-time 10 best film list in a poll of critics conducted in 1982 by the egghead British magazine, *Sight & Sound*. The classic 1958 psychological thriller came in at No. 9.

(A crank minority of critics insist *North by Northwest* is Hitchcock's finest. That film, however, had little depth of character and only stands out for its ingeniously plotted storyline, although it is in no way superior to *Vertigo's* plot convolutions.)

It's a Wonderful Life was his favorite child, *The Glenn Miller Story* and *Bend of the River* were his wealthiest offspring, but *Vertigo* was the kid who went away to Harvard on a full scholarship.

Vertigo would have been a classic of *film noir*, except that it was shot in glorious Technicolor. Besides being his best film, it also contained the absolutely kinkiest role in a career that knew no kink except when Hitchcock twisted him into psychosexual knots. While it's overkill to call Jimmy a voyeur in *Rear Window*, it's understatement to call him sexually obsessed in *Vertigo*. With ill-concealed delight, Hitchcock turned the boy next door into the sexual compulsive down the street. The film displays the usually girl-shy actor at his horniest.

At the advanced age of 50, Jimmy was still boyish and sexy enough to make us believe Kim Novak, a former beauty contest winner in real life, would fall for him before falling to her death. Jimmy's retired police detective returns the affection in spades.

A wealthy friend from boyhood hires Stewart, who has left the force because of a disabling fear of heights (the title phobia), to trail his suicidal wife, whose delusions lead her to believe she's the reincarnation of a courtesan who committed suicide a century earlier at 26, the same age as Novak's character.

Jimmy falls in love with his employer's wife and fails miserably at his assignment, because in mid-picture Novak falls to her death from a bell tower. After a guilt-tripping coroner's inquest that makes the Margaret Chase Smith hearings seem like an interrogation by a reporter from *Entertainment Tonight*, Stewart suffers a nervous breakdown and is committed to a mental institution. Hitchcock just couldn't resist subjecting Everyman to psychosis. Or as the psychiatrist explains to Jimmy's Girl Friday, Barbara Bel Geddes, Jimmy's burnt-out case is suffering from "acute melancholia with a guilt complex."

Out of the booby hatch but not cured of clinical depression, Jimmy finds himself paralyzed and tormented by the death of the woman he was hired to protect. Then one day, he sees a dead (pun intended) ringer for Novak, except unlike the blonde aristocrat he fell in love with, this doppelgänger has brown hair, bushy eyebrows, awful fashion sense, and a blue-collar accent. And she's a salesgirl at Magnin's living in a cheapie residential hotel instead of the original's Nob Hill high-rise. The cinematographer even manages to make her look fatter than the dead woman, even though both roles are of course played by Novak.

Hitchcock is at his slyest as he turns Jimmy into a tyrannical

Henry Higgins, a fashion and makeup dictator who buys clothes and orders a full cosmetic makeover to turn the badly dressed brunette into the image of his dead blond bombshell. Stewart is so obsessed with his late love he refuses even to kiss her reincarnation until he has transformed her into the original object of his desire.

Then an antique necklace owned by the dead woman shows up around Novak's neck, and Jimmy, the retired sleuth, instantly detects he's been set up. The women are one and the same. Jimmy was hired to serve as a witness to the apparent suicide of his friend's real wife, who was actually murdered for her money by her husband.

When Jimmy discovers he's been the stooge in this homicidal charade, he becomes as enraged as he once was obsessed with both incarnations of Novak. His treatment of her by today's standards would be considered spousal abuse if they were married. He drags her back to the scene of the faked suicide, the belltower, where a nun suddenly appears out of the shadows, scaring Novak's character, who finally falls to her death.

Although he didn't adopt a Polish-German accent or balloon up to 50 pounds over ideal weight (neither of which Jimmy could have done even had he wanted to), his decision to play a sex-obsessed, clinically depressed gumshoe was as profound a choice as any Meryl's Sophie Zawistowska or De Niro's Jake La Motta ever made.

Vertigo may be unique among pop films of the 1950s because it had an unhappy ending. In all of Hitchcock's other films, the hero overcomes all obstacles. Just before *Vertigo* fades to *noir*, Jimmy is left standing at the belltower portal, staring down at the corpse of the woman he has lost twice.

Although Novak didn't have a lot of competition from her other films, critics agree the modestly gifted actress did her best work in *Vertigo*. By 1956, two years before *Vertigo*, she was the No. 1 box-office star in America, but the actress felt intimidated when she showed up on the San Francisco set and confronted two masters of the cinema.

In the 1987 PBS special—the one Jimmy gave up $4 million to appear in—Novak warmly recalled how at least one of these masters made her life easier. "Jimmy made me feel like I belonged. He had a wonderful way of making you feel that he'd never met anybody like you before. In the weeks ahead, he looked after me. He was like the boy next door, my father and brother I wished I had had. He had a natural kindness and sensitivity," she said of our Saint Jim.

Despite the paternal and brotherly references, Novak made some genuine Freudian slips when she added in a *TV Guide* interview, "He was sexy, a term overused then as now; but I tell you that he was the sexiest man who played opposite me in 30 years. And if you ask me why, I'll tell you it was that boyish charm, that enchanting innocence." Novak like Grace Kelly, was 24 when she co-starred with the sexiest man alive, who had by then hit the half-century mark.

It was maturity and monogamy rather than innocence that kept Jimmy from falling for Novak, who was "romantically linked," in the quaint phrase of the time, with other famous studs like Cary Grant, Frank Sinatra, Aly Khan (Rita Hayworth's ex and the disinherited heir to the Muslim equivalent of the papacy), and the son of the Dominican Republic's hefty *el jefe*, dictator Rafael Trujillo. The latter liasion may have allowed her to commiserate with Jimmy in 1958 when another ludicrous Congressional assault on Hollywood mores saw Novak denounced on the House floor for accepting an expensive sports car from the young playboy. Plus, unasked, in 1986 Novak told me in her trailer on the set of of the nighttime soap *Falcon Crest* that she had been one of JFK's conquests. (Thanks for sharing, Kim, but the editor of the TV listings magazine I did the interview for refused to publish her claim to a dalliance with the Casanova of Camelot. Finally I get to spill my guts.)

To his credit, and for the sake of his 44-year marriage, there was never even a whisper in the dishiest of tabloids of a similar affair between Novak and her "sexiest leading man" in 30 years. Jimmy's daughter Kelly, not in the least embarrassed to discuss the touchy subject of a parent's sexuality, summed up his post-bachelor reputation: "The public has never seen Jimmy Stewart behave indecently. He hasn't had noisy, messy love affairs; he didn't leave his wife for another woman, etc."

The other master on the set didn't follow the solicitous example Jimmy set.

Supremely insecure despite her box-office clout, Novak suffered Hitchcock's notorious habit of refusing to give actors instructions other than where to hit their marks. When she asked him for her motivation in a crucial scene, Hitchcock replied, "Kim, it's *only* a movie."

Sexy, fatherly Jimmy was willing to play Stanislavsky to her Trilby. After the director's snub, she turned to Jimmy for help. "What do you think he wants me to do?" she asked frantically. Jimmy put his arm on her shoulder—purely platonically—and said, "There, there now, Kim. If Hitch didn't think that you were right for the part he wouldn't have signed you to do it in the first place. You must believe in yourself." The box office king found himself reassuring the shaky box office queen.

That anecdote has to be the ultimate rebuttal to film snobs who claim Jimmy was always playing himself on screen. His character in *Vertigo* would have been all over the vulnerable actress like a cheap leisure suit. Instead, Jimmy generously played armchair psychotherapist-daddy-brother.

Not only did Jimmy fail to hit on the voluptuous movie star, Hitch didn't either, despite the claim of biographer Donald Spoto in *The Art of Alfred Hitchcock* that the director sexually harassed many of his leading ladies, especially the blond ones, for whom he seemed to have a special fetish.

Jimmy's next film and next pairing with Novak was as disastrous artistically as their first collaboration was glorious. *Bell, Book and Candle* was a soporific comedy that plays like a two-hour TV reunion special of *Bewitched*, only less humorous than the lamest sitcom. 1959's *Anatomy of a Murder*, was even more sexually explicit than the over-the-top eroticism of *Vertigo*. Jimmy plays a down-on-his-luck defense attorney who agrees to defend Army officer Ben Gazzara, on trial for murdering the man who raped his wife, (Lee Remick), although the prosecution insists the rape of Gazzara's slatternly spouse was actually consensual sex.

In an era when a married Ricky and Lucy were still relegated to twin beds, *Anatomy of Murder* didn't just push the sexual envelope, it tore the thing into little pieces. In the climactic courtroom scene, Jimmy holds up Remick's panties and uses the term "semen-stained" to prove it was rape and not a one-afternoon stand.

The movie, directed by Otto Preminger, a Hitchcock wannabe, is a minor classic. But at least one viewer was not impressed. In fact, he was outraged.

Alexander Stewart once again came out of Mama Rose retirement to weigh in on his son's career. As Jimmy recalled with wry amusement in a 1970 *TV Guide* interview, "Good guy, my dad. Called me up just after I finished *Anatomy of a Murder*. 'What about that new picture of yours, son?' " Alexander casually asked. Then whammied him with, " 'I understand it's dirty. Sounds pretty dirty to me. I'm telling all my friends not to go.' " A customer had told Alexander it involved a rape case, and Alexander was treating his 51-year-old son like a teenager who had gotten his girlfriend pregnant.

In fact, after his conversation with the reporter, Alexander marched over to the local newspaper and actually took out an ad that said, "I'd like all of you to know my son has made an off-color picture, and I'm very sorry about it."

Eventually, dad the fan overcame dad the Hays Code enforcer and sneaked into a drive-in movie theater in nearby Homer City a month after he had threatened to boycott the film along with all his friends, substantially cutting into Jimmy's profit participation. Jimmy quoted his father as saying post-screening, "Son, don't tell anybody, but I saw it and I think it's the best picture you ever made."

The Academy voters agreed, and Jimmy won his fifth and final nomination, losing out to his *Greatest Show on Earth* lord of the three rings, Charlton Heston for *Ben-Hur*. The prestigious and arty Venice Film Festival made amends by giving Stewart its top prize that year, which praised his role for its "poetic originality and refined formality." Poetic? Refined? The Serenissima's citation must have lost something in translation from the Italian. No mention was made of unlaundered underwear, which did, however, justify the festival's singling out the ground-breaking film for its originality.

For a change, Jimmy was not as generous when judging the work of his best friend's kid, Peter Fonda. A year before the *TV Guide* interview he was asked to rate recent movies. His clipped speech sounded like George Bush doing an impression of Siskel or Ebert. Jimmy seemed to be an avid filmgoer who kept *au courant* on the current crop of films. Maybe he had to, since he was still fully employed in the industry. His praise and condemnation suggested that he wasn't a prude, but that he had zero tolerance for the glorification of drug use. "Saw *The Graduate*. Loved it. Saw *Blow-up*. Yes, I, ahh . . . a well-made thing. Saw *Easy Rider*. Didn't like it much. Not well-made."

In 1959, like God after six days of overtime, Jimmy could have rested on the seventh day of the decade in which he created his best works and made his most money. Except for a run-in with an extortionate trucker and the Torquemada from Maine, Jimmy had reason to be pleased with his creations. According to the *Guinness Book of the Movies*, Jimmy was *the* highest paid actor of the decade, earning "$1 million plus per film." (Interestingly, for an industry notorious for underpaying women relative to men, in the previous decade Betty Grable was No. 1, although at a measly $800,000 per year, not per picture. Maybe the box office dominance by a female during the war years can be explained by the fact that much of the male competition, including Jimmy, was in uniform instead of costume.)

Adding to this happiest time, Jimmy's wife remained the love of his life despite a certain lust for blood on Gloria's part. Fatherhood also continued to enchant him, although one of his animal-loving daughters would admit mom could be a serial killer when it came to four-legged fans.

Chapter 33

White Huntress, Black Heart

Few knew how ironic it was in 1982 when Mr. and Mrs. Stewart went to Washington to receive an award for Outstanding Contributions to the Conservation of Wild Life from the African Wildlife Leadership Foundation. In 1962 the couple also spent several nights as guests of William Holden at the huge game preserve in Africa to which the actor had devoted his life and fortune.

Gloria was a major benefactor and fund-raiser for the acquisition of the L.A. Zoo's Great Ape house. She and Jimmy visited their daughter Kelly in Rwanda, where she was studying the endangered mountain gorilla under the tutelage of Dian Fossey, who would be immortalized by Sigourney Weaver in her Oscar-nominated role in *Gorillas in the Mist*. Mrs. Stewart sat on the boards of the Greater Los Angeles Zoo Association, the L.A. County Museum of Natural History, and the African Wildlife Leadership Foundation. The zoo was one of her favorite charities, Mrs. Stewart explained, because she was an "ardent conservationist and animal lover." By 1992, Jimmy boasted to *TV Guide* that he had been on 16 safaris; his wife, on 22.

While on a photographic safari in Kenya in 1979, Jimmy starred in a documentary, *A Tale of Africa*, in which he sadly noted the absence of once numerous rhinos and elephants, the victims of poachers . . . and *the victims of two future "ardent conservationists and animal lovers," Mr. and Mrs. James Stewart of Beverly Hills and Kenya.*

In the summer of 1996 while researching Stewart's life at the Academy of Motion Picture Arts & Science's Margaret Herrick Library in Beverly Hills, I came across an original letter that had somehow found its way into the library's archives. The letter not only looked original (not a photocopy), but it also appeared to be genuine, filled with typos, bad punctuation, and the uneven lines typical of a manual typewriter, circa 1962.

That was the year the letter, dated August 14, was typed by the future preservationist, Mrs. Stewart. Despite her aristocratic pedigree, Gloria, Jimmy's "thoroughbred," represented a phenomenon unique to this day: the socialite as Rambo. In her typewritten letter to someone unnamed she wrote without compunction, "Jimmy got an elephant, rhinoceros *[sic]* (damned near killed him—it was three paces from him when he *dropped* it) and an Eland *[sic]*, a big, big one which is a very good trophy, and a leopard."

Her son Michael, 16, she went on, "got a lion, buffalo, and a leopard in one day. It was even more fun this time," she said of what was apparently an annual blood-letting in the bush. "After the first safari, you lose interest in shooting and you get fussy. I turned down three leopards. I loved every second of it. Were on safari almost a month. Spent a couple nights in Holden's Safari Club." (Holden would have been horrified if he had known of the slaughter.)

A year later, there was no need to dig up private correspondence in dusty archives. Jimmy repeated almost verbatim to *L.A. Times* TV columnist Cecil Wilson the contents of Gloria's letter, mentioning that while in Kenya he had shot another elephant, an eland, and a charging rhinoceros at three paces. His wife shot an elephant, leopard, and water buck. Jimmy's story differed only slightly from his wife's correspondence.

Jimmy said he had never gone on safari until his wife dragged him to Africa because he was "too lazy." More likely, the man who as a 10-year-old couldn't bring himself to kill a homicidal mutt had never gone hunting—other than with cap guns and his two stepsons in the hills of Beverly—because he didn't share his wife's Hemingwayesque lust for annihilating endangered species.

"It wasn't until I was married that my wife dragged me to exciting things and places, to travel, wildlife, the outdoors, fishing and hunting. We hunted for a year, then gave it up. You get a respect for the animals." You get the feeling that Jimmy, the guy who fed chateaubriand to Gloria's dog during their courtship, gently persuaded his bloodthirsty spouse to trade in her Uzi for a Leica.

After I spoke to their daughter, Kelly, who edits the *Gorilla Conservation Newsletter* in Davis, Calif., she confirmed that her parents were briefly wild animal hunters.

"When Mom and Dad first went to Africa in the early sixties," she told me, "they went on a hunting safari because that's what one did in those days in the early sixties." Not Bill Holden, who had already seen the writing on the wilderness, and was desperately trying to save, not shoot, wildlife.

"After a couple of trips, Mom and Dad realized that they would rather watch the animals than kill them, and so they started going on photographic safaris. In a sense, they learned where their real sensibilities lay. The switch from hunter to photographer/conservationist is a very common path," the former Cambridge zoologist said. "In good hunters, as opposed to mere trophy collectors, the attraction of hunting is based on a love of being out in nature, being near wild animals, sitting under the stars at night, and so on." And killing a few fat water buffalo from time to time.

Dr. Stewart also insists her kindly father didn't disarm her gun-toting mom. "As far as I know, Mom and Dad's shift from gun to camera was mutual. One did not have to persuade the other to leave the guns behind."

In fact, Professor Harcourt's fascination with nature and her doctorate from one of the great universities of the world are attributable to her mother's influence, not her father's workaholism, she believes. "Dad probably passed on somewhat of a work ethic to me. However, my academic career is more based on the intense interest and passion for wildlife, biology, and anthropology that my mother inspired in me. This arose from her love of wildlife and Africa,'' once Gloria became a one-woman advocate of gun control.

In 1981, the Stewarts visited their daughter during her stay with Dian Fossey in Rwanda. Stewart, who could charm human gorillas like L.B. Mayer and Margaret Chase Smith, found he had the same effect on the real thing. "Kelly was studying mountain gorillas in Rwanda. I visited her there. Right off, I discovered I was too old for those frisky gorillas,'' he said in Jhan Robbin's oral history. "Hairy things with long arms that kept pounding their chest. They weigh about 800 pounds apiece. Once, I was focusing my camera near a clump of trees when six feet from me, I noticed this gorilla. Now he wasn't doing much. Just staring. I kind of stared back. It's a good thing I had fast film.'' The gorilla was probably working up the nerve to ask for an autograph from his favorite movie star.

There were much scarier escapes in the bush. Once a hyena ate Jimmy's 8mm camera. It was probably the most indigestible film until *Showgirls*. Another time he admitted he was "terrified'' when he stepped on a cobra and "it reared up and hissed. It was my fault because I wasn't watching where I was going.''

In 1970, Jimmy, by then an ardent conservationist, regressed and did a bit of poaching. He brought back from Africa a dying bush baby in his airplane carry-on bag. He was warned that the adorable arboreal creature, which looks like a cross between a panda and a kitten, would not last a month in L.A.'s relatively harsh climate. But the animal was clearly dying, and Jimmy nursed it back to health in the backyard of his Beverly Hills mansion.

It must have been great to be James Stewart's daughter. Kelly recalls playing with the bush baby who was named Davey. "Dad designed for the bush baby a beautiful cage that was so big, you could walk around in it—shades of architecture! It was out in the garden. We had Davey for five years. He died of a kidney infection.''

Jimmy apparently felt secure enough in his credentials as a conservationist to display evidence of his earlier crimes against nature by mounting trophies from his first two safaris in the basement, a *TV Guide* reporter noticed in a 1970 visit to the house. There was also photographic proof: a framed picture showed Jimmy proudly holding the carcass of a magnificent lion. In the interview, Jimmy seemed to contradict his daughter when he claimed that his bloodlust evaporated before his wife's. A Texas oil baron and his wife, Frank and Bess Johnson, "first hooked" him on the bloodsport in the mid 1950s, Jimmy said. Since then, the only shooting *he* did was with a camera. "Decided to leave *that other part* to Gloria," Jimmy reportedly mumbles in the interview.

All of this is hardly on the magnitude of the scandal caused 15 years ago when another alleged conservationist, Prince Philip, was photographed beside the literally thousands of game animals he and his aristocratic pals had slaughtered during a single weekend in the country. But it does show that our Saint Jim did have lapses. As in the case of Saint Louis the Pious, the 13th century King of France and liquidator of the Paris ghetto, canonization can often conceal catastrophe.

Jimmy's film career from the 1960s on matched the unfortunate choices of his African massacres. Unlike Cary Grant, who gracefully entered semi-retirement as a perfume salesman for Fabergé or Garbo who strolled on Park Avenue when those stars saw the writing on the screen, Jimmy remained a workaholic. His congenital work ethic kept him toiling in projects unworthy of his talent or track record.

In a profession where "over 40" means over the hill, Jimmy as he floundered past his 50s found the number of A-list scripts he had been offered dropping like a failing student's GPA.

Airport '77.

Need we say more? We do. The compulsion to work made him ignore his exquisite taste in films to star in a sequel to a sequel. And on the few occasions when he worked with major directors like John Ford, they were regrettably Ford's (and Jimmy's) minor efforts. It was as though Babe Ruth had been traded to the minors. In his otherwise hagiographic 1973 filmography, Dennis John Hall calls their first collaboration, 1961's *Two Rode Together*, "sub-standard horse opera." Ford and

Jimmy's work a year later in the comic Western, *The Man Who Shot Liberty Valance*, was an improvement, although its plot was a rip-off of *Destry Rides Again*. And Jimmy, the No. 1 box-office star of the previous decade, found himself playing *third* banana to Lee Marvin and John Wayne. Jimmy wasn't even one of the title characters! A huge commercial hit, even this film was considered unworthy of the master, Ford. Pauline Kael, the Antichrist Will Rogers of film criticism, a woman who never met a film she didn't hate, called the comedy "a heavy-spirited piece of nostalgia."

By the late 1960s, Jimmy had resorted to slumming with the star of no-brainer comedies that made his attempts to resurrect the sophisticated farces of the 1930s seem superannuated. His co-star in 1968's *Bandolero!* was none other than Jerry Lewis's alter ego, Dean Martin, the pair whose Jim Carrey-like slapstick had put Jimmy's late 1940s farces out to pasture. Fond of his leading lady as usual, Jimmy was too generous about Raquel Welch, who never made the transition from bad joke to screen star. Jimmy predicted big things for her. "I think she plays a Mexican girl in the picture. I think she's going to stack up all right." The use of the term "stack" may have been a Freudian slip. Jimmy was no male chauvinist and much too polite to consciously use a sexist pun referring to Welch's physical endowments. Or as a talk show host once introduced his next guest, "Here they are, Raquel Welch."

In 1970, Jimmy enjoyed a happier if not much more commercially successful pairing with his best friend, Henry Fonda, in *The Cheyenne Social Club*. If he hadn't died nine years earlier, Alexander would have definitely boycotted this one, even though Jimmy lamely insisted it was a "family film." If it was indeed family fare, the storyline suggests he had clairvoyant knowledge of the Fleiss family since the Western took place in a whorehouse. Stewart and Fonda, two dim-witted cowpokes, inherit the establishment without knowing what's going on upstairs. Jimmy's justification for appearing in such G-rated smut suggests that if he hadn't been a Presbyterian he would have made a crackerjack casuist. Describing the plot, he told *Coronet* magazine, "It's about these two cowboys who inherit a spread. When they get there they discover they've inherited—aah, it's a bawdy house is what it is.'' Yet while he conceded the film was set "in a house of ill repute," he still believed, "I think it is a kind of *family* house of ill repute, because it's all comedy.''

When his film career finally hit the skids, he invaded what has been called the "elephant burial ground of fading movie stars," prime time television.

1971's eponymously titled sitcom, *The Jimmy Stewart Show*, immediately hit the remainder bin of the Nielsens and was cancelled in less than a year, even counting summer reruns. Two years later, the 90-minute Grisham-esque *Hawkins* cast Jimmy in the title role of a small town attorney who somehow gets enmeshed in big city cases. (So the show could stay cheaply ensconced in a Los Angeles studio.) Unlike his foray into lauqh-track land, *Hawkins* was actually a hit, but in 1973, aged 65, the usually tireless Jimmy found the 18-hour days unbearable. So he did something that must have had Alexander turning over in his grave. He walked away from the series after less than a year. It was one thing to do a cameo in a spot of trifle like *Airport '77*, it was another to carry a 90-minute show, even though it ran only every third week in rotation with *Shaft* and *The New CBS Tuesday Night Movies*.

Back on the big screen, his career reached a sad end when he traded in glorious Grace and co-dependent Kim for a leading lady who was literally a bitch in 1978's *The Magic of Lassie*.

But these regrettable big and small screen follies were nothing compared to the genuine tragedy that permanently altered the happy lives of Jimmy and Gloria and the kids, especially one of them.

Chapter 34
The War He Didn't Win

There is an uncredited photo in Jimmy Stewart's file at the Academy library in Beverly Hills dated June 16, 1951. In this case, a wire photo is worth much more than a thousand words. It speaks volumes of the love that suffused the Stewart household.

The photo is also heart-breaking, since we know the tragic end of one of its subjects, Ronald McLean, Jimmy's stepson. Ronnie is 6 years old in the photo. He is seated next to his mom and is just as beautiful as the socialite, down to the sculpted nose, deep-set eyes, and voluptuous lips. While his brother hams it up by looking straight into the camera, there's a far-off look in Ronnie's eyes as he gazes on his mother. Jimmy and Gloria each hold one of the infant twin girls in the picture.

In June 1969, shortly after his 25th birthday, Lt. Ronald McLean of the U.S. Marine Corps, described as a "tall handsome lad," by the *New York Times*, "died instantly from a Viet Cong machine gun blast."

Jimmy's stepson was leading a patrol of the 3rd Marine Division from Vandergrift combat base in the Quay Tri province, the *Times* reported, when he ran into a Viet Cong patrol.

His death was especially maddening because he was due to finish his tour of duty in Vietnam within two months.

"His mother and I were so proud of him," Jimmy told the *Times*.

It was scant consolation that Ronnie received the Silver Star, the third highest decoration in the Marines. When a *Times* reporter referred to the loss as a tragedy, Jimmy gently corrected him. "There's our son," he said, pointing to a photo of the handsome Marine in Vietnam, "eight months before he was killed. He wanted to be a Marine. He was a good Marine. I think of him all the time. It was a terrible *loss*, but I don't see it as a tragedy. He said he didn't want to be drafted. He wanted to be a Marine. He became a good Marine. He conducted himself honorably on the field of battle. You can't consider that a tragedy."

In a gentler version of Alexander Stewart's pushiness, you get the feeling Jimmy prodded Ronald to excel just as much but less noisily than his own father had pushed him. A quote suggests Ronald's academic record was discussed in the Stewart household, and his grades were an issue, but a minor one Jimmy didn't harass his stepson about.

Recalling his own academic floundering at Princeton, Jimmy commented, "He was a good boy, not a very good student, but a very good boy. He tried hard, for us, to graduate from college, and when he did, he enlisted in the Marines. He was a fine Marine and on the field of battle he conducted himself in a gallant manner. I don't think that's tragic."

Jimmy was intimately involved in his stepson's life. More than one visitor commented that he treated both stepkids like little princes. One said he felt the "boys were truly his own." They were in everything but name.

During a USO tour of Vietnam a year before Ronald's death, Jimmy visited his stepson. It was one of three trips the Stewarts made to that sinkhole of American lives and money. The other Marines didn't recognize the tall scarecrow who was visiting Lieutenant McLean, but they went nuts over Gloria without knowing she was Mrs. James Stewart. "She was the instant mother to everyone there. Even the Vietnamese kids tagged along with her everywhere," the *New York Times* said. (Jimmy's other son was classified 4-F because of his asthma.)

Ronald's death never undermined Jimmy's rock-ribbed Republicanism. He played golf with Nixon *after* Watergate and campaigned for his good friend from the Dream Factory, Ronald

Reagan, in 1976, even though by that time polls showed the incumbent, President Ford, was a shoo-in for the nomination. A friend, however, said Jimmy once confided he felt Ronald had paid "the ultimate price of war" and hinted at his bitterness over the useless waste of lives.

Jimmy's lifelong Republicanism doesn't seem to square with our concept of Saint Jim. His daughter, Kelly, agrees. As she writes in this book's *Afterword*, Jimmy was a Republican of the old school, which Kelly says believed in "indivdualism, hard work, decency," not the reactionary welfare program for the rich it has become. As to why gentle Jim supported the only war America ever lost, she explains, "I think Dad was a hawk in Vietnam because of old-fashioned patriotism: he belived that you should do what your country asked you to especially in times of conflict."

Gloria's reaction was bizarre, although her behavior after the death of her son makes perfect psychological sense. After the death of a loved one, psychologists say that often the predominant emotion is anger, not grief—even when someone dies of natural causes, as opposed to being the victim of a handgun or Nixon's disastrous policy in Vietnam. Often, this anger is directed at inappropriate targets.

Instead of calling Nixon up (the well-connected Stewarts probably had the Oval Office's private line), she vented her fury at the church the couple had been attending ever since Jimmy found religion after he got married. Gloria was incensed when the church organist failed to show up for the funeral service. Gloria said, "I got mad with my church. On the day of the service for Ron, the organist forgot to come. There wasn't any music. I don't go to chunch anymore. But Jimmy does. Jimmy's a believer."

Indeed, Jimmy's religiosity after marriage was deeply felt. As late as 1993, he was still narrating a Christmas poem at an SRO service held at his church. Gloria did not attend these events, which were advertised by the church in *Daily Variety*. Like good Calvinists, the church elders had the *chutzpah* to charge a $5 admission to their Jimmy Stewart show, even though it was part of an actual religious service.

By 1993, Jimmy was practically stone-deaf, with hearing aids sticking out of both ears. It was typical of his generosity that he would continue to narrate a Christmas service he probably couldn't even hear.

A man (or a woman, in Kim Novak's case) was genuinely blessed to have James Stewart for a friend. In one of his best-selling memoirs, *The Moon is a Balloon*, David Niven said of their mutual friend, Errol Flynn, "You could always count on Erroll . . . to let you down."

Jimmy's behavior was the antithesis of Flynn's except when it came to their wild bachelor days together, which continued after Flynn got married and stopped immediately after Jimmy said I do.

When a friend from college got into trouble decades later, Jimmy volunteered to lend his unassailable integrity and credibility to a man whose Fortune 500 company was desperately in need of both.

In 1978, Leonard Firestone, Jimmy's longtime pal, was in deep doo-doo. His company's Firestone 500 tire was so poorly manufactured it resulted in the largest tire recall in the history of the business.

With all his bucks, Jimmy rarely deigned to do a commercial, but when Firestone personally asked him to do a series of TV commercials for the company in the wake of the recall scandal, Jimmy said yes immediately. Firestone's request was the moral equivalent of asking Mother Teresa to become the spokeswoman for Union Carbide after the Bhophal disaster.

Jimmy never stiffed a friend and never forgot his roots. In 1992, Indiana, Pennsylvania, asked him to come home for the dedication of a *bronze* statue of the actor in front of the courthouse. A subscription drive failed to raise enough funds, and the statue ended up being constructed of fiberglass which a meteorologist predicted would self-destruct within 18 months in Pennsylvania's rainy climate. Jimmy accepted the invitation anyway and spent three glamorous days in the boondocks with his wife, glad-handing people he didn't know. As he later explained, everyone in his family and all his old friends had died by then.

A year later, Gloria, with the grudging consent of her husband, was still living up to her reputation as the "Hollywood hostess with the mostest." They opened their home on his 85th birthday to 40 friends, including Ronald Reagan. Like a good Calvinist, Jimmy charged admission to the event with proceeds going to their favorite two-legged charity, St. John's Hospital and (Mental) Health Center in Santa Monica, Calif.

When his 85th birthday was advertised by the hospital to raise more money, it was inundated with 10,000 birthday cards from all over the world.

In 1980, the doldrums of Jimmy's career were dramatically churned up by the ultimate accolade the industry can bestow on a golden oldie, the AFI Life Achievement Award. It was about time. (Seven recipients had already been honored on the annual awards show, whose highly rated TV broadcast earns the American Film Institute almost all of its operating bucks.)

Jimmy had to play eighth fiddle to men whose contributions to the cinema were only arguably more important than Jimmy's. You could argue that Hitchcock, Ford, and Orson Welles deserved to be first in line, but James Cagney before James Stewart?

Jimmy was too gracious to comment on having to wait eight years to receive an award he so richly deserved. The event, held at the Beverly Wilshire Hotel, right down the block from his house, was filled with lavish encomia from colleagues like Henry Fonda and just plain fans like Dustin Hoffman, who gave a speech even though he had never worked with Stewart. Paraphrasing Prince Philip's salute at another of the innumerable charity events Jimmy coughed up $1,000 a plate for, Hoffman said simply, "Thank you for being Jimmy Stewart."

The self-effacing 78-year-old must have had even his ego tweaked just a bit when Princess Grace, dressed in royal purple, referred to his days as a stud muffin. Even though Gloria was sitting on the other side of him, Princess Grace, seated on the other, said, "I remember that Hitchcock asked for another take of our love scenes in *Rear Window*." Her Serene Highness dryly added, "Jimmy never complained about being required to do take after take." Kelly may have been as frustrated during filming as the infatuated girlfriend she played in *Rear Window*. Jimmy had been married five years by the time they worked together, and he never suffered a 7 or even 44-year itch. His was a strictly hands-off approach to his leading ladies when the camera wasn't rolling, as Kim Novak would later say with noticeable regret.

A few years after those hosannas Jimmy proved that he deserved the moniker Saint Jim. In an incident that sounds like a publicist's dream but was actually a story in the *Los Angeles Times* on May 21, 1982, Jimmy and Gloria were two of thousands of pilgrims and tourists checking out St. Peter's Square in Rome. Once a week, the head of the Holy See wades into this sea of humanity to press the flesh. Hundreds of thousands of papal fans show up for the Big One.

Throwing security precautions to the wind, Pope John Paul II was working the crowd when he suddenly halted his papal procession after spotting a handsome elderly gentleman and his attractive wife.

His Holiness said to Jimmy, "I just want to tell you I'm a huge fan."

Five years later, the Academy of Motion Picture Arts & Sciences finally got around to giving Jimmy its version of a lifetime achievement award. Often, this thanks-for-nothing Oscar is given to major stars who through an oversight of its membership never got around to voting the actor or actress an Oscar for an actual film. (Garbo, Cary Grant.) Jimmy didn't come cap in hand to the 57th Annual Academy Awards. He had already won a bona fide Oscar for acting, one out of five nominations.

With virtually no career and retired, Jimmy still made headlines, although not the kind even the biggest publicity hound would want. In his 80s, Jimmy began to suffer a series of minor heart and skin ailments which never resulted in more than a few days in the hospital before he was back at the office, autographing 500 fans' photos a week. It was testament to his popularity that every single hospital trip made the newspapers around the world, even though none of them was serious. The only ailing, fading celebrity who gets that kind of hospital notoriety is Elizabeth Taylor, and she has major health problems.

Tragically there was one hospital trip Jimmy barely survived, and he wasn't even sick.

Epilogue
Fade Out Gracefully

In 1994, Gloria Stewart was crazy with worry. Her husband had just had a pacemaker implanted, and Jimmy was also concerned, but not for the same reason. He was worried about what Gloria would do after he was gone.

A close friend of Gloria's, whose own mother had recently had a pacemaker installed, told told me she got round-the-clock phone calls from a distracted Gloria wanting to know all the details of the operation, what to expect, the long-term prognosis, etc. "Gloria called me to ask how my mother reacted to the pacemaker because her husband was having one put in," a Beverly Hills socialite who asked not to be identified told me.

Based on her experience with her 98-year-old mother, the socialite jokingly added, "Stop worrying. Jimmy'll bury us all."

Jimmy did bury Gloria.

On February 16, 1994, Gloria's lifetime of chain-smoking caught up with her and she died of lung cancer. The socialite remembers that she wasn't sick long. "She was always saying, 'What am I going to do without Papa?' She called him Papa. Then suddenly she was gone."

During Gloria's brief illness, Nancy Reagan turned out to

be as good a friend to her as Jimmy was to just about everyone. In her obituary, the *L.A. Times* reported that Mrs. Reagan visited Gloria "every few days" during the last of them.

Upon her death the former President released a statement to the press: "Gloria was one of our dearest friends for more than 40 years. Nancy visited with Gloria every few days. She was touched by Gloria's tremendous courage and strength. We are saddened today and send our deepest sympathies to Jimmy and the entire family." Although the statement was attributed to the 40th President of the United States, by then Reagan was in the final stages of Alzheimer's. It was probably Gloria's friend, Nancy, who generated the press release.

To say Jimmy was distracted by the death of his wife . . . well, facile puns fail me here. No, they don't. Jimmy worshipped the ground Gloria gardened on. When the house next door came up for sale in the late '60s, he snapped it up for a then whopping $500,000 and promptly tore it down so Gloria would have more room for the garden she loved only slightly less than her family.

Her Beverly Hills friend on Gloria's Candide-like obsession: "She loved to grow her own vegetables. He bought a beautiful half-million-dollar house just to tear it down because she asked him to. She used to give everybody in the neighborhood vegetables. She really loved it. She did all the gardening herself. She never hired a gardener."

Her friend should know, since she ran the employment agency that supplied the Stewart household with its meager staff of two, which shrank to one maid after Gloria's passing.

Jimmy's daughter Kelly implied that the socialite was exaggerating when she said he kept the house exactly as her mother left it, a living shrine to his adored wife. And for once, Jimmy's affability betrayed him. He should have threatened to shoot Gloria and mount her on the wall like one of their trophies if she didn't stop smoking like a chimney. He loved Gloria not wisely but so well he didn't have the heart to nag.

Kelly: "He retired from public and social life after Mom died, and I don't think that will change. He never begged Mom to stop smoking. He never mentioned her smoking. The house looks the same as when Mom was alive in the sense that the housekeeper, Anne Coyle, makes sure it's well taken care of. The garden, in particular, is beautiful, and the house is full of its flowers. Mom's spirit carries on.''

Jimmy's one and only publicist for the last 40 years was less optimistic about his favorite client. In a rare moment of candor for a press agent, the genial John Strauss, 83, told me, "The spark just went out of his life when Gloria died. He doesn't go out anymore. Before Gloria died, they went out on the town almost every night,'' usually to raise funds for one of the half dozen charities they supported.

"Dad is in sound health for an 88-year-old,'' Kelly told me in 1996. His daughter should have talked to the housekeeper, who told a mutual friend of hers and mine, "Mr. Stewart is so lost without Mrs. Stewart, he told me that when his pacemaker wears out, he's not having it replaced.''

Fans might have taken comfort in that fact, since the typical lifetime of a pacemaker is seven years. Admirers were grateful for his longevity even if he was not.

Jimmy didn't have to wait for the batteries to run out to be reunited with his much-missed wife. On the morning of July 2, 1997, he died quietly in the upstairs bedroom of the home he had shared with his wife for over 40 years. Cause of death was attributed to a blood clot in his lungs and cardiac arrest. He was 89, the same age as his father when he died in 1961.

His stepson, Michael McLean, read a brief statement outside the home where Jimmy had raised him and his siblings with vigorous affection and kid-glove discipline. "The family would like to thank the public for the support and affection they gave to our father over these many years. It always meant a great deal to him and to his family as well.'' Per his father's request, McLean asked fans and friends not to waste money on flowers. He suggested donations to two of the many charities his stepfather had supported, St. John's Hospital in Santa Monica, California, and the African Wildlife Foundation in Washington, D.C. Even in death, Jimmy remained the thrifty Yankee with a social conscience and gratitude toward fans. Jimmy's funeral took place on July 7, 1997, at the Beverly Hills Presbyterian Church, where he had married Gloria and worshipped for half a century. The gathering was more star-studded than the Oscars, with lifetime friends like Nancy Reagan, Bob Hope and Lew Wasserman, the studio chief who made his fortune, paying their last respects.

But it was his daughter, Dr. Kelly Harcourt, who gave the most moving eulogy. She recalled the closing lines of *It's a Wonderful Life,* which held that no man is a failure who has friends. Suppressing a tear, Dr. Harcourt said, "Here's to our father. The richest man in town."

Ironically, unlike George Baily, who was rich in friends not finances, Jimmy, with his oil wells and airlines, was one of the richest men in Beverly Hills in both senses of the word.

Inevitably, Jimmy's passing made headlines around the world. A banner headline surrounded by quotation marks in the *Los Angeles Times* said, "America Lost a National Treasure." The quote came from the President of the United States. Clinton wasn't the only Commander-in-Chief whose affection Jimmy commanded. Ronald Reagan had called him the "boy next door, open, kind and honest." Harry Truman, perhaps the least sentimental Chief Executive, said after a screening of *It's a Wonderful Life,* "If Bess and I had a son, we'd want him to be just like Jimmy Stewart." The film industry's top lobbyist, Jack Valenti, said, "I think God is going to enjoy Jimmy's companionship."

And why not? Everyone else—from Popes to princesses—did.

Afterword

by Kelly Stewart Harcourt

Author's note: When I spoke to Jimmy's daughter, Dr. Kelly Harcourt, in the summer of 1996, I asked her to put in writing why she thought her father was one of the most beloved men on the planet. A private person, Dr. Harcourt seemed hesitant at first, but perhaps she remembered her father's lecture to treat fans as partners, not customers. And what is a biographer, but a fan with a word processor? Her insightful response showed she was one of her father's biggest fans. Dr. Harcourt, who is a professor of anthropology at the University of California, Davis, said via fax:

There are times when I have been taken aback by the adoration and love that the American public shows toward my father. I think that basically it's because he has never let them down. He has never acted in real life in a way that contradicted the public's image of him. [The public that hadn't seen *Vertigo*, at least.]

He has never behaved without grace. I think his lack of ostentation and pretension has been key. He does not throw money around in a showy manner like so many famous glitterati do. He has not acted like a spoiled brat, for example, by demanding extra luxuries or attention on movie sets or by being "difficult" or "temperamental" to work with. He and Mom did not run with an ostentatious crowd. Their close friends all share a remarkable lack of pretension. The public has never seen Jimmy Stewart behave indecently. He hasn't had noisy, messy love affairs; he didn't leave his wife for another woman, etc.

I believe my father was a Republican because of the values Republicanism *used* to stand for: individualism, hard work, decency, etc. I do not think that the modern-day Republicanism of greed, short-sightedness, mean-spiritedness, etc., are at all compatible with my father's spirit or beliefs. Mr. Smith would fight them tooth and nail! I must stress that this is my own analysis (as you can probably guess, I'm a Democrat). I did not get any of this from Dad. We never talked politics.

Dad has always seen the public as the basis of his career, as his bread and butter. He has always felt very grateful to his fans and has always treated them with respect and affection. He does not think he's better than they are, and people can read that sort of attitude. I have never seen Dad refuse to sign an autograph or be rude to a fan, no matter how tired he was, how late it was.

Last, but not least, Dad *is* a damned good actor. I don't think he would be as loved as he is if he weren't so incredibly talented.

The most important lesson I learned from Dad was to be nice to people.

—Dr. Kelly Stewart Harcourt,
Davis, California, 1996

Selected Films of Jimmy Stewart

The Murder Man (1935)
Spencer Tracy, Virginia Bruce

Rose Marie (1936)
Jeanette MacDonald, Nelson Eddy

Next Time We Love (1936)
Margaret Sullavan, Ray Milland

Wife vs. Secretary (1936)
Clark Gable, Jean Harlow

Small Town Girl (1936)
Janet Gaynor, Robert Taylor

Speed (1936)
Una Merkel, Ted Healy

The Gorgeous Hussy (1936)
Joan Crawford, Robert Taylor

Born To Dance (1936)
Eleanor Powell, Virginia Bruce

After the Thin Man (1936)
William Powell, Myrna Loy

Seventh Heaven (1937)
Simone Simon, Jean Hersholt

The Last Gangster (1937)
Edward G. Robinson, Rose Stradner

Navy Blue and Gold (1937)
Robert Young, Florence Rice

Of Human Hearts (1938)
Walter Huston, Gene Reynolds

Vivacious Lady (1938)
Ginger Rogers, James Ellison

The Shopworn Angel (1938)
Margaret Sullavan, Walter Pidgeon

You Can't Take It With You (1938)
Jean Arthur, Lionel Barrymore

Made For Each Other (1939)
Carole Lombard, Charles Coburn

The Ice Follies of 1939
Joan Crawford, Lew Ayres

It's a Wonderful World (1939)
Claudette Colbert, Guy Kibbee

Mr. Smith Goes to Washington (1939) (Oscar nominee)
Jean Arthur, Claude Rains

Destry Rides Again (1939)
Marlene Dietrich, Brian Donlevy

The Shop Around the Corner (1940)
Margaret Sullavan, Frank Morgan

The Mortal Storm (1940)
Margaret Sullavan, Robert Young

No Time For Comedy (1940)
Rosalind Russell, Genevieve Tobin

The Philadelphia Story (1940) (Oscar winner)
Katharine Hepburn, Cary Grant

Come Live With Me (1941)
Hedy Lamarr, Ian Hunter

Pot O' Gold (1941)
Paulette Goddard, Horace Heidt

Ziegfeld Girl (1941)
Judy Garland, Hedy Lamarr

It's a Wonderful Life (1946) (Oscar nominee)
Donna Reed, Lionel Barrymore

Magic Town (1947)
Jane Wyman, Kent Smith

Call Northside 777 (1948)
Richard Conte, Lee J. Cobb

On Our Merry Way (A Miracle Can Happen) (1948)
Burgess Meredith, Paulette Goddard

Rope (1948)
John Dall, Farley Granger

You Gotta Stay Happy (1948)
Joan Fontaine, Eddie Albert

The Stratton Story (1949)
June Allyson, Frank Morgan

Malaya (1949)
Spencer Tracy, Valentina Cortesa

Winchester '73 (1950)
Shelley Winters, Dan Duryea

Broken Arrow (1950)
Jeff Chandler, Debra Paget

The Jackpot (1950)
Barbara Hale, James Gleason

Harvey (1950) (Oscar nominee)
Josephine Hull, Pegg Dow

No Highway in the Sky (1951)
Marlene Dietrich, Glynis Johns

The Greatest Show on Earth (1951)
Charlton Heston, Betty Hutton

Bend of the River (1952)
Arthur Kennedy, Julia Adams

Carbine Williams (1952)
Jean Hagen, Wendell Corey

The Naked Spur (1953)
Janet Leigh, Ralph Meeker

Thunder Bay (1953)
Joanne Dru, Gilbert Roland

The Glenn Miller Story (1954)
June Allyson, Charles Drake

Rear Window (1954)
Grace Kelly, Wendell Corey

The Far Country (1954)
Ruth Roman, Corinne Calvet

Strategic Air Command (1955)
June Allyson, Frank Lovejoy

The Man From Laramie (1955)
Arthur Kennedy, Donald Crisp

The Man Who Knew Too Much (1956)
Doris Day, Brenda De Banzie

The Spirit of St. Louis (1957)
Murray Hamilton, Patricia Smith

Night Passage (1957)
Audie Murphy, Dan Duryea

Vertigo (1958)
Kim Novak, Barbara Bel Geddes

Bell, Book and Candle (1958)
Kim Novak, Jack Lemmon

Anatomy of a Murder (1959) (Oscar nominee)
Lee Remick, Ben Gazzara

The FBI Story (1959)
Vera Miles, Murray Hamilton

The Mountain Road (1960)
Lisa Lu, Glenn Corbett

Two Rode Together (1961)
Richard Widmark, Shirley Jones

The Man Who Shot Liberty Valance (1962)
John Wayne, Vera Miles

Mr. Hobbs Takes a Vacation (1962)
Maureen O'Hara, Fabian

How the West Was Won (1962)
Carroll Baker, Gregory Peck

Take Her, She's Mine (1963)
Sandra Dee, Audrey Meadows

Cheyenne Autumn (1964)
Richard Widmark, Carroll Baker

Dear Brigitte (1965)
Brigitte Bardot, Glynis Johns

Shenandoah (1965)
Doug McClure, Glenn Corbet

The Rare Breed (1965)
Maureen O'Hara, Brian Keith

Flight of the Phoenix (1965)
Richard Attenborough, Peter Finch

Firecreek (1967)
Henry Fonda, Inger Stevens

Bandolero! (1968)
Dean Martin, Raquel Welch

The Cheyenne Social Club (1970)
Henry Fonda, Shirley Jones

Fools' Parade (1971)
George Kennedy, Anne Baxter

That's Entertainment (1974)
co-narrator

The Shootist (1976)
John Wayne, Lauren Bacall

Airport 77 (1977)
Jack Lemmon, Olivia de Havilland

The Big Sleep (1978)
Robert Mitchum, Sarah Miles

The Magic of Lassie (1978)
Alice Faye, Mickey Rooney

An American Tail: Fievel Goes West (1991)
(voice of animated character)

TV SERIES

The Jimmy Stewart Show (1971–1972)

Hawkins (1973–1974)

About the Author

Frank Sanello is the author of biographies on Tom Cruise, Steven Spielberg, Sharon Stone, Will Smith, and the upcoming *Eddie Murphy: The Life and Times of a Comic on the Edge*. As a journalist for the past 25 years, he has written for the *Chicago Tribune,* the *New York Times Syndicate,* the *Washington Post, People, Cosmo* and *Penthouse*. He was also the film critic for the *Los Angeles Daily News* and a business reporter for UPI.

A native of Joliet, Illinois, Sanello graduated from the University of Chicago with honors and earned a Master's Degree from UCLA's film school. His hobbies include gourmet-cooking, weight-training and kick-boxing. He holds a purple belt in Tae Kwon Do.

He lives in Los Angeles with three dogs and five cats.